FLORIDA'S FOOD FOREST COOKBOOK

400 Healthy, No-Waste Recipes for 20 Popular Perennial Plants

AMANDA ALDERS PIKE, PHD, ATR-BC

Pineapple Press

Essex, Connecticut

Pineapple Press

An imprint of The Globe Pequot Publishing Group, Inc.
64 South Main Street
Essex, CT 06426
www.globepequot.com

British Library Cataloguing in Publication Information available

Library of Congress Cataloging-in-Publication Data

Names: Pike, Amanda Alders author
Title: Florida's food forest cookbook : 400 healthy, no-waste recipes for 20 popular perennial plants / Amanda Alders Pike, PhD, ATR-BC.
Description: Essex, Connecticut : Pineapple Press, [2026] | Includes bibliographical references and index.
Identifiers: LCCN 2025030075 (print) | LCCN 2025030076 (ebook) | ISBN 9781683344681 paperback | ISBN 9781683343745 epub
Subjects: LCSH: Cooking--Florida | LCGFT: Cookbooks
Classification: LCC TX715 .P634 2026 (print) | LCC TX715 (ebook) | DDC 641.59759—dc23/eng/20250707
LC record available at https://lccn.loc.gov/2025030075
LC ebook record available at https://lccn.loc.gov/2025030076

Printed in India

To James and Wesley: You inspire me to do better and try harder every day.
Thank you, my loves.

May we be grateful, humble, and devoted to one another.
May our sense of purpose inspire contentment, health and a long life. **Hara hachi bu**.

CONTENTS

FIGURES

ACKNOWLEDGMENTS

I would like to extend my deepest gratitude to the incredible individuals who contributed to the creation of this cookbook. Your passion, creativity, and dedication to sustainable living have been invaluable. While the world drowns in wheat, rice, and corn recipes, we are foraging forward to much needed but largely undocumented territories! For the majority of our human history, we have relied on sustainable ingredients and simple preparation. Yet, those beautiful recipes based on abundance were often passed down through oral traditions . . . it only takes one generation to lose millennia of knowledge! We have forgotten how to create and eat from a perennial paradise. Remembering is a collective process!

First and foremost: **Thank you** to all the recipe testers. This year has been a doozy! Even through hurricanes, tornadoes, and flooding, you harvested, cooked, and baked! Your willingness to experiment, share feedback, and provide thoughtful suggestions has made each recipe more refined and enjoyable. Your time, energy, and expertise are deeply appreciated. To those who generously shared their own recipes, zero-waste ideas, and homegrown ingredients, your contributions were the soul of this book. I am truly inspired by your commitment to permaculture, food forestry, and the garden-to-table ethos. Throughout the process of shaping this cookbook, you became my heroes.

For me, this book is more than just a collection of recipes—it's the fingerprint of a community committed to nurturing not only the land but also the relationships which keep us nourished. This experience has been transformative for me in so many ways. I am deeply humbled by the support, love, and wisdom that you have all brought to this project. From the bottom of my heart, thank you for being a part of this shared, ancestral journey.

Sincerely,
Amanda ("Mama Manda")

CONTRIBUTORS

Melanie Adams
OnOurOwnHomestead.com
Hastings, FL

April C. Ruth
Bradenton, FL

Sebastien Goodman
Jupiter, FL

Angela Holmes
Jupiter, FL

Kimberly Nieves
Winter Springs, FL

Tanja Vidovic
Floyd, VA

Carly Reo
Stuart, FL

Michelle Ott
St. Petersburg, FL

Kami Conklin
Mount Dora, FL

Javiera Correa
Jupiter, FL

Cassandra Lyle
Jupiter, FL

Jenn Rivera
Debary, FL

Jan and Time Letzring
Port Orange, FL

Leslie Highsmith
Tampa, FL

David Stack
Stack's Urban Harvest
Oakland Park

Niquelle Averkamp
Loxahatchee Groves, FL

Ana Anabella
Jupiter, FL

Tina Warren
Orange Park, FL

Kacie Wasserman
Jupiter, FL

Vivian Tiegen
Jupiter, FL

Rachel Hardy
Indianapolis, IN

Angela Foldi
Hastings, FL

Adina Benitez
Naples, FL

Rebecca Grohall
Fellsmere, FL

Elyse Schwartz
Palm Beach Gardens, FL

Jessica Clardy
Jacksonville, FL

Michele Farkas
Boyton Beach, FL

Sue-Ann Cowan
Jupiter, FL

James Pike
Jupiter, FL

Michael Neimes
Jacksonville, FL

Ana Lozada
Jupiter, FL

Susan Cecilia
Jupiter, FL

PoShan Wong Rabade
Miami Springs, FL

Marilyn Munoz
Jupiter, FL

Ellen Morris
Hobe Sound, FL

Nicole Romero
Rosemaryandaloe.com
Palm Beach Gardens, FL

Pam Miller
Jupiter, FL

Ana Anabella
Jupiter, FL

Cecilia Kathy
Weston, FL

Nicole Rawley
Myakka City, FL

Kumari Kelly and Hope
Skinner
Pigeon Pea Project
Blue Kitchen, Inc
Winter Park, FL

Vanessa Harvey
Port St. Lucie, FL

Lis Iswari
Ocean Breeze, FL

Liztere Fiol
Tampa, FL

Molly Trapuzzano
Cocoa, FL

Amy Friedrichs
Palm City, FL

Susan Hahn
Boca Raton, FL

Kelly Walker
Jupiter, FL

Elizabeth Collado
West Palm Beach, FL

Cori Campbell
Wimauma, FL

Robyn Lieberman
Tequesta, FL

Susan Jeck
Cocoa, FL

Wendy Geller
Chuluota, FL

Jay Reynolds
Bokeelia, FL

Myrelie Colon
Miami, FL

Catina Davidson
Titusville, FL

Mary Jo Sharp
Osteen, FL

Adrian Avedisian
Coconut Creek, FL

Michaelle Rodriguez
Ft. Pierce, FL

Michelle Manfredi Hall
Yacht Charter Broker
Www.worldwideboat.com
Jupiter, FL

Ally Sauber
Jupiter Farms, FL

Samantha (and Emily) Gestal
Palm Beach Gardens, FL

Jessie Bastos
Davie, FL

Ana Martinez
Jupiter, FL

Kerrie Williams
Lake Worth, FL

Alissa Zemering, ATR,
LCAT
www.masteringtheartof
aging.com
Palm Beach, FL

Tony Fraser
Maryborough, QLD,
Australia

George Lambert
Jupiter, FL

Terry Lastella
Jupiter, FL

Priya Vardheesh
(Sripriya Varadheeswaran)
The Healing Forest
www.ojhus.com
Ft. Pierce, FL

Jan Comos
West Palm Beach, FL

Natalie McAlhany
Rocking Chair Homestead
Vero Beach, FL

Char Magnifico
Vero Beach, FL

Tina Tolle
Beverly Hills, FL

Ellen Morris
SunshineLens.com
Hobe Sound, FL

Adrienne Cizek
Hollywood, FL

Robyn Lieberman
Tequesta FL

Lonnie Reid
The Reid Farm
Deland, FL

Kathleen Gibson-Dee
Lotus Wood, LLC
Terra Ceia, FL

Tammie Ferguson
Bartow, FL

Aliris Loperena
Tampa, FL

Brandy Maldoon
Jupiter Farms, FL

Ken Stevens
Jupiter Farms, FL

Laura Wortzel
West Palm Beach, FL

Sarah Kniffin
Jupiter, FL

Brielle Murch
Everything Earth Tribe
Boca Raton, FL

Holly Worth
Jupiter, FL

Lisa Russo
Leaves for Life: Tropical Teas
for Health and Well-Being
Englewood, FL

Nancy Brackett
Sanford, FL

Corinna Britten
Boca Raton, FL
Rebecca Schiebel
Delray Beach, FL

Elana Smith
Jupiter, FL
www.oneworld-zerowaste.com

Chunxiao Zhang
"Seven"
Jupiter, FL

Jack Sandquist
Jupiter, FL
urbanabundance.com

Lea Kulas
Clearwater, FL
southernbiophilliacurban
farm.com

Sharah Macklin
Palm Beach Gardens, FL

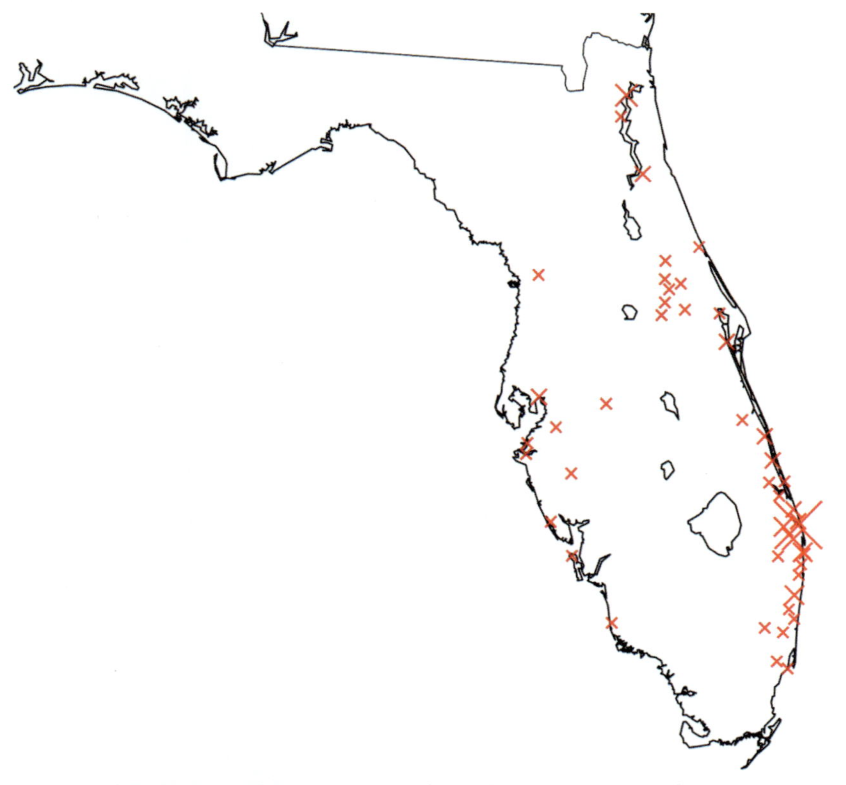

Figure 1. Florida Contributors. Size of X indicates density of participation.
NOTE: NW contribution limited due to hurricane season impacts.

FROM VISION TO TABLE: GROW, PLAN, COOK

WHY HAVE A FOOD FOREST COOKBOOK?
Health, Wealth and Happiness

We all deserve to live our best life. Health and happiness are not obscure luxuries meant only for a select few. If you're like me, joy comes naturally when you're gathered with loved ones, sharing stories and laughter over a table of wholesome, flavorful food. This ritual of enjoying abundant, nourishing meals together represents a cherished tradition, embodying the "good life" many crave. Yet, for most, a home-cooked meal made with homegrown ingredients—and the health it brings—is increasingly rare. This cookbook serves as a back-to-basics manifesto for garden-to-table living.

The perennial plants I've included in this book come together in layers to create a yard so lush it resembles Eden—where fruits, vegetables, seeds, and nuts naturally flow into your kitchen, just waiting to be enjoyed. With Florida's abundant rain and sunshine, food grows year-round in this layered *food forest* through the *permaculture* style of gardening. This approach to food cultivation is gaining popularity because it works *with* nature rather than *against* it. As you grow the *perennial* plants for the 400 recipes in this book, your food forest will serve as a calming oasis amid the chaos of modern life.

Plants Featured in This Cookbook

Avocado	Guava	Oak
Banana	Jackfruit	Papaya
Blue Butterfly Pea	Katuk	Pigeon Pea
Chaya	Mango	Seminole Pumpkin
Coconut	Money Tree	Sweet Potato
Cocoplum	Moringa	Tropical Almond
Coffee	Mulberry	

These 20 plants are ones that grow quickly and easily. They yield abundantly while costing very little to acquire. No pesticides, herbicides, or chemical fertilizers are needed to get these plants to produce.

I live in South Florida, and while many of the 20 plants in this cookbook thrive throughout Florida, some require Zone 10 or higher. Each plant profile includes substitutes for a wider gardening zone (see lower left section). If a plant grows well indoors, I note it in the *Other Uses* section. Many tropical edibles have dwarf varieties that thrive near a south-facing window or hydroponics. I've even grown some, like katuk, in my living-room fish tank as an aquaponic shortcut.

Take jackfruit, for example—some varieties have seeds with up to three times the protein of wheat, making them an excellent base for flavorful bread. When minced, they resemble rice in both texture and taste. Roasted, they take on a nutty, popcorn-like crunch. They are so versatile!

Cultivating Abundance

My family is my world—just as I'm sure yours is to you—I want my family to be healthy and happy. Unfortunately, the American standard-of-living and scarcity mindset has imposed upon us a constant "busy-ness." Health and savings plummet as millions of us eat low-quality food on the go, developing expensive illnesses.[1,2,3] In 2022, nearly a million people died due to the standard American diet.[4]

If current trends continue by 2030, three-quarters of Americans will be overweight or obese, and half will have diabetes.[5] Wheat, rice, corn, and cane sugar are limited or entirely omitted from the recipes in this cookbook. These heavily subsidized ingredients dominate global diets, but their overuse has contributed to chronic health issues and environmental degradation.[6,7]

How we spend our money is our greatest power as a populace. Saving money, by growing your own produce and cooking homemade food, means you avoid funding those who profit from a sick society. A food forest is more than just a garden—it's a legacy to pass down to your children. It embodies tradition, values, knowledge, culture, and time-tested recipes. This form of generational wealth strengthens a family by providing the greatest asset possible: health.[8]

Along these lines, land ownership has always been synonymous with inheritable wealth because of the renewable natural resources.[9] Creating a food forest implies acquiring land which inevitably appreciates in today's rapidly populated world. Having crops on that land buffers the family from inflated grocery bills while bolstering the economic value of the landscape. Compared to annuals, perennials in a landscape have a deep root system and accumulate more nutrients over longer periods, benefiting your health more dramatically.

The 20 plants featured for the recipes are *long-lived* perennials. Plant them once, harvest hundreds of times. Many of these plants will be producing for decades. In fact, many will produce well-beyond two or even three lifetimes, saving multiple generations time, effort, and money.

Cooking Up a Business

Simply eating a homegrown meal means you get to know crops intimately. Plant-based trademarks, patents, inventions, and business ventures become natural dinner conversations. In the recipe pages, I list research on patent opportunities and easy business startups. The $ symbol marks recipes that may qualify as cottage food, requiring no license or permit and allowing direct or mail-order sales. Double check the cottage-food laws in your area to meet local criteria. Appendix D lists eco-friendly ideas for packaging cottage foods to sell. Essentially, you can get paid to eat healthier, simply by sharing portions.

Crunchy, crispy food textures are the most popular in America. Two of the most profitable businesses for food manufacturers are cookies and cereal. Both turn inexpensive ingredients into pricey commodities with a long shelf life. For instance, the average American consumes 10 pounds of cereal a year.[10] Similarly, Americans average about 300 cookies per person per year, which translates to about 22 pounds of cookies annually.[11] So if you want to create a cottage food business with homegrown produce, crunchy, crispy goods are the top choices! It's easy to create homegrown, homemade cereal and cookies along with crackers, freeze-dried or dehydrated fruits, nuts, seeds, and veggies. These easy-to-market cottage food products are included in the recipes.

Zero-Waste. Saving money can be as valuable as making money. The top way to save is waste less. Within this cookbook, I aim to show you how to use *every* plant part. This zero-waste approach reduces food waste and offers significant cost savings. Some of the most nutrient-dense parts of a plant are often the very part discarded. For nearly all of the 20 plants I feature, more than one plant part can be eaten (flowers, fruit, roots, bark, leaves, seeds).

Even "garbage" can be wealth generative in a food forest. For instance, through composting, kitchen scraps can regrow food like sweet potatoes and pumpkins. They can also break down into "black gold"—nutrient-dense soil that nourishes crops in the food forest or can be sold as premium fertilizer. Food is the largest contributor to landfills today.[12] A full 90% of America's food-based garbage can be composted into potent natural fertilizer or used for pet and livestock feed. In the plant profile sheets and notes, I outline how to use the plant as a fertilizer and which plants can be fed to animals and how.

Stories, Traditions, and Recipes

Stories and traditions are more than memories—they are a form of wealth, enriching our lives by passing down wisdom, culture, and connection. Kitchens and dining tables are hubs for this kind of bonding, offering hope and life lessons during even the most challenging times. While preparing meals, we learn to share stress-free family time, appreciate ingredients, and strengthen relationships—all while saving money.

In each plant profile, I include storytelling resources to help spark meaningful family dialogue. Stories give us a shared cultural heritage, and across the world, one belief is nearly universal: The "Eden" in our most cherished stories was not a series of raised beds or row crops—it was a forest garden.[13, 14] This aligns with nostalgic ideas of the "good old days," when food was abundant, effortless, and deeply connected to nature. Trees are the backbone of paradise, and for that reason, they take center stage in this cookbook. Layered trees in a forest create cooling shade and nutrient-rich soil, producing fruits, vegetables, nuts, and seeds that are more flavorful and wholesome than anything store-bought.

Because the kitchen is the heart of the home—where birthdays, holidays, and celebrations come to life—I've included "classic dishes" reimagined with food forest ingredients. In Appendix A, you'll find a list of holidays paired with familiar recipes, each given a nourishing, homegrown twist.

Blue Zone Wisdom and Longevity Foods

The way a society treats its children reflects its wisdom. In America, many of our kids are sick. Research shows that regular family meals significantly enhance both mental and physical well-being for all ages, with particularly profound benefits for children.[15, 16] Yet, for most families, home-cooked meals feel like an unattainable luxury. Instead, fast food and sedentary lifestyles have fueled a crisis—childhood obesity is soaring, bringing with it an epidemic of chronic disease, preventable youth deaths, and crushing healthcare costs.[17] Diet-related ill-nesses now account for a staggering portion of the U.S. economy, with healthcare spending nearing 20% of GDP.[18] Families with sick children bear the heaviest burden, facing pro-longed and costly management of chronic conditions.[19]

We can do better and be wiser by looking to "blue zones"—areas of the world where people are living to over 100 disease-free thanks to their food culture and tight-knit life-style.[20] The "fountain of youth," as it turns out, is diet and lifestyle. These cultures have cracked the code. They garden together, cook together and eat meals together, and, as a result, they live longer and are happier. We can do this too!

Although there are numerous pockets of the world that can be considered "blue zones," five have gotten a lot of attention. Coincidentally, these five places are located a similar dis-tance from the equator as Florida. (1) **Okinawa, Japan**; (2) **Nicoya, Costa Rica**; (3) **Ikaria, Greece**; (4) **Loma Linda, California**; and (5) **Sardina, Italy**. This means Floridians can grow what these blue zones grow. The plants I have chosen for this cookbook are common across the blue zones. In Appendix C, I provide design ideas for how to lay out your food forest in thematic blue zone sections.

Similarly, each of recipes in this book are inspired by (*but not limited to*) one of these 5 regional traditions where quality-of-life and longevity are high. Blue zone recipes are easy. They average just six ingredients or fewer and are garden fresh.[20] Based on this inspiration, you will notice three things about the recipes in this book: (1) They are limited to six ingredients, (2) They promote health through a rainbow of phyto-nutrient colors, and (3) Each featured perennial is the bulk of the recipe—A banana recipe is mostly bananas, for instance. My goal is for these simple recipes to come together effortlessly and be easy to memorize, providing the tools we need to push back against the toxic tsunami flooding our families' bodies.[21]

For me, the most important "blue zone" takeaway is: **Eat with loved ones daily from the garden by keeping recipes simple and easy**. Beside each recipe, you will notice

Figure 2. Image of Healthy Mealtime. Left: Robert Pike and grandson harvesting pigeon peas. Middle: Lis Iswari's daughter rolling out dough. Right: Nicole Romero showing papaya use in herbalism.

a flag representing a blue zone region. In my family, we created a themed weekly menu inspired by the blue zones, bringing a touch of global tradition to our meals. Each day draws from a different region known for longevity: *Mediterranean Monday* (Italian dishes from Sardinia), *Taco Tuesday* (Latin American flavors from Nicoya, Costa Rica), *Okinawa Wednesday* (Asian-inspired recipes from Okinawa, Japan), *Thankful Thursday* (Fusion cuisine inspired by Loma Linda, California), and *Fancy Friday* (European flavors from Ikaria, Greece). You'll notice this same order reflected in each recipe section.

This five-day theme keeps meals varied, exciting, and adaptable to our food forest ingredients and preferences. On weekends, I usually make a big stew or finish leftovers, giving me time to harvest and prep food for the week ahead.

ENSURING HARVESTS: FOOD FOREST PLANNING

In a food forest, understanding **macro-, micro-,** and **phytonutrients** is helpful for decreasing for even eliminating certain groceries. When planning out your food forest, it's important to know that you need **calories** to stay *alive* (macronutrients) but you need **vitamins** and **minerals** to stay *disease-free* (micronutrients). If you're sick, you need *medicine* (phytonutrients).

Figure 3. Food Forest Nutrition Pyramid. Macronutrients are the majority of what we eat. Growing macronutrients in a food forest means you can decrease grocery bills.

Many of the crops I've chosen to feature in this book offer all three types of nutrients: macro, micro and phyto, depending on which plant part is harvested or how the plant is prepared.

In the blue zones, the centenarians eat mostly fresh produce. To mirror this, I am listing crops that can easily yield the meal portions blue zones enjoy. For instance, the ideal is to have a food forest that provides the following blue-zone-based, minimum daily amounts for each person in your family:

- **Macronutrients**: ½ cup high-protein beans, 2½ cups of starchy vegetables, and ¼ cup of nuts, seeds, or other fat sources;
- **Micronutrients and Phytonutrients**: 3 cups of cooked greens, herbs, and colorful veggies along with 1½ cups fresh fruit.

Additionally, once you understand a plant's food category (i.e., macro, micro, phyto) and type (e.g., starch, protein, fat), then you can substitute. An unripe, boiled green banana can be a substitute for potato—both are pure starch. Coconut oil can be a substitute for butter—both are types of delicious saturated fat. Pigeon peas can replace soybeans—both are very high protein. Unripe papaya can be a substitute for zucchini or cabbage while semi-ripe papaya can be a substitute for carrots. In the plant profile sheets, I list substitutes and comparable plants to help you make these culinary connections.

Using Natives to Grow Food

Many new gardeners in Florida worry about the sandy soil. Interplanting crops under native tree canopies solves most of the concerns about irrigation, weeding, fertilizing, and more. Native tree root systems prevent erosion, allowing soils to stay moist longer, and the leaves create fertile soil while blocking weeds.

Each plant profile in the cookbook includes native companion plants, with a focus on edible natives to enhance your harvests. Native trees also support beneficial insects, transforming your food forest into a thriving butterfly garden. To highlight their ecological role, I list the number of caterpillars each native plant hosts (in parentheses), as caterpillars are the foundation of an ecosystem.[22] If a crop is a host plant for moths or butterflies, I include a butterfly symbol on the plant profile (top right).

HOW TO USE THIS COOKBOOK
Food as Medicine

Historically, recipes served a *health* purpose. Food combining can help the body absorb nutrients. The Blue Zones have mastered the art of food combining for optimal nutrition. For example, cooking greens helps reduce anti-nutrients like oxalic acid, making nutrients more accessible. In Ikaria, Greece, it's common to squeeze citrus juice over cooked greens—a simple yet powerful practice. The vitamin C enhances plant-based iron absorption in the body. Likewise, soaking dried beans in water overnight, like the Nicoyan Costa Ricans do, helps to remove phytic acid, which can bind up minerals such as calcium. These culinary traditions are nuggets of wisdom I consulted in depth for each of the recipes.

Preventing or even healing disease with nourishing food is time and cost efficient. About 60% of adult Americans have at least one chronic disease, and 40% have two or more.[23] In the U.S., managing disease symptoms (e.g., with medication, appointments, research, and scheduling), seeking accurate diagnosis, and attempting to find adequate treatment are all immensely time-consuming.[23]

Micronutrient deficiencies are often the critical variable in whether or not diseases like cancer develop.[24] Millions of Americans are deficient in critical nutrients like iron, calcium, magnesium, vitamin A, and zinc.[25] When selecting the crops for this cookbook, I prioritized nutrient-rich ones which could address these common American deficiencies. In each plant profile, I list the nutrients each plant offers. If a plant is an "excellent" source of iron, for instance, I put it under the "20%+ DV" category on the plant profile. If it is a "good" source of iron, I put it under the "10%+ DV" category.

Cooking to Sleep Well. Sleep is one of the most important variables in life. In the recipe pages, I mention if a recipe may aid sleep (such as by containing tryptophan or aiding digestion). If you're like me, you want to sleep soundly, and meal choices influence this! Some recipes are tailor-made to decrease our stress levels and allow our bodies to deeply relax. I include this symbol if a recipe may aid sleep: **Z** (as in ZZzzzzz). Across the blue zones,

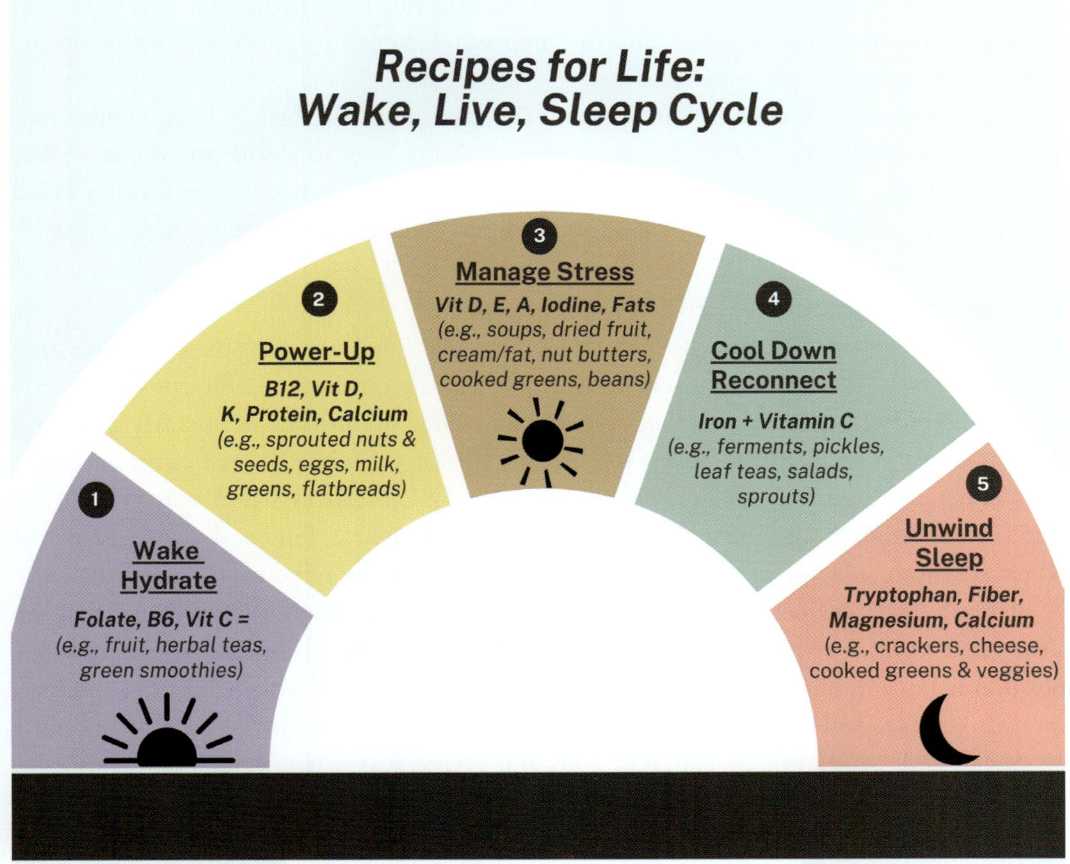

Figure 4. Recipes for Life. Sleep is the foundation of good health. Certain nutrients aid sleep.

certain foods are consumed at specific times of day to aid energy levels and also promote rest.[26] I consulted these trends when creating this cookbook.

Super-Foods: Greens. Who doesn't want to live a long, healthy, happy life? Among those studying longevity, cooked greens are considered the most vital addition to the diet. Cooked greens are called the "elixir of life," restoring virility and providing therapeutic nutrients. Plants that offer both a wheat alternative and a leafy green are a jackpot in efficient food forestry. However, to eat greens every day, you need a mountain of leaves—a tireless resource. For this reason, I offer numerous plant options for bottomless leafy greens and many varied recipes to enjoy them. For those just getting started, tea and soup can be very easy ways to incorporate cooked greens.

Teas and Soup. In life we all look for shortcuts. The easiest way to improve nutrition without increasing calories is to drink tea in between meals. Most tea just takes 5 minutes to make and so I list a tea (or infusion) recipe for every plant in this cookbook. Also, offering tea is cross-culturally a sign of hospitality. You only need a few leaves, flowers, or herbs to create several cups of tea. You can make your own blends with dried fruits, leaves, and even nuts! Mix and match the tea ingredients!

The only difference between soup broth and tea is aroma—broth is typically more savory, while tea leans sweeter. Both are considered caregiver gifts, offering first lines of defense in healing, by providing hydration and essential nutrients. Most viral infections simply need time and fluids to pass,[27] and the high water content supports circulation so the body can maximize its immune response.

The tea and soup recipes in this book offer a simple, low-risk form of kitchen medicine. Simmering and steeping extracts nutrients, making them easier to absorb and digest—a key factor in whether food is truly medicinal. For that reason, broth-based soup is often called "food for the soul," and I include a soup (or porridge) recipe for each plant in this book.

Replacing Groceries: 80/20 Principle

In business there is a concept called the 80/20 principle, meaning that 80% of profits come from just 20% of efforts. The principle can help us figure out how to efficiently get maximum benefits with minimal cost. Let's plan for efficiency in our food forests! My goal with this cookbook is to focus on what will yield the most food with the least effort and time. Most American food is simply a wheat product. Go to a U.S. grocery store and what do you get? Cereal, bread, pasta, pastries, crackers—nearly all are wheat. Find and plant a perennial wheat substitute and you can immediately replace the majority of your groceries. Efficient!

Bread. Bread is one of the most nourishing and versatile foods, appearing in countless shapes and forms. The phrase "give us this day our daily bread" historically referred to flatbread in many cultures. Flatbread is among the most versatile and easiest breads to produce, even in a home garden, and has been a cornerstone of diets across civilizations.[28] Popular foods like pizza crust, tortillas, pancakes, pitas, and even crackers, chips, cakes, and cookies—favorites worldwide—are all forms of flatbread. Even with leavened loaves, many cultures slice bread thinly to create flatbread versions. It's surprising how many foods and dishes are simple variations of a single idea.

You don't need wheat to make bread. Within this cookbook, I provide at least one flatbread recipe per plant. The most basic bread is just flour and water. Flour is just a word for a powder made by drying and then grinding down roots, seeds, nuts, grains or legumes. To make flour, and other bread-related items, I reference three tools repeatedly throughout the cookbook: (1) a **dehydrator**, (2) *high-powered* **blender** (I recommend Vitamix), (3) a **food processor** (I recommend Cuisinart with the spiralizer feature), and (4) **compostable parchment paper** (banana leaves work the best).

Any type of flour can be used to make bread. For the result to be true "bread," though, it must be a protein-carbohydrate balance because this is "sustenance." So if you have a pure starch, to create the balance for bread, you would add a protein (e.g., egg, nuts, protein leaves, or seeds). Using a blender makes this simple—for instance, just purée a boiled green banana with two eggs and pour the batter on a griddle.

Sourdough. Fermented sourdough flatbread recipes are among the oldest known. Just consider this excerpt referenced cross-culturally and even within several distinct religions (Ezekiel 4:9): *"Take thou also unto thee . . . barley, and beans, and lentils, and millet, and fitches, and put them in one vessel, and make thee bread thereof . . ."*

This verse is recommending fermenting a *wide variety* of content. This process melds a spectrum of nutrients and amino acids, helping to provide bread that is a "complete protein." Simply purée your harvest with equal parts water to feed to your sourdough starter: Boiled green banana, cooked sweet potato, soaked pigeon pea or even soaked jackfruit seeds—all are great to feed to a starter. Experiment! Fermentation makes nutrients more bioavailable and more readily absorbable.

Using Flatbread to Create Variety. Flatbread is also an easy stepping stone to other recipes. The difference between flatbread and crackers or chips is just size and moisture level. By toasting and breaking flatbread into pieces, you have a cracker or chip. By adding several eggs (or psyllium husk), you can transform flatbread into buns or muffins. With extra fat (such as from nuts) and sweeteners (like dried fruit) you have a cookie.

Figure 5. Feeding Sourdough. Left: Spent coffee grounds; Middle: Purple sweet potato; Right: Pigeon Pea. STEPS: Soak or boil, purée with equal parts water. Stir thoroughly into starter. Fermentation visible between 4 and 12 hours.

Slice a thin flatbread into strips and you have linguine pasta. Any of the flatbread recipes can become a pizza with a bit of marinara and cheese. Sandwiches have filling between two flatbreads, while tortillas are simply stuffed and folded in half to make tacos. Use the flatbread recipes in this cookbook to the fullest: Stuff them, toast them, or layer them! Layers of flatbread easily become a lasagna or, when sweetened, a "crepe-stack cake."

Creating Your Weekly Menu

I've included hundreds of recipes in this cookbook. You don't need to master or even try them all. Pick which ones excite you the most. The majority of people repeat the same few meals every few days, including the healthiest people.[29] This makes menu planning easy! When creating a menu and harvest schedule, planning out five full days of different meals is often enough to keep it interesting—just a mere 15 recipes!

The people in your family may have different nutritional needs. Kids often need more fat and protein than adults, and women tend to need less protein but more iron than men— up to 4× the iron.[30] To make sure each family member gets enough of what their body is craving, I try to set out a buffet-style meal so loved ones can plate their own portions. By having a few options on the table and empty plates presented, individual family members feel in control. The options can be pretty simple: Chopped fresh or dried fruit, flatbread, cooked beans, sautéed greens, pickles, tea—each person can decide what and how much goes on the plate or in their glass. In Appendix B, you will find a list of easy-to-memorize recipes that can be applied universally across plants so you can keep a stock of ready-to-eat therapeutic foods for your loved ones.

Safety, Symbols, and Dietary Needs

All **recipes are ovo-lacto vegetarian and gluten-free.** On each plant profile, I list anti-nutrients as well as any health cautions. Please review these carefully. Try new foods early in the day with company in case you have a reaction. Many tropical fruits are latex allergens: Banana, papaya, chaya, and even avocado are prime examples. The goal of this book is to boost health, so the safety aspects are as important as the fun aspects. Also, many people may not be aware of an allergen before trying a new food. Making crafts, using plant parts for dye or woodworking allows exposure. If your skin reacts poorly to touching a plant part, investigate further before eating it. The *Other Uses* category provides ideas for crafting especially when engaging young children.

You'll notice a few symbols by the plant profiles and recipe pages. Several I have already mentioned and explained. However, I've listed the symbols below for quick reference:

- *V* indicates a recipe is vegan-friendly;
- *$* indicates a recipe may be a sellable "cottage food";
- *Z* indicates that a recipe may aid sleep (as in ZZzzzzz);
- **Butterfly** symbol indicates the plant is a caterpillar host;
- **Florida peninsula** symbol indicates native status, variety, or cultivar; and
- **Shield colors** relate to safety and skill levels, as shown in Figure 6.

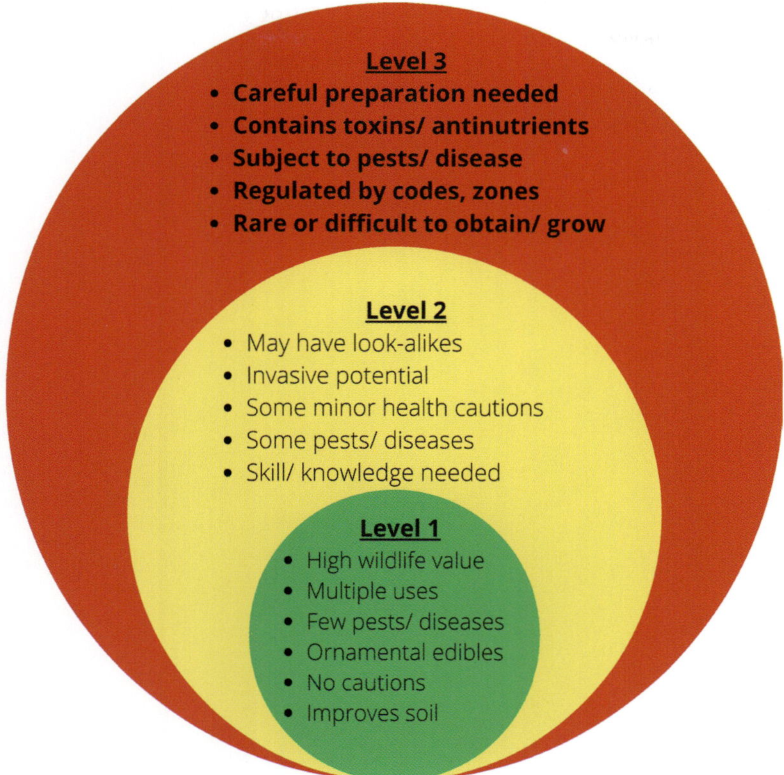

Figure 6. Levels Color Codes *Note:* This color code relates to those established in the book *Transforming Florida Yards: A Regional Food Forest Guide.*

Cooking for Joy and Well-Being

As you dive into the recipes, I sincerely hope you find inspiration. Make your own versions . . . experiment . . . host potlucks! Bringing a neighbor a pie or jar of preserves is as endearing today as it was 100 years ago. There's something magical about sharing nourishing food and laughter—it brightens the world and brings us closer together.

The warmth of community can be nurtured through the simple yet powerful act of sharing food and heartfelt connection. Tea and cracker parties, finger foods with flavorful dips, and charcuterie boards are effortless to set up, and even a young food forest can provide these. Best of all, these dishes can be prepared in advance and served cold, making entertaining both simple and stress-free.

Together, with this cookbook, let's create a life where stepping into the garden means effortlessly harvesting fresh produce and creating nourishment for ourselves and our loved ones. May these recipes be the start of a journey toward lowered grocery bills, boosted well-being, and always having plenty to share. If you need encouragement or have questions: Reach out on my Facebook page, *Transforming Florida Yards*, or Instagram, *@florida_food_forests*.

I can't wait to see your beautiful creations.

400 RECIPES FOR 20 PERENNIAL PLANTS

Avocado
Persea americana
Lauraceae Family

ZONE/ SEASON	SIZE H*W	SUN/ SOIL
9-12/ all yr	30+ft*30+ft dwarf options	full-part/ well-draining

STAPLE CROP INFO
Balanced protein/carb seed & oil in fruit
Edible leaves, seed & fruit
Called "green gold" & "butter pear." Considered the world's healthiest fruit. Seed carb averages 50+% & protein averages 7+%. The pulp yields up to 25% cooking oil similar in nutrition to olive oil - rich in oleic acid. Hypolipidemic effects.

PROPAGATE/ PRUNE	PESTS/DISEASE	WATER/ WIND	LIFESPAN	MAX STAPLE YIELD
Cleft graft/after harvest	scale/rot, scab, anthracnose, Laurel wilt	wet feet kills/ Brittle - block wind	6+yr to fruit; Lives 400+ yrs fast growth rate	Up to 300 fruit per yer

STORYTELLING

A pair of avocados is said to represent a couple, living & growing together, teaching a spiritual lesson about true love. Beauty is not merely physical—the avocado's wrinkled outer skin hides silky, luscious flesh, symbolizing the less visible depths of heart, mind, & soul. Mayans planted avocado trees over loved ones' graves, creating ancestral, cosmological landscapes & sacred forests. Planting avocado orchards mirrors romantic matchmaking, resulting in love's alchemy through proximity, the pairing of A & B types, & the delicate timing of flowers opening & closing. Today, avocados are dubbed a "superfood," & "avocado mania" is sweeping the U.S. As prices soar, debates rage over how many avocado toasts it takes to afford a home. Food choices—driven by convenience & fads—often impact us financially in ways we overlook. For those growing avocados in Florida backyards, free luxury produce awaits! Top-tier Super Bowl & Cinco de Mayo party food! Selling extra avocados is easy—the fruit is ideal for farm-to-market sales, with no processing or packaging required.

HEALTH CAUTIONS	VARIETY & HEALTH	HEALTH FEATURES	20%+ DV NUTRITION	10%+ DV NUTRITION
Latex/ tree-pollen allergen; Unripe = toxic	Mexican(20% oil) Guatemalan(12%) West Indian(5%)	Pulp = Lutein & zeaxanthin (eye health)	Tryptophan (pulp) Vit C, K, Folate (pulp) Fiber (seed)	Potassium (pulp) Vit B2,3,5,6,E (pulp) Magnesium (pulp)

FOOD FOREST PLANNING

- # to Plant/ Spacing: 2+/Plant A+B by season, 15ft apart
- Wildlife Info: Persin (highest in leaf)-toxic for livestock
- Native Companion (host): Oak (395) - wind block
- Comparables: Olive (8-10); Chayote (9-12)
- Notable Varieties: Self-sterile. Cross-pollinate A & B
  - Fall/Winter: Lula(A), Monroe(B), Hall(A), Oro N(B)
  - Spring/Summer: Donnie(A), Brodgon(A/B)
  - Dwarf (Ok for Pots): Wurtz (Summer, A/B)

Ripens off tree. Ripe fruit are slightly soft.

Breakfast, Lunch, & Dinner Entrees

Peak avocado season in Florida is summer-winter. Open an avocado by cutting lengthwise. Twist apart halves. Citrus acid prevents browning (acidulants-1 tbsp per avocado). Prolonged cooking causes pulp bitterness—avoid. Cook at or below 350°F for max of 30 min. Avocado seed nutrients are similar to corn. Anti-nutrients are thermolabile - cooking removes them.

<u>NOTES</u>

Sue-Ann's Stuffed Avocado   Z

Preheat oven to 350°F. Halve 3 avocados & remove seeds. Spoon ½ tbsp marinara into each cavity. Match egg size to seed cavity (e.g., quail, duck). Crack an egg into each half. Sprinkle with salt, pepper, & smoked paprika. Bake 15 min or until whites set. Top with herbs (e.g., rosemary).

To-Go Breakfast "Liquado"   V

Purée until smooth: ½ cup coconut milk, pulp from 2 avocados (2 cups), ½ cup frozen pineapple, ½ cup ripe frozen banana, pinch sea salt, 1 tbsp honey & 2–3 cups water. Makes 5 servings. Packed with anti-inflammatory, digestion & immune-boosting benefits.

Sushi   Z,V

Peel & grate/"rice" 1 cup boiled green banana. Mix with 1 tbsp rice vinegar, ½ tbsp honey & ¼ tsp salt. Toss 2 avocado wedges with 2 tbsp citrus juice & a pinch of salt. Press banana "rice" onto nori using wet fingers. Fill with avocado. Roll tightly. Chill 10 min. Slice with a serrated knife.

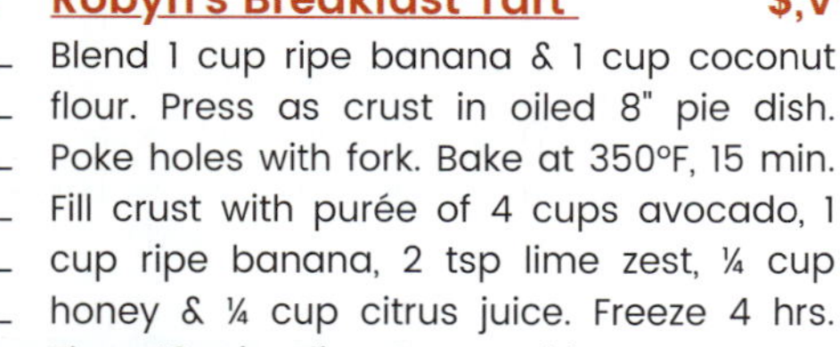

Robyn's Breakfast Tart $,V

Blend 1 cup ripe banana & 1 cup coconut flour. Press as crust in oiled 8" pie dish. Poke holes with fork. Bake at 350°F, 15 min. Fill crust with purée of 4 cups avocado, 1 cup ripe banana, 2 tsp lime zest, ¼ cup honey & ¼ cup citrus juice. Freeze 4 hrs. Thaw 10 min. Slice. Serve cold.

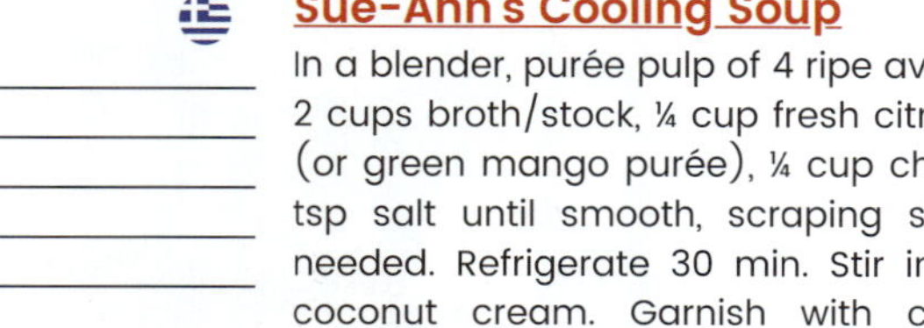

Sue-Ann's Cooling Soup   V

In a blender, purée pulp of 4 ripe avocados, 2 cups broth/stock, ¼ cup fresh citrus juice (or green mango purée), ¼ cup chives & 1 tsp salt until smooth, scraping sides as needed. Refrigerate 30 min. Stir in ¼ cup coconut cream. Garnish with chopped chives.

Appetizers, Snacks, & Sides

Mexican varieties have greater cold resistance (-6°C), followed by Guatemalan & West Indian "races." FL varieties are hybrids. Don't refrigerate when unripe—can cause "watery" texture. Thaw frozen, ripe avocado in 1 cup water with 1 tbsp vinegar to prevent browning. For flour, chop seed, soak 12 hrs, peel off skin, & boil 35+ min. Dry & grind (4 mo shelf life or freeze 6+ mo).

NOTES

Wesley's Deviled Eggs   Z

Hard boil 4 eggs & cut in half. Purée yolks with pulp of 2 avocados, 2 tbsp citrus juice, 2 tsp honey mustard & ⅛ tsp salt. Pipe or spoon into egg whites. If too thick to pipe, add ½ tsp water to thin. Arrange on a platter. Top with chives. *Extra filling can be used as dip or spread.

James & Nancy's Guacamole   V

Toss diced pulp of 4 avocados with 1 tbsp citrus juice, 1 tsp garlic powder, ⅛ tsp salt, 1 tbsp minced onion & 1 tbsp minced basil. Gently mash. Serve with flatbread. *Variation: Press guac into pre-baked pie crust. Top with crumbled queso fresco or feta. Chill 10 min. Slice.

Adriana's Pickled Avocado   Z,V

Mix 2 cups vinegar, 2 cups water, 4 tbsp maple syrup, 1 tbsp salt & 3 tbsp pickling spices. Simmer, stirring until dissolved. Cool. Dice 5 large, ripe but firm avocados into 1-inch cubes & fill 3 quart jars. Pour brine to fully cover avocado. Refrigerate 24 hrs. Serve chilled.

Tina's Goddess Salad   Z,V

Dice 4 avocados. Toss with 1 cup chopped herbs (e.g., dill, cranberry hibiscus, basil) & 2 tbsp toasted nuts (e.g., pine). Drizzle with dressing. To make dressing: Purée pulp of 1 avocado with 1 tbsp basil, ¼ tsp salt & 1 tbsp vinegar, gradually adding ½ cup water until very smooth.

Sourdough Flatbread   Z,$,V

Peel outer husk off 5+ avocado seeds. Chop into ½" cubes. Soak 12 hrs. Strain. Boil 50 min in fresh water. Strain. Purée with equal parts fresh water. (*Optional: Feed to starter 6 hrs.) Mix 1 cup seed purée with 2 eggs. Pour 2 tbsp rounds onto a well-oiled, medium-hot pan. Cook 5 min. Flip. Repeat.

Drinks, Desserts, & Dips

Avocado pulp is soothing to the digestive lining. Mexican avocado leaf & peel tea is valued in folk healing for flu, bronchitis, menstruation pain, diabetes, & rheumatism symptoms. Often compared to widely marketed mate tea, the leaves are also used in rituals & ceremonies, symbolizing physical & spiritual wellness. Other avocado varieties may have higher persin levels, making them less suitable.

NOTES

Lea & Robyn's Ice Cream   V

Purée 3 frozen, diced avocados (3 cups), ¼ cup honey, 3 tbsp citrus juice, ½ cup cold coconut cream & ¼ tsp oil-based peppermint flavoring until smooth. Add 1+ tbsp cold coconut milk as needed to blend. Fold in ¼ cup mini chocolate chips. *Variation: Add 2 tbsp cocoa powder.

Toasted Leaf & Peel Tea $,V

Wash equal parts Mexican avocado tree leaves & peels. Dry in oven at 200ºF until crisp. Toast at 350ºF for 2–3 min until fragrant. Crush. Steep 1 tsp in 1 cup boiling water for 3 min. Anise flavor. Used in folk healing for anti-inflammatory & antimicrobial properties.

Mica & Robyn's Pie $,V

Purée 1 cup coconut flour with 1 cup ripe banana. Press as crust in oiled 8" pie dish. Poke holes & bake at 350ºF, 15 min. Fill with purée of 4 cups avocado, 3 tbsp maple syrup, 1 tsp vanilla powder & 1 cup melted chocolate. Top with banana slices dipped in maple syrup. Chill 4 hrs. Serve cold.

Holly & Sue-Ann's Spread   Z,V

Purée pulp from 4 ripe avocados with 3 tbsp lemon juice, 1 tbsp white miso (or 1 tbsp nutritional yeast & ⅛ tsp salt) & 1 tbsp olive oil. Spread on flatbread. Top with herbs & fresh cracked pepper. *Variation: Omit lemon juice, oil & miso. Use ¼ cup Greek yogurt.

Cold-Press Oil   V

Purée 6 avocados. Spread ¼-inch thick in a clean pan. Place in a warm (95ºF–113ºF) area for 2 days. Stir 2x daily. Scrape dried pulp into cheesecloth & squeeze firmly until no more oil drips (about 6 tbsp). Strain oil. Refrigerate. Use leftover pulp in teas or smoothies. Smoke point: 520ºF.

Other Uses

Blue Zone centenarians average 1½ cups of low-sugar "fruits" daily. Avocados are rich in omega-3 fatty acids & vital nutrients, promoting healthy skin & hair. Year-round harvests are possible with planning. For good production, plant A & B tree types for each fruiting season (winter, spring, summer, fall). "A" types are pollen-receptive in A.M. & shed in P.M., while "B" types shed in A.M. & are receptive in P.M.

<u>**NOTES**</u>

Walking Stick

Choose a 1½–2" thick, 4–5 ft long avocado branch. Dry in shade several wks. Whittle off bark, carving spirals or patterns. Sand smooth. Apply avocado oil with cloth. Let soak 24 hrs. Wipe off excess & reapply as needed for a protective finish. *Variation: Carve a genealogy staff, as used in Genesis.

Sue-Ann's Hair/ Face Mask

Mash ½ overripe avocado (black skin, soft to touch) into a paste. Apply to face or hair. Leave 15–20 min, then rinse with warm water. Rich in fatty acids, vitamins E & C & antioxidants—hydrates & nourishes.

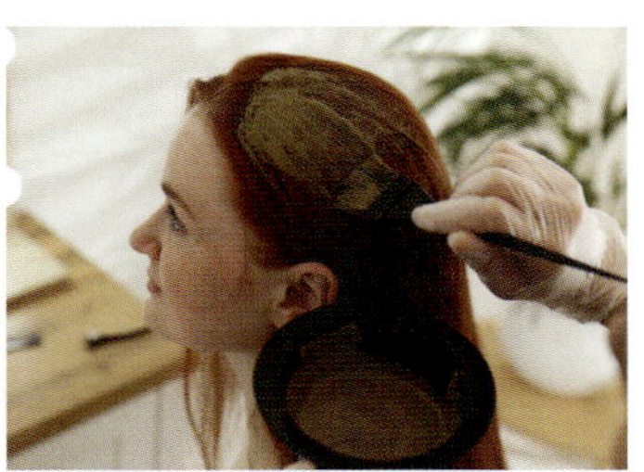

Seed Whittling Craft

Dry several halved avocado seeds at 95°F for 2 days until hard. Peel skin. Carve out center with a whittling or butter knife. Shape into a tiny bowl. Sand smooth. Use to store jewelry, beads, gems & trinkets. *NOTE: Not suitable for liquids or food.

Potpourri

Use 10–15 dried Mexican avocado leaves, known for their subtle anise-like aroma. Oven-dry at 150°F for 2–3 hrs. Place whole or crumbled leaves in small bowls or sachets around home for a natural, earthy scent.

Pink Seed/ Peel Dye

In a stainless steel pot, simmer 3 chopped avocado seeds & peels in 4 cups water for 1 hr. Cool. Strain. Pre-soak natural fabric in high-protein milk (1-hr soak, air-dry, repeat). Simmer fabric in seed liquid 1 hr. Cool. Wring. Rinse. Dry. *Variation: Use as watercolor for painting.

Banana

Musa spp.
Musaceae Family

ZONE/ SEASON	SIZE H*W	SUN/ SOIL
7a-10/ all yr	16ft*6ft dwarf options	60%+ sun/ pH 6-7 (lime)

STAPLE CROP INFO

Pure starch fruit
Edible flower, stem & fruit
Fruit is 80-90% starch unripe. Cooked like potato. The world's 4th most important staple crop. Green banana flour is a gluten-free wheat alternative. Used like "plantain" when unripe. Resistant starch. Low glycemic index. A functional food.

PROPAGATE/ PRUNE	PESTS/DISEASE	WATER/ WIND	LIFESPAN	MAX STAPLE YIELD
Sword suckers/ Divide in winter	Beetles, weevils, aphids/ Fungus, viruses, wilt,	brief flood- ok; mulch 3-6"/ shelter from wind	1-2 yrs to fruit; lives 25+ yrs fast growth rate	15k lbs per yr/ acre; 500 plants per acre

STORYTELLING

Shaped like the growing crescent moon & as yellow as the sun, bananas symbolize divine generosity—an abundance bestowed day & night. Described in religious texts as integral to a paradise of "layered trees," the reward & blessing of plentiful fruits prevent a life of toil & labor. Rich in potassium, the "salt of intelligence," bananas are considered brain food. Smart couples ready to marry & start a family know pregnancy & childbirth mean hungry mouths. That's why many cultures create wedding arches with gifted banana trees. Bananas are an ideal baby food! They also replace potatoes, oil, egg, & sugar in many recipes, creating healthy culinary options. Similarly, savvy warm-weather farmers grow bananas over potatoes. Above-ground starches avoid the destruction caused by tilling—no more back-breaking digging! Growing your own bananas takes a stand for social justice to prevent banana mafias!

HEALTH CAUTIONS	VARIETY & HEALTH	HEALTH FEATURES	20%+ DV NUTRITION	10%+ DV NUTRITION
Tannin in unripe-boil 15 min; latex	Overripe = tyramine/ migraine trigger	Ripe bananas eaten for dry cough, & ulcers	Fiber (blossom, peel) Vit B6 (ripe, peel) Vit K, Potassium (green)	Copper (unripe) Magnesium (unripe) Vit A & C (ripe)

Cook (e.g., boil) to eat green. Hang to ripen.

FOOD FOREST PLANNING

- **# to Plant/ Spacing:** 10+/ clumps of 3 pups 6ft apart
- **Wildlife Info:** Harvest when plump & green to protect
- **Native Companion (host):** Seagrape (15) =windbreak
- **Comparables:** Cassava (8-11), Mamoncillo (9-12)
- **Notable Varieties:** 1000s of varieties, sizes, & fruit color
  - **Cold Hardy:** Orinoco, Rajapuri, Blue Java
  - **Dwarf (8ft):** Dwarf Red, Rajapuri
  - **Disease-Resistant:** FHIA01-03, Apple, Mysore

Breakfast, Lunch, & Dinner Entrees

In Florida, peak banana season is spring-fall. In the recipes, "green banana" & "plantain" are interchangeable. Magnesium & resistant starch in unripe bananas aid sleep. To cook green banana, cut off peel ends. Make a slit along the peel's length. Then microwave for 7 min or boil 15 min to leach tannins. Drain, cool, & peel. For flour: Dry at 140°F (60°C) for 12 hrs. Grind into flour & store airtight.

NOTES
____
____
____
____
____
____
____

Wes' Gnocci — Z,$,V

Whip 5 peeled green bananas (boiled 15 min) in a food processor until a ball forms. If too sticky, chill 30 min. Form tiny balls. Roll down a fork to imprint. Toast in oven at 400°F for 5–10 min until browned. Mix with sun-dried tomatoes in oil & Pecorino (or tofu). Drizzle with sweet balsamic.

Tortillas — Z,$,V

Boil green bananas with a slit in the peel & ends cut off for 15 min. Drain. Peel. Cool. Whip in a food processor until a ball forms. If too sticky, refrigerate 30 min. Form small balls, press into tortillas & cook on a medium-hot griddle 5 min per side or until browned. Top with favorites.

Tammie's "Fried Rice" — Z,$

Grate 2½ cups boiled, peeled green banana. Mix with 1 tbsp soy sauce, ¼ cup pre-boiled peas & ¼ cup chopped chives. Scramble 1 egg in ½ tbsp oil. Chop. Slide egg & oil onto the "rice." Gently mix. *NOTE: Dried "rice" is sellable.

James' Latke Waffles — $,V

Mix 4 cups grated, boiled, peeled green banana with 3 eggs, 1 tsp salt & 3 tbsp melted oil. Spoon onto an oiled griddle & press as waffle. *Variation: Whip batter in food processor, chill 30 min & drop spoonfuls into hot broth as "matzo balls." Simmer gently 15 min.

Susie & Holly's Breakfast Bites

In a high-speed blender, purée 4 cups ripe banana with 6 eggs, ¼ tsp nutmeg & ¼ tsp salt. Pour into an oiled 8" square pan. Top with ½ cup crushed nuts. Bake at 350°F for 1 hr until firm. Cool. Slice. Drizzle with honey. *Variation: Pour 2 tbsp batter on oiled, medium-hot pan as pancakes.

Appetizers, Snacks, & Sides

Wash banana peel thoroughly before use. The peel is rich in antioxidants & dopamine, aiding sleep. The banana stem's pure white inner core & male florets are also edible & can be added to pickle recipes. For florets, remove paper-like covers (calyx) & match-like center thread (pistil). For "mints," dehydrate 2 tsp rounds of 1 cup ripe banana puréed with 1 tsp peppermint.

NOTES

Char's "Potato" Salad   Z,V

Chop 4 cups boiled (15 min), peeled green banana into ½" cubes. Toss with 1 tsp salt, ½ cup vinaigrette & 1½ cups washed, minced mixed herbs (e.g., basil, chives, society garlic, mint, longevity spinach, aibika).

Michael's Mashed "Potatoes"   Z

Purée 2 large boiled (15 min), peeled green bananas with 2 tbsp butter, ⅓ cup milk & ⅓ cup sour cream. Add salt to taste. Top with chopped herbs of choice (e.g., oregano, chives, cilantro). *Variation: Purée with 1 cup milk for soup.

Banana Floret Curry   V

Peel flower layers. For each floret, discard the hard pistil & calyx. Chop banana flower heart. Blanch heart & florets in boiling water 5 min. Drain. Sauté 10 min in Japanese BBQ sauce. *Option: Serve on bao bun (e.g., Puree 1 cup green banana, 2 eggs. Form 2-tbsp rounds. Steam in microwave 1-2 min.)

Kerrie's "Bacon"   Z,$,V

Wash 3 yellow-speckled bananas. Peel. Tear peels into strips. Scrape off white layer with spoon. Marinate 20+ min in 2 tbsp soy sauce, 1 tsp ground cumin & ½ tbsp maple syrup. Spritz with oil. Broil or toast 10 min until crisp. Cool 5 min on rack. *Variation: Shred peel & prepare "pulled pork" style.

Sebastien's Fries   Z,V

Slice 10 boiled, peeled green bananas into wedges. Toss with a drizzle of oil. Sprinkle with sea salt & mix in ¼ cup chopped Cuban oregano & rosemary. Broil 20 min on an oiled cookie sheet, flipping after 10 min. Finish with a squeeze of lemon or lime. Serve with condiment of choice.

Drinks, Desserts, & Dips

½ banana replaces 1 egg in recipes—an effective binder! Replace 1 cup oil with ½ cup ripe banana purée—it retains moisture! As bananas ripen, fiber, vitamins & minerals decrease, but overripe bananas work as a sugar substitute. Replace 1 cup sugar with 1 cup puréed banana. For a marshmallow substitute, cut barely ripe bananas into cubes, skewer & toast over a flame or grill.

NOTES

Wesley's "Ice Cream" — V

In a high-speed blender, purée 4 cups peeled, frozen, very ripe bananas with 1 cup frozen berries (e.g., mulberries, Mysore raspberries or blueberries) covered with full-fat nut milk. Serve immediately. *Variation: Use a Yonanas machine. Omit milk. Alternate berries & bananas.

James' Baked Banana Liquado — V

Peel 10 large bananas. Place in a pan. Top with 3 tbsp melted coconut oil & 3 tsp cinnamon. Bake at 350°F for 30 min. *Variation: For a smoothie, purée 1 cup baked banana (cold), ½ cup frozen avocado, 2 tbsp cacao, 2 tbsp mint & cold nut milk to the 3-cup mark on blender.

Susie's Sleepy-time Tea — Z,$,V

Slice a very ripe banana (peel included) into thin pieces, discarding ends. Place in a pan with 2 ginger slices & 2 cups water. Bring to a boil, turn off heat, cover & steep 5 min. Strain, dilute & sweeten to taste. *Optional: Add 1 tbsp chopped banana leaf for extra nutrients.

FL Cranberry Sauce/Jam — V

Simmer, stirring 1 cup chopped roselle calyces in ½ cup juice (e.g., orange, passionfruit) for 10 min until softened. Add 3 cups puréed ripe banana, ½ tsp orange zest, 1 tbsp maple syrup & 2 tsp pumpkin pie spice. Simmer 5 min. *Variation: Add ½ tsp agar. Pour into crust as pie.

Natalie & Wesley's Muffins — $,V

Purée 5 cups ripe banana, 1 cup nut butter, 2 tsp vanilla, ½ tsp salt & ¼ cup cocoa powder. Pour into an oiled cupcake mold. Bake at 350°F for 35 min. *Variation: Add icing—pipe purée of 1 cup ripe banana & ¼ cup melted chocolate.

Other Uses

Bananas grow as houseplants! Leaves are rich in antioxidants & used for weaving baskets, mats & even wound bandages due to their cooling sensation & ability to repel germs & microbes. The peel is high in antioxidants, antibacterial & antibiotic compounds, & has astringent properties. Fertilize plants with potash to boost potassium. Mashed banana with honey, frozen, makes a soothing throat lozenge.

NOTES

Fodder
Banana leaves are beneficial fodder for goats, sheep, cattle, rabbits & chickens. They supplement feed. Rich in nutrients & fiber, banana leaves aid digestion but should be given in moderation. For smaller animals, tear or chop large leaves.

Parchment, Container & Wrap
Clean & trim banana leaf. Fold or roll to form containers. Use the midrib (central vein) as toothpicks to secure shapes. Rich in antioxidants that help preserve food. Excellent nonstick parchment paper! Also used as a wound bandage (e.g., for burns). Aids healing.

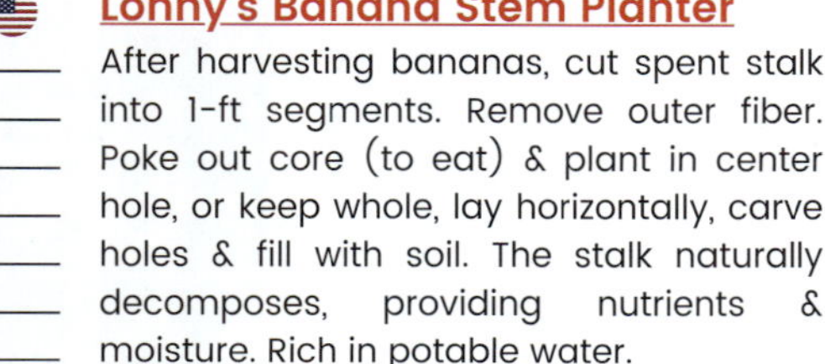

Banana Blossom & Peel Dye
Peel sturdy outer petals of banana flower, cover with water & boil 60 min to extract black dye. Banana peels can be used similarly, but color varies by banana type (red, purple, blue or black).

Lonny's Banana Stem Planter
After harvesting bananas, cut spent stalk into 1-ft segments. Remove outer fiber. Poke out core (to eat) & plant in center hole, or keep whole, lay horizontally, carve holes & fill with soil. The stalk naturally decomposes, providing nutrients & moisture. Rich in potable water.

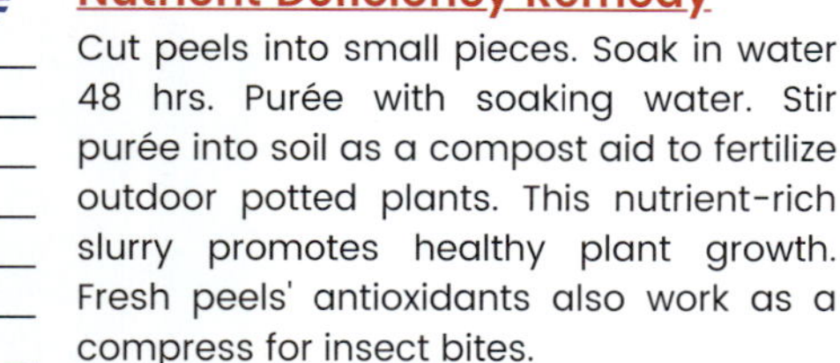

Nutrient Deficiency Remedy
Cut peels into small pieces. Soak in water 48 hrs. Purée with soaking water. Stir purée into soil as a compost aid to fertilize outdoor potted plants. This nutrient-rich slurry promotes healthy plant growth. Fresh peels' antioxidants also work as a compress for insect bites.

Butterfly Pea

Clitoria ternatea
Fabaceae Family

ZONE/ SEASON	SIZE H*W	SUN/ SOIL
9b-12/	8ft*1ft	60%+ sun
all yr	cover crop	any, clay-ok

STAPLE CROP INFO

Protein in seed
Edible flower, leaves, shoots, pods & seed
High protein, gourmet flowers, leaves, & pods. White & light blue flowers highest in protein (18%). Seed meal contains up to 50% protein & 10% oil. Rich in fiber. Leaves are up to 20% protein. Rich in bioactive compounds useful in pharmaceuticals.

PROPAGATE/ PRUNE	PESTS/DISEASE	WATER/ WIND	LIFESPAN	MAX STAPLE YIELD
Scarify seed/ Divide-fall	acorn weevil/ wilt, canker, rot	drought tolerant/ wind tolerant	90 days to flower; lives 5 yrs; fast growth rate	2k lbs yrly plant matter per acre; root-seed

STORYTELLING

After food, shelter, & love, stories are what we crave most in life. Origin stories tend to be a crowd pleasing favorite! Blue butterfly pea tea is like a time-traveling storyteller, its deep blue essence encapsulating the beauty of a heavenly, cerulean sky. Its instant pH, color-changing dye creates a vivid vision of cosmic star births—serene nebula transformations & swirls! Chemistry made visible. Some even cite biodynamic agriculture, linking the planet Venus to butterfly pea's ability to enhance "aura" & graceful aging. Included in many cultures' prayer rituals, this ancient plant is mentioned in all Ayurveda scriptures as 'Aparajita,' meaning "undefeated winner in the battles of life." So named for its power to calm the soul, sharpen the mind, & heal the body. Used for boosting memory, it's likened to a warm hug from ancestors, helping us cultivate wisdom & illustrating Corinthians themes: "bloom where you are planted." Indeed, butterfly pea improves poor soils as a nitrogen fixer & elevates humble food to haute cuisine with rare hues & shapes.

HEALTH CAUTIONS	VARIETY & HEALTH	HEALTH FEATURES	20%+ DV NUTRITION	10%+ DV NUTRITION
Avoid if pregnant; Aids menses. Look-alike=*C. mariana*	7 flower colors; 9 anthocyanins (blue flowers)	Used as brain tonic: mood, memory & sleep	Magnesium (seed) Vit C, A (leaf, flower) Folate (leaf, pod)	Protein (leaf, pod, flower) Calcium (seed, leaf) Magnesium (leaf, pod)

Young pods are easier to digest (#2 on L).

FOOD FOREST PLANNING

- **# to Plant / Spacing:** 20+, plant 1 per sq ft for coverage
- **Wildlife Info:** Bunnies love; catepillar host; ideal fodder
- **Native Companion (host):** Fig (29)-deciduous trellis
- **Comparables:** Lablab (9-11); Alfalfa (4-11)
- **Notable Varieties:** Single & double flowers types for all
  - **Blue/ Violet:** Highest protein
  - **Pink:** Highest content of β-carotene
  - **White:** Used in religious ceremonies

Breakfast, Lunch, & Dinner Entrees

In Florida, peak butterfly pea season is spring-fall. It's a nutrient-dense, easily grown legume. Young shoots, leaves, flowers & tender pods are eaten as vegetables. Considered a functional food, it enhances health & reduces disease risk. Used as an anti-cancer, anti-diabetic, anti-cholesterol, anti-inflammatory, anti-microbial & anti-parasitic herb. Empty bean pods serve as "snow pea" substitutes.

NOTES

Cori's Green "Minestrone"   V

Boil 1 cup diced, peeled green banana for 15 min, 1 cup blue butterfly pods (e.g., 2" young, pliable, seedless) for 10 min & 1 cup blue butterfly leaves for 5 min. Drain all. Rinse & chop. In 1 tbsp oil, sauté ¼ cup diced onion. Add leaves, pods & 4 cups seasoned broth of choice. Simmer 20 min.

Black "Beans"   Z,V

Soak 2 cups deshelled, mature, dried blue butterfly seeds in 4 cups water for 24 hrs. Strain. Rinse. Boil in 6 cups water for 60–90 min or until soft. Turn off heat. Stir in 1 tsp salt, 2 tbsp oil & ¼ cup pineapple juice. *NOTE: Like many beans, these are used in folk healing as a gentle laxative.

Serenity Smoothie   V

Steep 1 cup (about 10) fresh blue butterfly pea flowers in 1 cup hot water for 5 min. Cool. Purée tea with flowers, ¼ cup frozen banana, 1 tbsp coconut cream, ½ tsp cinnamon & ½ tsp ground cardamom. *NOTE: Known for nootropic properties. Used in folk healing to reduce anxiety.

Blue "Rice"   Z,V

Steep 1½ cups butterfly pea flowers in 2 cups hot water for 10 min. Strain. Microwave a green banana/plantain with ends cut off & a slit in the peel for 7 min or until peel blackens. Peel. Grate to "rice" 1 cup. Pour blue butterfly pea tea over the "rice." Simmer 1 min. Steep 30 min. Strain & serve.

St. John's Fiber Crepe Cake $

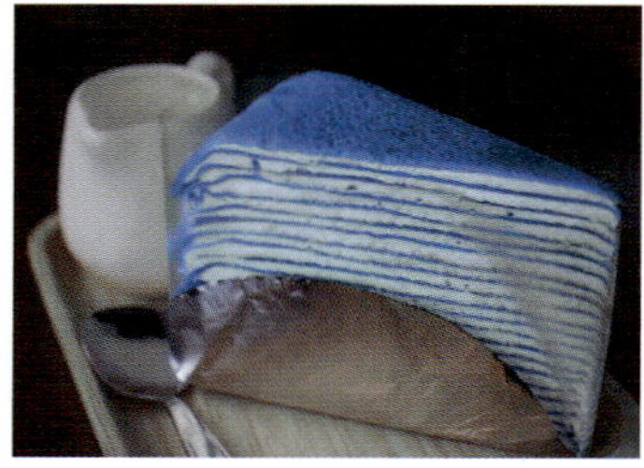

Steep 20 flowers in 2 cups hot water. Strain. Whip 1 cup coconut flour, 1 tbsp psyllium powder, 1 tbsp oil, ½ tsp salt & 1 tbsp honey. Add hot tea (form ball). Roll out circles. Layer with coconut cream. Chill 4 hrs. Dust top with 1 tsp (dry/grind 25) flowers. Slice. Purée spent flowers with syrup to drizzle.

Appetizers, Snacks, & Sides

Western food is mostly white, tan, or brown. Blue- & purple-colored foods are rare in nature & the least commonly eaten. However, this nutrient color is considered "anti-aging." Research shows the 'violet' blue butterfly variant has the highest protein content. Protein is highest in butterfly pea seeds, followed by flowers & leaves. Seed caloric content is 500 cal/100 g.

NOTES

Dyed Eggs   Z

Boil 6 eggs. Peel. Brew tea with 3 cups (30) fresh butterfly pea flowers in 4 cups boiling water. Cool. Add peeled eggs. Soak overnight, turning after a few hrs. Use a slotted spoon to remove eggs. Air dry on a soft towel. *Variation: Add 3 tbsp vinegar for pink eggs.

Kami's Chimichurri   Z,V

Boil 1 cup chopped blue butterfly pea leaves for 5 min. Strain. In a food processor, pulse with 2 minced chili peppers, 2 tbsp oregano, 3 minced garlic cloves & ⅓ cup red wine vinaigrette. Add 1+ tbsp water as needed. *Variation: Add 3 tbsp minced raw cranberry hibiscus leaves.

Mary Jo's Butterfly Curry   V

Boil 1 cup young blue butterfly pea pods (e.g., 2", pliable, seedless) & ½ cup de-stemmed blue butterfly pea leaves 5 min. Drain. Add 1 cup coconut milk, ¼" peeled, grated ginger & ½ tsp salt. Stir in pods & leaves. Simmer 15 min. Cool. *Optional: Garnish with ¼ cup fresh, washed flowers.

Spinach Pinwheels   Z,V

Purée 1 cup cottage cheese, 2 eggs, 1 tsp Italian seasoning & ¼ tsp garlic salt. Spread as rectangle on parchment. Bake at 325°F, 30 min until firm but pliable. Chop & boil 5 cups raw *C. ternatea* leaves 5 min. Squeeze dry. Spread on "flatbread." Roll into log. Slice ¼" thick. Top with Parmesan. Broil 5 min.

Angela's Pea Soup   V

Soak 2 cups shelled green *C. ternatea* peas in 4 cups water overnight. Strain & rinse. Boil for 40 min in 6 cups water. Strain. Purée with 2 garlic cloves, 3 tbsp nutritional yeast, 1 cup water & 1 cup salted broth of choice. Add more water if needed. Garnish with fresh oregano, boiled peas & 1 tsp lemon juice.

Drinks, Desserts, & Dips

Blue flowers are among the most important sources of polyphenols & have strong antioxidant capacity. They bloom from early spring through autumn. To germinate: Soak seeds in 2 oz water & 1 tsp H_2O_2 (household peroxide) for chemical scarification. Leave in liquid until sprouted, refreshing the liquid if a bacterial smell occurs.

Chocolate Chip Cookies $,V

Purée 2 cups cooked blue butterfly "beans" (deshelled, soaked 24 hrs, strained, boiled 90 min) with ½ cup nut butter, 3 tbsp maple syrup, ¼ cup cocoa & ¼ tsp salt. Add 1+ tbsp water as needed to purée. Fold in ⅔ cup chocolate chips. Form drop cookies on oiled pan. Bake at 350°F, 10 min. Cool 5 min.

Mocktail V

Brew ¼ cup dried (or 20 fresh) butterfly pea flowers in 2 cups boiling water for 10 min. Strain & cool. Pour into ice cube molds. Freeze overnight. Muddle 3 mint leaves in a glass. Add blue ice cubes. Pour in ½ cup fizzy water, then ½ cup pineapple juice. Serve with lemon.

Sue-Ann's Butterfly Jello Z,V

Simmer 7½ tsp agar & 1 cup water 3 min. Steep blue tea: 4 cups (40) fresh flowers in 8½ cups hot water 5 min. Strain. Simmer with agar & ¼ cup maple syrup 3 min. Divide into 3: (1) Blue (2) Pink—add 1+ tbsp citrus juice (3) Teal—add ½ cup nut milk. Layer in 10-cup mold. Firm layers 10 min in freezer.

Brain Tonic V

Blend 1 cup wilted blue butterfly pea leaves (3 cups raw, boiled 3 min, strained) with ¼" peeled ginger, 1½ cups water, ½ tbsp honey & 1–2 tbsp coconut yogurt to thicken. Serve chilled over ice. Stir if settling occurs.

Catina's Blue "Love Potion" V

Wash & dry 15 butterfly pea flowers. Remove calyx & stamen. Add flowers & 1 tbsp washed, chopped fresh butterfly pea roots to 750 ml low-acid white wine (e.g., Viognier, Chenin Blanc, Pinot Grigio). Steep 48 hrs in fridge. Strain. *Used in folk healing for menstrual pain (emmenagogue).

Other Uses

Grown as a houseplant! The entire vine is believed to benefit the central nervous system in Ayurveda; roots & seeds are used as a 'nerve tonic,' while flowers, leaves & pods aid sleep. Leaves & flowers boost the immune system. Petal & leaf juice is used as dye, for insect bites & skin problems; to promote hair growth & cover grays; as a pink-eye treatment; a skin/anti-itch wash; & an aid to digestion.

NOTES

Animal Fodder/Ground Cover

Plant scarified seeds ¼" deep every sq ft for full coverage. Harvest in 8–12 wks for hay/silage. Suitable for cattle, sheep, goats & horses. High-protein, easy-to-digest fodder. Summer annual or sub/tropical perennial. Nitrogen fixer & green manure.

Hammered Leaf & Flower Print

Place leaves & flowers between paper or fabric. Hammer firmly & evenly over the entire surface. Pound until pigments release & transfer for a botanical print. Let dry in shade. Rub off any plant matter. Avoid direct light (pigment will fade).

Nicole's Herbal Supplements

Remove calyx & stamen from 100 flowers. Dehydrate at 95°F–113°F. Grind into fine powder in a blender. *Optional: Use 1 mm sieve. Fill capsules (e.g., 50) with an encapsulation device. Store in airtight container, away from direct light. Max 1 per day for 2 wks.

Nematode Repellent

Boil 1 cup chopped roots in 1 gallon water for 15 min. Cool. Strain. Pour over 4x8 ft garden bed or pond. Mosquito & nematode larvicide. Inhibits hatching of up to 93% of eggs. Root extracts are sold commercially in Australia (e.g., Sero-XR).

Butterfly Host Plant

Host plant for the Long-tailed Skipper butterfly: Plant blue butterfly pea in a sunny spot. Provide a trellis. The skipper lays eggs on the leaves & caterpillars feed on the plant. Avoid pesticides to support butterfly growth & transformation. Inspect leaves for eggs before harvesting.

Chaya

Cnidoscolus aconitifolius
Euphorbiaceae Family

ZONE/ SEASON	SIZE H*W	SUN/ SOIL
9b-11/	12ft*12ft	60%+ sun/
all yr	coppice 2ft	pH 6+=low HCN

STAPLE CROP INFO

Protein leaf
Edible leaf
Considered top-tier sustainable protein crop. Protein content (in dried leaf) is up to 30% & is comparable to meat; called "Green Deer." A fierce crop that grows without irrigation or weeding. Guaranteed success. Highly productive investment.

PROPAGATE/ PRUNE	PESTS/DISEASE	WATER/ WIND	LIFESPAN	MAX STAPLE YIELD
cutting-spring/ prune yr round	Mites, white-fly, aphids/ CsCMV	drought - ok/ needs wind break	1+ yrs to harvest; lives 20+ yrs; fast growth rate	5k lbs per yr (dry leaf)/ acre

STORYTELLING

Take after French royalty—have greens at every meal as part of your beauty routine. Chaya's 'superfood' nutritional status has ancient Mayan origins & is believed to help hair & nails grow strong. Mayan grandmothers sang while boiling this tree spinach to time the cooking. Provides up to 3x the nutrients of any other land-based vegetable. Nicknamed 'hospital too far' & is used for health problems like insomnia, anemia & virility. You've got holiday greens covered! Replace collards with fresh, organic chaya for New Year's; fill your Lent & Easter garden with chaya cuttings in spring! In fact, as a perennial evergreen that grows wild, you'll never find an easier row crop. Pest & disease-free. Flowering chaya hedges create organized, ornamental garden lines & perfect living fences. A wall of nutrients in today's food-desert & food-swamp era! Thrives in both arid & rainy regions, full or part sun. Ensures food security despite climate change. As a bonus, this plant is HOA-friendly: no fruit drop & easily pruned to shape! Attracts butterflies with flowers!

HEALTH CAUTIONS	VARIETY & HEALTH	HEALTH FEATURES	20%+ DV NUTRITION	10%+ DV NUTRITION
Raw contains cyanide compound (HCN); latex allergen	Large leaves=part sun; 27-42 mg HCN (in 100g raw)	High in L-arginine = immune health	Calcium, Vit A, C Phosphorus Iron, Potassium	Protein Fiber Vit B1, B2, B3

Edible boiled in steel 15+ min uncovered.

FOOD FOREST PLANNING

- # to Plant/ Spacing: 5+/ plant 5ft apart for leaf yield
- Wildlife Info: White flowers attract butterflies
- Native Companion (host): Live oak (6-10)-alkaline soil
- Comparables (zone):Abikia(8-11); Stinging Nettle(3-10)
- Notable Varieties: Syn *C. chayamansa* (debated)
  - *C. chayamansa*: Maple-like leaves (i.e., Redonda)
  - *Cnidoscolus aconitifolius*: Five-lobe star-like (i.e., Estrella)
  - Picuda: Sets seed, seedlings have stinging hairs

Breakfast, Lunch, & Dinner Entrees

In Florida, peak chaya season is spring-fall. As with stinging nettle, wear gloves to avoid sap/hairs. Toxic raw: Cyanide substances in the leaf bind with B12. Linamarase, the enzyme that removes the cyanide compound, activates best in water. To ensure safety, chop leaves and BOIL UNCOVERED IN A STEEL POT AT LEAST 15 MINUTES IN A WELL-VENTILATED AREA. No aluminum pot (creates toxic broth). Do not hover over pot or breathe steam.

NOTES
____
____
____
____
____
____
____

JC's Chaya Pie   Z

Purée 1 cup each: ripe banana & coconut flour. Form as crust in 8" pie dish. Poke holes. Blind bake for 15 min at 350°F. Fill with 5 cups finely chopped chaya (10 cups raw, boiled 20 min, strained & squeezed dry), 1 cup grated Parmesan, 1 tsp salt & 3 eggs. Bake at 350°F for 50 min.

Nancy's Green Taquito   Z

____
____
____
____
____
____
____

Boil 16 large maple-leaf chaya 15 min. Drain & dry. Use 1 cup mozzarella cheese. Place 1 tbsp in each leaf. Roll as tiny burritos. Place on oiled pan. Spritz with oil & salt. Broil 5 min until crisp. *Variation: Cover parchment with a solid layer of boiled leaves. Top with cheese. Broil 5 min. Roll & slice as pinwheels.

Cori's Bird Nest   Z

____
____
____
____
____
____
____

Boil 5 cups chopped chaya 15 min. Drain & squeeze out liquid. Toss with 1 cup shredded Parmesan. Pack thinly as a crust/nest in 12 oiled muffin cups. Crack 12 eggs, 1 per center of each "nest." Top with 3 chopped garlic cloves & 2 tbsp onion. Spritz with oil & sprinkle with salt. Bake at 350°F, 15–20 min.

Sarah's Creamed Spinach   Z,V

____
____
____
____
____
____
____

Boil 4 cups chopped chaya for 15 min. Drain. Boil 2 cups cashews in 4 cups water for 3 min. Drain. Purée cashews with 3 cups water, 2 tsp salt, 3 tbsp nutritional yeast, 2 tbsp vinegar & 4 garlic cloves. Toss with chaya. Bake in oiled dish at 350°F for 30 min until bubbly.

Brandy's Naked Spanokapitas Z,$

____
____
____
____
____
____
____

Boil 5 cups finely chopped chaya for 15 min. Drain & squeeze out liquid. Mix or pulse with 5 eggs, ½ tsp salt, 2 tsp lemon pepper & ½ cup feta cheese. In well-oiled cast iron, spread & press mixture gently. Bake at 400°F for 30 min. Cut into wedges/triangles.

Appetizers, Snacks, & Sides

Blue zone centenarians average 3 cups of greens & veggies daily. Chaya provides an endless supply & is a treasure chest of vitamins. Far superior to spinach: 78% more protein, 111% more fiber, 100% more iron & 242% more vit C. Boiled chaya improves blood circulation, aids weight loss, lowers cholesterol, stimulates the liver, improves digestion & alleviates constipation.

<u>NOTES</u>

Wesley's "Spinach Pasta"   Z,$,V

Use a pasta cutter to slice jumbo chaya leaves into fettuccini strips or tightly roll leaves & julienne into thin strips. Boil for 15 min. Strain. Sauté for 1 min in oil with a pinch of salt. Toss with marinara, chopped basil & olives. Top with nutritional yeast. *NOTE: Dried "pasta" is sellable.

Cecilia's Spinach Tortilla   Z,$

Purée 1½ cups chaya (boiled for 15 min, strained) with 3 eggs, 1 tsp salt & 1 tbsp chives. Ladle ½ cup purée into oiled pan on medium-high. Tilt pan to coat evenly. Flip when bubbles surface. Cook for 3 min more. Repeat. Makes 4 tortillas. *Variation: Use pasta machine to slice tortilla into fettuccini.

David's "Spinach" Gomae   Z,V

Boil 3 cups chopped chaya for 15 min. Drain & squeeze. Form ½ tbsp balls. In a blender, purée 2 tbsp soy sauce, 2 tbsp vinegar & 2 tbsp sesame oil. Drizzle over balls. Top with sesame seeds & coconut cream (or sour cream). *Variation: Place ball in miso-based broth for soup.

"Spinach" Casserole   Z,V

Sauté ¼ cup mushrooms in oil for 5 min. Purée with 1 cup coconut milk, ¼ tsp salt & ½ cup green banana (boiled for 15 min, peeled). Toss with 4 cups chaya (boiled for 15 min, strained). Bake at 350°F for 50 min. Top with 1½ cups crispy onions. Bake for 5 min more.

Chaya Salad   Z,V

In 2 tbsp oil, sauté for 5 min: ¼ cup chopped onions, 3 cups finely chopped chaya (boiled for 15 min, strained—approx. 6 cups raw), 2 tbsp capers & 2 tbsp raisins. Serve warm. *Variation: Omit raisins & top with pomegranates after sautéing.

Drinks, Desserts, & Dips

Chaya's health benefits have led many to call for commercialized products, mass cultivation & adoption as a horticultural crop. Chaya contains higher nitrogen ($\delta15N$) levels than deer meat, potentially offering greater muscle health benefits. Boiling chaya increases the bioavailability of calcium, phosphorus & iron. Salted water helps preserve calcium & potassium.

NOTES

"Spinach" Pate   Z,V

Boil 5 cups finely chopped chaya for 15 min. Drain & squeeze dry. Purée 1 cup pumpkin seeds with ⅓ cup warm water, 2 tbsp rosemary, 2 tbsp vinegar, 2 cloves garlic & 1 tsp salt. In a food processor, pulse purée with chaya. Serve with crackers.

Pura Vida Tea Slushy   V

Boil 1 cup chopped chaya for 20 min in 2 cups water. Cool in fridge overnight. Strain. Purée the chaya tea with 1 cup frozen, chopped pineapple, 1 tbsp agave syrup & ½ tbsp lime juice (or passionfruit). Rub rim of glass with a slice of lime & salt &/or tajín spice. Pour in slushy mixture. *High in Vit C.

Elizabeth's Energy Balls   Z,$,V

In a food processor, pulse ¼ cup dried minced pumpkin seeds & ¼ tsp salt until coarse flour forms. Add ½ cup pitted, soaked dates, a squeeze of citrus juice, ½ tsp zest & 3 cups chaya (boiled for 15 min, drained & liquid squeezed out, 6 cups raw). Form ½ tbsp balls. Top with minced pumpkin seeds.

Peppermint Pudding   Z,V

Boil 2 cups chopped chaya leaves in 2 cups coconut milk for 25 min. Purée with ½ cup banana & 1 tsp peppermint extract in oil. Cool. Stir in ¼ cup chia seeds. Set in fridge overnight. Top with toasted coconut.

Mint "Float"   Z,V

Boil 2 cups chopped chaya for 25 min in 2 cups coconut milk. Strain. Cool overnight in fridge. Purée with ½ cup chopped, frozen ripe mango, ¼ cup mint leaves & 1" ginger. Top with small dollop of honey-sweetened coconut yogurt frozen as "ice cream." Makes 2 servings.

Other Uses

Chronic malnutrition affects half of all children under five. Everyone in the family should eat greens daily. Craft time can help kids get used to greens. Water from boiling chaya leaves yields a vibrant green dye for textiles & watercolor paint. Cyanotype paper can be used to test hydrogen cyanide levels and ensure safety.

NOTES

Butterfly Garden Hedge
To form a dense hedge or living fence, space chaya cuttings 1½ ft apart. Prune every 6 months to under 4 ft to encourage thick growth & create an effective enclosure. Plant in hedgerows around the home or along walkways. Intercrop with caterpillar host plants (e.g., goldenrod, milkweed).

Chicken Feed
Use freshly boiled or puréed/dried (150+°F, 24 hrs; eliminates hydrogen cyanide to safe level under 0.20 mg/L) chaya leaves as fodder. Significantly boosts chicken health (heart & liver mass, red blood cell count, reduced mortality). Increases egg production & darkens yolks.

Fertilizer
Make compost/mulch with shredded chaya branches & leaves. High in minerals & nitrogen to fertilize demanding vegetable gardens. *NOTE: Cyanogenic glycosides are reportedly NOT absorbed by plants, soil, or water. Must be shredded—branches will root, so no chop & drop!

Pimple Remedy
Chaya stem sap is applied directly to pimples/warts for anti-inflammatory & anti-microbial benefits & proteolytic (protein-digesting) enzymes. Leave on for 5 min, then wash off. *NOTE: Some may be sensitive to the sap. Avoid sap contact with mouth, eyes, genitals, nose, or inner ears.

Nail Strengthener
Boil chaya leaves for 15 min, uncovered. Strain. Dry with ventilation at 150+°F for 12–24 hrs. Grind. Use 1 tsp per 1 cup as a nutritional supplement in citrus-based drinks. Rich in essential amino acids.

Coconut

Cocos nucifera
Arecaceae Family

ZONE/ SEASON	SIZE H*W	SUN/ SOIL
10-12/ all yr	98ft*10ft dwarf options	full-part/ saline- ok

STAPLE CROP INFO

Balanced protein/carb & oil in "meat"
Edible water, sap, root, stem & fruit/seed
The oil offers a true "fat." Solid under 70F like butter (87% saturated). Coconut flour has as much or more protein than wheat, rice or corn. $1/2$ cup of coconut flour offers 8g of protein. One coconut yields $1/2$ cup flour, $1/4$ cup oil, 1 cup cream & 1 cup milk.

PROPAGATE/ PRUNE	PESTS/DISEASE	WATER/ WIND	LIFESPAN	MAX STAPLE YIELD
seed-yr round/ remove dead fronds	beetles, mites/ rot, lethal yellowing	brief flood- ok/ wind break	5+ yrs to fruit; lives up to 100 yrs; fast growth rate	75+ coconuts yrly per tree; 5k per acre

STORYTELLING

Some interpret the coconut's 3 dots as a face—ancestral eyes & mouth blessing the food within. Others see the dots as symbolizing the holy trinity—food for cleansing body, heart, & soul! Still, others dub the coconut a "3-generations tree," providing all necessities for 100 years. Water, flour, oil, sugar, milk, cream, fruit, & vegetables—all from one source! Considered one of the top-10 most useful trees, coconuts make an ideal housewarming gift, baby food & elderly pension. Providing free food to millions, coconut is called "God's chosen tree of life." Root to seed edible. For 1/3rd of the world, coconut holds a higher food status than cow. A heavenly wonder of nature, coconut pre-dates humans, floats across seas to new shores, & grows without aid—as if divinely guided. The coconut market has grown 300% in 20 years. Savvy entrepreneurs make money selling sprouted "Queen's bread," heart-of-palm "millionaire's salads," or simply offering refreshing coconut water from a young coconut.

HEALTH CAUTIONS	VARIETY & HEALTH	HEALTH FEATURES	20%+ DV NUTRITION	10%+ DV NUTRITION
Drupe - rare allergen; falling coconuts kill	No tempeh from meat! Bongkrekic acid (BA) Risk	MCT oil=50% lauric acid; like mother's milk	Copper (meat) Manganese (meat) Fiber (meat, sprout)	Folate (sprout) Potassium (meat) Selenium (meat)

Root to seed edible (at all stages).

FOOD FOREST PLANNING

- # to Plant/ Spacing: 15+/ plant 20ft apart
- Wildlife Info: Invasive risk near flowing waterways **Native**
- Companion(host): Goldenrod (82) - pollinators
- Comparables(zone):Paradise Tree(9-12), Cocoa(10-12)
- Notable Varieties: Over 100 cultivars/ varieties
  - Highest Yield: Malayan Tall - produces up to 80 yrs
  - Dwarf (10-20ft): Fiji, Malayan - bears at 5ft/ 5 yrs
  - Disease-resistant: Maypan - resilient hybrid

Breakfast, Lunch, & Dinner Entrees

In Florida, peak coconut season is summer-fall. About 20 coconuts are needed to make a 5 lb bag of flour. Tools matter! A green coconut hole "puncher" & dried coconut "dehusker" make life easier. Use the dehusker to remove the husk, then tap around the "equator" line with a hammer, rotating until it cracks. To remove the meat, use a scraper or hit the shell with a hammer until it shatters.

NOTES

Bread Sculpture   Z,$,V

Blend 1 cup coconut flour & 1 tbsp psyllium powder. Add ½ tbsp melted coconut oil, 1 tbsp lemon juice, ½ cup ripe banana purée & 1+ tbsp hot water (if needed). Rest 30 min. Form shapes (e.g., crescent, heart, braid, wreath, star). Glaze with jam. Bake at 350°F for 30 min. *Optional: Add 2 eggs.

Sarah's "Ceviche"   Z,V

Open a young coconut. Scoop out 1 cup soft, jelly-like meat with a spoon. Chop. Mix with 2 tbsp chopped red onion, 2 tbsp finely chopped cilantro or culantro & 1 tbsp sliced Everglades/cherry tomatoes. Marinate in ¼ cup lime juice for 30+ min. Sprinkle with salt to taste.

Coconut "Rice"   Z,V

Toast 1 cup full-fat shredded coconut in a dry pan. Simmer covered in 1 cup water, 1 tbsp soy/aminos sauce, 1 tsp grated, peeled ginger, 1 tbsp vinegar & 3 tbsp nutritional yeast for 15 min, stirring until softened & water dissolves. Top with 2 tbsp chopped chives & serve.

Sue-Ann's Ambrosia Salad   V

In a large bowl, gently combine 1 cup coconut flakes, 1 cup cold coconut cream, 1 tbsp honey & 1 cup mixed dried &/or fresh fruit (e.g., pineapple, papaya, raisins, banana, mango, oranges, cherry). Chill 30 min before serving.

Mel & Ellen's "N'Oatmeal"   V

In medium-hot pan, toast ½ cup dry, shredded full-fat coconut. Simmer in ¼ cup full-fat coconut milk, ¼ tsp ground cinnamon & ⅛ tsp salt 10 min. Add purée of ¼ cup coconut milk & ½ cup ripe banana. Simmer 2 min. Top with 2 tsp maple syrup, banana & coconut.

Appetizers, Snacks, & Sides

Nearly every part of the coconut is edible, including the sugar-rich sap of the flowers. Opening a coconut is a treat—the water is rich in electrolytes & combats dehydration from heat & illness. Fermented coconut water turns into a fun jelly, but the real nutrition lies in the meat, sprout & heart. Coconut flour has high liquid absorption (1:1 flour-to-liquid ratio works best).

Vanilla Coconut Biscotti   Z,$,V

Purée 3 cups ripe banana, 2 tbsp maple syrup, 3 cups coconut flour, ½ tsp salt & 1 tsp vanilla until smooth. Bake in oiled 9"x5" loaf pan at 350°F for 50 min or until firm. Cool. Turn out. Slice. Dry on oiled sheet 4 hrs at 170°F. *Variation: Keep mix raw. Coat spoonfuls in melted chocolate as "Mounds."

Marilyn's Millionaire's Salad   Z,V

Cut open a sprouted coconut with a 6" green stalk. Chop the coconut "apple" ball (1 cup). Halve the stalk & pull out the sweet, white core (½ cup). Chop core. Slice & toss with 3 tbsp chives, ¼ cup mixed ripe & unripe mango, ¼ tsp salt & 1 diced avocado.

Ginger "Biscuit" Snaps   Z,$,V

Whip 1 cup coconut flour with ⅔ cup ripe banana, 1 tbsp coconut oil, 1 tbsp molasses (or kuromitsu), 1 tbsp grated ginger & ½ tsp salt. Add 1+ tbsp water if too dry. Form 24 1-tbsp drop cookies & press flat to ¼" thick. Bake 20 min at 350°F. Cool. *Variation: Roll dough in parchment, chill 1 hr, slice cookies.

Coconut "Granola Cereal" $,V

In a food processor, whip 1 cup ripe banana with 1 tbsp cocoa powder, ½ tsp salt, 1 tbsp maple syrup & 1 tsp cinnamon. Pour over 2 cups full-fat shredded coconut. Squish into clumps. Drop clumps onto an oiled sheet. Dry at 170°F for 4 hrs or until crisp.

Jan's Coconut Yogurt   Z,V

Purée 2 cups young coconut "jelly" with 2 tbsp vegan yogurt as a starter. Stir well. Ferment for 7 hrs at 113°F. Optional: Strain with cheesecloth. Refrigerate 12 hrs to thicken to cream cheese consistency. *Variation: Stir in 2 tsp vanilla powder, 2 tbsp honey & a pinch of salt.

Drinks, Desserts, & Dips

A mineral-rich food at any stage of maturity, but mature coconut meat has more protein, fiber, fat & carbohydrates. Harvest all coconuts before hurricanes for safety. Green coconut water eases upset stomachs & morning sickness, while mature coconut water helps ferment dough. Simmer 1 cup coconut milk with ½ tsp agar & ½ tsp vanilla powder for 5 min to make a delightful "panna cotta."

NOTES

Evelyn's "Rice" Pudding   V

Blend 3 eggs, ¼ cup maple syrup, 3½ cups full-fat coconut milk & 1 tsp ground nutmeg. In a 2 qt casserole dish, stir blend with 1½ cups shredded coconut & ½ cup raisins. Set casserole in a baking pan filled with hot water. Bake at 325ºF for 1½ hrs, stirring after 30 min. Top with raisins & nutmeg.

Milk, Flour, Cream, Oil   V

Cover 1½ cups dried, shredded coconut with boiling water for 10 min. Cool 10 min. Purée & strain through cloth. Keep pulp for meal/flour. Let cream rise overnight in fridge. Scoop out cream. To make oil, simmer cream on low to evaporate water. Oil smoke point: 350ºF.

Wesley's Fruit Sandwich   V

Open a sprouted coconut. Using a spoon, pop out the sprouted ball. Slice into disks. Smear two disks with coconut cream. Add sliced fruit to the creamed side of one & form a sandwich by combining the two creamy disks. Cut in halves & secure with skewered berries.

Candied "Apple"   V

Open a coconut once roots have emerged. Use a spoon to pry out the "apple." Wash & dry exterior. Poke a skewer into the base. Paint exterior with melted chocolate & roll in dried shredded coconut. Eat immediately.

Nicole's Coconut "Coffee" $,V

Uproot a young sprouted coconut. Cut off roots, wash & scrub. Chop into ¼-inch pieces. Dry at 200ºF for 1 hour or until crisp. Toast at 350ºF until fragrant. Steep 1 tbsp in 1 cup water or grind. Brew like coffee with a pinch of cardamom & cinnamon. Used for digestion & anti-inflammation.

Other Uses

Sprouted coconuts make a suitable houseplant. Dried husk is an excellent tinder/firestarter & shells are used for charcoal. Husk fibers make strong rope. Palm leaves are woven into roofs, baskets & hats. Sugar is harvested by cutting coconut flower buds before they open to collect sap, which is boiled until it crystallizes. Fresh coconut water is sterile & has been used intravenously.

Elana's "Butter" $,V

Purée 3 cups melted coconut oil with ½ tsp ground turmeric, ¼ cup nutritional yeast & ½ tsp salt. Pour into parchment-lined molds. Refrigerate for 2 hrs. De-mold & wrap in parchment. *Variation: Liquidize dry, shredded full-fat coconut in food processor, scraping sides & puréeing until smooth.

Coconut Face Drawing

Dehusk a dry coconut. Use chalk or charcoal to mark 3 holes as a mouth & 2 eyes. This aligns with many folk stories. Opening the coconut symbolizes opening the mind to spiritual knowledge, growth & enlightenment, unveiling hidden wisdom.

Foot Cream

Melt ½ cup coconut oil & 2 tbsp beeswax in a double boiler. Once melted, remove from heat & add 10 drops peppermint essential oil. Stir well. Pour into a 4 oz mold. Let cool & solidify. De-mold & use as a lotion bar. Apply daily for foot health.

Eco-friendly Plant Pot

Dehusk coconut with a dehusker. Tap along the center of the shell with a hammer to crack open. For soil drainage, poke holes through the 3 "eyes" or leave solid for water-loving plants. Fill with soil & plant seedling.

Butterfly Host Plant

The Monk Skipper butterfly lays eggs on coconut palm leaves. Avoid pruning during egg-laying season (spring-summer). Prune in late fall & avoid disturbing leaf bases where eggs are laid.

Cocoplum

Chrysobalanus icaco
Chrysobalanaceae

ZONE/ SEASON	SIZE H*W	SUN/ SOIL
9b-12b/	6+ft*6+ftft	full-part/
All year	easily shaped	sand - ok

STAPLE CROP INFO

Protein & oil in seeds
Edible fruits, leaves & seeds
A valued medicinal & food. A kitchen garden staple! Seed is 21% oil (14% linoleic & linolenic acids). Protein content of the seeds (31%) is comparable to hemp. Tastes like coconut & plum combined!

PROPAGATE/ PRUNE	PESTS/DISEASE	WATER/ WIND	LIFESPAN	MAX STAPLE YIELD
Tip cutting/ shape in winter	Scales/ sooty mold, canker	brief flood- ok/ wind break	2+ yrs to fruit; lives 50+ yrs moderate growth rate	6k lbs per yr per acre

STORYTELLING

A Florida native that provides critical habitats for wildlife like gopher tortoises, cocoplum is a hurricane-resistant favorite. As an all-in-one plant, it offers fruit, protein-oil nuts, & medicinal leaves—considered ethnopharmacological in research! Cocoplum is an ideal living fence & used for hedges & labyrinths. Traditionally, labyrinths wind inward to a center & are legendary in Greek mythology for protecting children. Cocoplum bushes can be tightly manicured to create this labyrinth experience. The name coco-"plum" ties it to holiday traditions! Fruiting even in the colder months, cocoplum matches the '3 friends in winter' motif in Chinese art (with pines & bamboos). Cocoplum snacks are perfect for sending to lonely loved ones during the holidays. Gift the potted plant or candy the marshmallowy fruit & nuts as "sugar plums"—a treat made famous in 16th-century nursery rhymes, Nutcracker ballets, & the 'Night Before Christmas' story!

HEALTH CAUTIONS	VARIETY & HEALTH	HEALTH FEATURES	20%+ DV NUTRITION	10%+ DV NUTRITION
Look-alike *Eugenia astringens*	Anthocyanin in purple fruit (e.g., Red Tip)	Linoleic & oleic acids in seeds; Leaf=antiobesity	Protein (seeds) Magnesium (seeds) Iron (fruit)	Vit C (fruit) Omega 3s (seed oil) Iron, calcium (seed)

FOOD FOREST PLANNING

- # to Plant/ Spacing: 20+/ plant 5ft apart for fruit
- Wildlife Info: Host plant; Seeds eaten by bird & tortoise
- Native Companion (host): Pine (171)
- Comparables(zone): Muscadine(5-10); Jambu(8-12)
- Notable Varieties: Horizontal = coastal groundcover
  - Horizontal(2-6ft): Largest fruit; pinkish white = ripe
  - Red Tip (25ft): Red on new leaves; purple = ripe
  - Green Tip (25ft): Purple or pinkish white = ripe

Ripe fruit are soft & plump & purple or white.

Breakfast, Lunch, & Dinner Entrees

In Florida, peak cocoplum season is in late spring. Harvest only very ripe fruit, as unripe fruit is astringent. For all recipes, remove the woody shell/husk from seed & pulp. Steps: With scissors, halve cocoplums & pop out edible seeds. Quarter fruit halves & cut the shell off the pulp. 2 cups whole fruit = 1 cup pulp & ¼ cup seeds. Soak seeds for 12 hrs to remove anti-nutrients (e.g., phytic acid).

<u>**NOTES**</u>

Plum & Ricotta Muffin   Z

Purée 1 cup cocoplum pulp, ¼ cup dehusked cocoplum seeds (soaked overnight & strained), 2 tbsp maple syrup, ¼ tsp salt, 2 tsp vanilla extract, ½ cup ricotta & 4 eggs. Bake in lined muffin molds for 25-35 min or until firm in center. *Variation: Add deseeded cocoplum "raisins."

Donut "Rosquillos"   Z,$

In a food processor, purée 1 cup dehusked cocoplum seeds (soaked 12 hrs & strained), ½ cup grated queso seco (or feta), 1 tsp cinnamon & 1 tbsp maple syrup. Add 1+ tbsp water if needed to form a thick batter. Pipe 3" rings & spritz with oil. Bake at 350ºF for 30 min or until crisp.

Sipping Soup   V

Steep covered in 1 ½ cups boiling water for 10 min: 3 sprigs torn basil, 1 tbsp society garlic, 2 bruised lemongrass stalks & ½ tsp turmeric. Strain broth. Purée 1 cup cocoplum pulp, ¼ cup dehusked seeds (soaked 12 hrs & strained) with broth until smooth. Simmer 5 min, stirring in ½ tsp salt.

Breakfast Cobbler $,V

Combine 5 cups cocoplum pulp with ¼ cup maple syrup, ¼ tsp salt, 3 tsp pumpkin pie spice & 2 tbsp coconut oil. Pour into an oiled 8" cast iron pan. Dollop top with purée of: 1 cup cocoplum seeds (soaked 12 hrs, strained) & 1 cup banana. Bake at 350ºF for 50 min.

JC's Stuffed Peppers   Z

Purée 1 cup cocoplum pulp, ¼ cup dehusked cocoplum seeds (soaked overnight & strained), 2 tsp maple syrup & ½ tsp salt until smooth. Add 1+ tbsp water as needed. Stuff sweet peppers, starfruit, or dates. Bake at 350ºF for 25 min. Top with grated cheese & broil for 5 min. Sprinkle with oregano.

Appetizers, Snacks, & Sides

Seeds are economically & medicinally valuable worldwide. Recognized as a functional food, they help prevent degenerative diseases, offering well-documented health benefits. Studies show the fruit contains anti-cancer & anti-diabetic bioactive compounds, and researchers encourage its use in culinary applications.

"Golden Acorn" Cookies — Z,$,V

Purée 1 cup ripe banana, ¼ cup cocoplum pulp, 1 cup dehusked cocoplum seeds (soaked 12 hrs, strained), 1 tsp vanilla, 2 tbsp maple syrup & ½ tsp salt. Fold in ¼ cup cocoplum seeds. Chill 30 min. Form drop cookies on oiled pan & press flat. Bake at 350°F for 30 min.

Salted Paradise Nuts — $,V

Cut 8-10 cups cocoplums in half. Use a butter knife to pop out the seed kernels. Cover with water & soak for 12 hrs. Strain & rinse. Sprinkle kernels with salt, spritz with oil & spread thinly on a baking pan. Dehydrate at 170°F for 2 hrs or until crisp, stirring after 1 hr. Toast at 325°F for 5 min until fragrant.

Pickled Plum "Umboshi" — Z,V

Wash 4 cups cocoplums. Pierce fruit & pit with a knife or skewer to allow water in. Soak for 12 hrs. Drain & rinse. Pat dry. Dissolve 3 tbsp sea salt in 1 quart water. Fill a quart jar with cocoplums & submerge in brine. Ferment for 2 wks, stirring daily. Refrigerate. Like olives.

Marilyn's Fiber Crackers — Z,$

Purée 1 cup dehusked cocoplum seeds (soaked 12 hrs, strained) with ½ cup water, 2 eggs, ½ tsp salt & 1 tbsp fresh oregano. Roll to ⅛ inch thickness between parchment. Bake 20 min at 325°F. Remove top parchment, cut into squares, & poke holes. Bake 30 min until crisp.

"Sugar" Plums — $,V

In a food processor, coarsely combine 1 cup cocoplum pulp, ¼ cup dehusked cocoplum seeds (soaked 12 hrs, strained), ½ cup soaked dates, ¼ tsp salt & 2 tsp cinnamon. Add 1+ tbsp coconut flour if needed to form a stiff dough. Chill. Roll 1-tbsp balls. Sprinkle tops with coconut sugar. Dry 6 hrs at 170°F.

Drinks, Desserts, & Dips

Fruit mass production is limited due to cocoplum's largely unknown value in the U.S. Research shows cocoplum leaves aid in normalizing insulin sensitivity & blood glucose while inhibiting weight gain from a high-fat diet. Seeds can be pressed for oil rich in linoleic & oleic acids, ideal for salad dressings or cosmetics (semi-drying, high saponification, iodine value, thermally unstable).

NOTES

Sebastien's "Apple" Butter   V

Toss 1 cup cocoplum pulp, ¼ cup de-husked cocoplum seeds (soaked overnight & strained) with 1 tbsp oil, ⅓ tsp salt & 2 tsp cinnamon. Sauté on low for 5 min. Puree with 1 ½ tbsp agave & ½ cup water, adding 1+ tbsp more if needed. Refrigerate. Use as a spread.

Cocoplum Hot Sauce   V

Simmer in 1 cup water for 5 min: 1 cup cocoplum pulp, ¼ cup de-husked cocoplum seeds (soaked overnight & strained), ¼ tsp salt & 2 medium-hot chili peppers. Cool. Puree with ½ cup vinegar & 1 tbsp maple syrup. Refrigerate. *Variation: Add ½ cup water for a pourable consistency, like Lizano.

Cocoplum Tea $,V

Rinse 1 cup cocoplum leaves & 5 cups fruit. Cut husk off fruit & seed. Soak seeds for 12 hrs. Strain. Dry leaves, seeds & fruit at 170°F for 3 hrs or until brittle. Pulse coarsely in blender. Steep 1 tsp mix of fruit, seed & leaves in 1 cup boiling water for 5 min. Strain. Used in folk healing for weight loss.

Cocoplum Pudding   V

Simmer in ½ cup water for 8 min: 1 cup cocoplum pulp, ¼ cup dehusked cocoplum seeds (soaked overnight & strained), ½ tsp vanilla extract. Cool. Purée. Add 1+ tbsp water as needed. Purée again with 3 tbsp cocoa powder, 3 tbsp maple syrup & ¼ tsp salt. Top with cream.

Cocoplum Milk/Flour/ Spice $,V

Simmer 2 cups dehusked cocoplum seeds (soaked overnight, strained) in 5 cups water. Cool slightly. Purée. Strain "milk" through cheesecloth. Blend milk with 2 tsp maple syrup & ¼ tsp salt. Dry pulp for spice/flour substitute.

Other Uses

Cocoplum is gaining popularity in home gardens as an ornamental plant, shade tree, or living fence, yet it holds significant untapped economic potential. The fruit is rich in medicinal anthocyanins & polyphenols. In traditional Brazilian medicine, the leaves, bark, & roots are used for inflammation & chronic disease prevention. It offers numerous opportunities for functional foods & natural health products.

NOTES

Topiary Hedge

Space 1.5-2 ft apart for a dense hedge in full sun to partial shade & well-drained, sandy soil. Ensure good air circulation between plants to prevent disease. Water regularly, but avoid waterlogging. Prune regularly to maintain a 3-5 ft height & shape for a uniform look.

Mini Fence/ Seedling Protector

Select 6 limbs, 1" thick & 2 ft long. Push limbs 6" deep into the ground, spaced 4" apart around the seedling. Weave 10 thin, flexible branches (½" thick, 2 ft long) horizontally between upright limbs to form a sturdy barrier.

Black Dye

Carefully peel outer cocoplum bark using a knife or peeler. Chop. Simmer 1 cup bark in 2 cups water for 1 hr. Add 2 tbsp iron vinegar (vinegar soaked with rusty nails) to darken. Strain. Use as watercolor or fabric dye.

Mini Torch

Cut 10 cocoplums in half. Pop out kernels. Skewer on a stick. Dry in the sun for several days. Store in a dry, cool place. When lit, kernels burn for 1-3 min with a steady flame. Seeds are rich in oil, making them flammable.

Butterfly Host Plant

Shoemaker butterfly caterpillars (*Prepona laertes*) feed on new cocoplum leaves. Adults are fast fliers. Males are territorial, attacking blue objects they mistake for rivals. Cocoplum also hosts the Io moth, Packard's white flannel moth, and morning-glory prominent moth.

Coffee

Coffea arabica
Rubiaceae Family

ZONE/ SEASON	SIZE H*W	SUN/ SOIL
10-12/ Nov-Mar	12ft*6ft best kept 6ft	35-65% sun/ well-draining

STAPLE CROP INFO

Balanced protein/carb seeds
Edible fruit, leaves & seed
Spent coffee grounds (SCG) are up to 17% protein, 40+% carbs & 7–15 % oil. A gluten-free & fiber-rich flour. SCG flour boosts antioxidants in baked goods & is called a nutraceutical - protective against chronic inflammation. Light roast best for flour.

PROPAGATE/ PRUNE	PESTS/DISEASE	WATER/ WIND	LIFESPAN	MAX STAPLE YIELD
seed-spring/ winter-trim to 6ft	borers, aphids/ wilt, rot, fungus	keep moist/ give wind break	3+ yrs to fruit; lives 100+ yrs fast growth rate	1lb yrly beans per plant/ 500 per acre

STORYTELLING

Only 3 places in life matter most: your home, work, & sanctuary. Coffee plays a role in each! As a symbol of hospitality, nothing is more traded except oil. Coffee brings people together, fosters a safe haven, & is the beverage of choice even among clergy! This pick-me-up has many benefits. Historically, doctors sent patients to coffee houses to treat health issues like constipation & attention deficit. Over time, coffee houses became "penny universities." Coffee beans are a functional food —rich in amino acids with positive effects on short-term memory. Pay for coffee & get interesting conversation & company free! Tight-knit bonds form over coffee. So do revolutions! France, Berlin, Budapest, & Venice— all used coffee houses to plot. Early Americans switched to coffee to protest British tea taxes. Coffee is political—even today. With wars, disrupted supply chains, & climate change, how will coffee imports fare? You don't need to read coffee grounds to know the future. Grow your own plants & brew your very own cup of joe!

HEALTH CAUTIONS	VARIETY & HEALTH	HEALTH FEATURES	20%+ DV NUTRITION	10%+ DV NUTRITION
Acrylamide-soak out; avoid caf after 12pm	1mg caffeine per lb=ideal max; Unfiltered raises LDL	Vasoconstrictor (bean); anti-inflammatory(leaf)	Vit C (leaves, husk) Magnesium(bean) Vit K (leaf)	Calcium, Iron(leaf) Protein, B3(beans) Potassium (beans)

Ripe fruit are plump & yellow, red or purplish.

FOOD FOREST PLANNING

- # to Plant/ Spacing: 10+/ plant 5ft apart for fruit
- Wildlife Info: Caffeine impacts aquatic ecosystems
- Native Companion (host): Oak (395)
- Comparables (zone): goji (5-10); yerba mate (9-11)
- Notable Varieties: Hybridizes with *Coffea canephora*
  - Yellow/Orange Cherry: Fruitier with honey notes
  - Red/ Purple: Robust flavor with high complexity
  - Dwarf: Caturra

Breakfast, Lunch, & Dinner Entrees

Peak coffee season in Florida is fall-spring. A winter delight! The average household produces over 1 lb of spent coffee grounds monthly. To make flour, steep 1 cup spent grounds in 2 cups boiling water for 30 min. Light roast is best to further decaffeinate & remove bitterness (acrylamide is water-soluble). Strain, rinse in hot water, & dry at 95-120°F for 24 hrs. If needed, finely grind in a high-speed blender. Store in fridge.

NOTES

Breakfast Coffee Cake

Purée 1 cup dry, finely ground SCG flour, 2 tbsp almond butter, ¼ tsp salt, ½ cup full-fat milk, 3 tbsp honey, & 3 eggs until smooth. Add 1+ tbsp water to purée if needed. Oil molds, fill halfway, & microwave mini bundts for 2 min (until firm) or full bundt for 6–8 min. Cool. Serve w/ cheese & jam.

Spinach Tortillas/Quesadillas

Boil 5 cups washed, chopped coffee leaves in 5 cups water for 5 min. Drain. Keep liquid as "green tea." Purée 1½ cups cooked greens, 3 eggs, ¼ tsp salt & 1 tbsp maple syrup. Ladle ½ cup purée on oiled pan over med-low heat. Tilt pan to coat. Cook 3 min each side. Flip. Fold in cheese & melt.

Black Sesame Fiber Crackers Z,$,V

Whip 1 cup dry, finely ground SCG flour, 1 tbsp psyllium powder & 1 tbsp nutritional yeast. Add 1 tbsp soy sauce & 1 cup hot, full-fat nut milk to form a ball. Roll ⅛" thick on parchment. Press w/ 1 tbsp "Everything Bagel" seasoning. Cut shapes. Dry at 170°F for 4 hrs until crisp. Serve w/ tart fruit & tofu.

Cheesy Grits & Extract Tea

Soak 2 cups fresh coffee beans w/ cherry 12 hrs. Strain. Pinch off cherry. Boil 1 cup beans in 4 cups water for 1 hr. Strain (keep liquid as coffee extract). In high-speed blender, purée beans in 2 cups water. Simmer on low 30 min, stirring often. Add ½ tsp salt, 1 tbsp butter, & 2 tbsp cheddar.

Spinach Muffins

Boil 5 cups washed, chopped coffee leaves for 5 min. Strain & squeeze dry. Keep liquid as "green tea." Mix 1½ cups spinach w/ 1½ cups almond flour, 3 tbsp feta, 3 beaten eggs, & ½ cup puréed ripe banana. Spoon into 6 oiled muffin tins. Bake at 350°F for 30 min or until firm. Cool before serving.

Appetizers, Snacks, & Sides

Coffee plants have edible leaves, jasmine-like flowers, & nutritious cherry husks with a citrus flavor! Coffee cherries help lower cholesterol, with 38% more antioxidants than pomegranates, 3x the iron of spinach, & 2x the potassium of bananas. The cherries can be ground into "flour," and the flowers can be dried & brewed into tea. The cherries contain 0.1-0.2% caffeine, about 1/10th of what's in the beans.

NOTES

Baked Cheese & Spinach

Boil 5 cups washed, chopped coffee leaves 5 min. Drain & squeeze dry. Keep liquid as "green tea." Mix spinach w/ 1 cup ricotta, 3 eggs, ⅓ cup Parmesan, ¼ tsp salt, ⅛ tsp pepper & pinch of nutmeg. Pour into oiled dish. Bake at 350°F for 30 min until set & golden. Cool slightly. Serve warm.

Coffee Leaf Liquado   V

Toast 3 tbsp fresh coffee leaves on stove over med heat. Boil 1 cup water & steep leaves for 3 min. Cool. Blend water/leaf combo w/ ¼ cup frozen mango pulp, ¼ cup frozen pineapple, 3 tbsp mint, & ¼ cup coconut cream. Serve cold.

"Matcha" Cookies $,V

Wash & dry 2 cups coffee leaves. Grind to fine powder in blender. Mix 2 tbsp powder w/ ½ cup almond flour, ½ cup puréed ripe banana, 1 tbsp maple syrup, 1 tbsp coconut oil, & 1 tsp vanilla. Form drop cookies & press flat. Bake at 350°F for 30 min until crisp. Cool.

Rebecca's Energy Bars $,V

Purée 1 cup dry, finely ground SCG flour, ½ cup ripe banana, ¼ tsp salt, ½ cup soaked, pitted dates, 1 tsp ground cardamom, & 1 tbsp melted coconut oil. Press into parchment-lined pan. Top w/ tiny chocolate chips. Bake at 350°F for 30 min. Slice. *Variation: Form cookies or "granola."

Spinach Omelette Bites

Boil 5 min 4 cups washed, finely chopped coffee leaves in 4 cups water. Drain & squeeze dry. Keep liquid as "green tea." Mix spinach, ¼ cup feta, 1 tbsp oregano, 3 eggs, & 1 tbsp milk. Heat 1 tbsp oil in pan on med, pour mix, & cook until set. Cut into cubes. Serve w/ toothpicks.

Drinks, Desserts, & Dips

Coffee grows on new shoots. Prune often & make year-round tea from caffeinated coffee leaves. 13mg/g caffeine (young leaves); 7.5mg/g (mature leaves). More caffeine & medicinal chlorogenic acid (CGA) than green tea! Floral taste with health-boosting mangiferin & theobromine. Coffee beans have 5mg caffeine per bean/100mg per cup. Coat roasted beans in chocolate for a treat!

NOTES

Chocolate Coffee Tart

Purée 1 cup dry, finely ground SCG flour, 1 cup soaked dates, & 1 tbsp coconut oil. Press "crust" into oiled 8" pan. Bake at 350ºF for 15 min. Simmer 2 cups brewed coffee & 2 cups milk on low. Mix 4 beaten eggs w/ ½ cup melted chocolate (warm, not hot) & add to simmer for 7 min. Pour into crust. Chill 8 hrs.

Harvested Coffee/ Cold-Brew　$

Harvest ripe coffee cherries. Soak 12 hrs. Pinch off cherry. Dry beans in oven at 170ºF for 1-2 hrs, stirring often. Cool. Pinch off silverskin. Roast at 350ºF for 5+ min until desired color (blonde, medium, dark roast), stirring often. Cool. Grind & brew 1 cup grounds in 4 cups water for 24 hrs in fridge.

Priya's Cascara Tea Jelly

Purée 1 cup fresh coffee cherry pulp w/ 2 cups water, 3 tbsp maple syrup, 2 tbsp lemon juice, & 1½ tsp agar. Pour into saucepan & simmer 5 min. Remove from heat. Pour into jello mold & let set overnight. Caffeinated.

Tina & Aliris' Brownies　$,V

Purée 1½ cups dry, finely ground SCG flour in 1 cup water, ½ cup ripe banana, 2 tbsp maple syrup, ¼ cup almond butter, 2 tsp vanilla, & ½ cup melted chocolate. Bake in oiled 8x8" pan at 350ºF for 30 min. Cool before slicing. *Variation: Omit water. Mix ingredients. Chill 4 hrs. Roll into "truffles."

Marilyn's Cherry Sauce

Soak 4 cups coffee beans overnight. Massage cherry off. Simmer covered on low 10 min: 1½ cups coffee cherries (cascara), ¼ cup water, & 1 tbsp lemon juice. Stir often until cherries are soft. Add more water if needed. Let cool. Blend w/ ¼ cup honey. Serve over fresh ricotta. Garnish w/ mint.

Other Uses

Suitable houseplant! Around 6 million tons of SCGs are generated in the U.S. yearly, with 75% ending up in landfills. Opportunities abound for entrepreneurs. For science lovers: The CYP1A2 gene influences caffeine tolerance. Caffeine, a therapeutic psychoactive drug, can interact with medications & reduce absorption of calcium, iron, & magnesium.

Animal/ Plant Feed

Ensure SCGs are rinsed & dried. Mix w/ animal feed at 10-15% for added nutrients. Cost-effective feed supplement. High C/N ratio. Add to compost piles at 20% of total or spread thin around acid-loving plants (e.g., blueberries) as mulch & slow-release nitrogen.

Solid Biofuel

Press grounds into small cakes or logs in a mold (e.g., muffin tin or pellet press). Dry thoroughly until hard & compact (e.g., in oven at 170°F for 2 hrs). Burn as biofuel. Ensure proper ventilation. Coffee grounds emit more particles than wood/sawdust.

Oyster Mushroom Substrate

Sterilize a liter canning jar & metal lid in oven at 350°F for 15 min. Add 60g spawn to spent grounds in jar. Poke 2 holes in lid & cover with micropore tape. Place in cool, dark place until grounds whiten. Top w/ grounds & repeat. For fruiting, place in indirect light. Replace lid w/ moist cloth.

Seven's Black Licorice Twists Z,$,V

Whip 1 cup dry, finely ground SCG flour & 1 tbsp psyllium powder. Add ½ tsp licorice extract, 1 tbsp melted coconut oil, & 2 tbsp honey. Pour into 1 cup hot water to form a ball. Roll out & cut into strands. Braid into 3-strands. Dry at 170°F for 4 hrs. Used in folk healing for digestive issues & cough.

Body/ Face Scrub

Mix ½ cup dried, spent coffee grounds & ¼ cup coconut oil. Massage onto damp skin to exfoliate. Rinse off. Antioxidants help fight free radicals, protecting against aging & stimulating blood flow for glowing skin.

Guava

Psidium spp.
Myrtaceae family

ZONE/ SEASON	SIZE H*W	SUN/ SOIL
9-12/ all yr	20+ft*20+ft dwarf options	full-part/ well-draining

STAPLE CROP INFO

Balanced protein/carb & oil seeds
Edible fruit, leaves & seeds
Seeds are nearly 30% of fruit weight. Dry seeds are up to 15% protein, 16% oil, & 13% starch. Guava seed oil is similar to sunflower seed. Offers Omega 3 & 6 & linolenic acid. Can bear fruit all year

PROPAGATE/ PRUNE	PESTS/DISEASE	WATER/ WIND	LIFESPAN	MAX STAPLE YIELD
airlayer in spring/ Prune heavily spring	fruit & whiteflies/ fungus	drought tolerant/ provide wind breaks	4+ yrs to fruit; lives 40+ yrs; fast growth rate	20k lbs per acre; 200 trees per acre

STORYTELLING

⅓ of Florida kids are food insecure or malnourished. With so many hungry mouths, what do you call a superfood that grows wild? While some say "an invasive" & offer plant poisons, others see a gift: Free food! Foraging can protect both health & ecosystems. Nicknamed "tropical apple," guava exceeds nearly all other crops in productivity, toughness, & adaptability. Yet, guava legend speaks of paradise turned hell. Long ago, in a land of abundance, colonists arrived seeking fertile soil for a cash crop: Guava. After plowing down natives' food forests & enslaving locals as farmhands, colonists forbade eating their row-crop "apples." A mother, exhausted from fieldwork, lost sight of her youngest, & the hungry child devoured a fruit. Caught red-handed, the child was sentenced to death, but his mother offered herself instead. After her execution, a bird descended, spreading seeds. Guava plants grew freely. The bird dropping guava seed is believed to be the mother ensuring her child & others are forever well-fed. Seed-grown trees fruit longest.

HEALTH CAUTIONS	VARIETY & HEALTH	HEALTH FEATURES	20%+ DV NUTRITION	10%+ DV NUTRITION
2 guavas daily = safe; rich in medicinals	Red fruit = Lycopene & triterpenes	Higher essential minerals than semolina (seed)	Vit C (fruit, peel) Fiber (seeds, fruit) Folate (fruit)	Vit A, Potassium (fruit) Iron, Zinc, Vit E (seeds) Protein (seeds)

FOOD FOREST PLANNING

- # to Plant/ Spacing: 2+/ plant 15ft apart
- Wildlife Info: Hosts 20+ caterpillar species; invasive risk
- Native Companion (host): Goldenrod (82)-pollinators
- Comparables (zone): passionfruit (5-12); apple (3-9)
- Notable Varieties: 140 species/ cultivars
  - *P. guajava* (10+ft): commercial, sweet-tart
  - *P. cattleianum* (6+ft): strawberry-like, cold hardy
  - *P. friedrichsthalianum* (6+ft): acidic, wetter soil

Edible when ripe, aromatic & slightly soft.

Breakfast, Lunch, & Dinner Entrees

Peak guava season in Florida is summer-fall. Ruby Supreme (*P. guajava*) may fruit year-round! Seed flour is easy to digest & nutritious. Phenolic content in seeds increases with baking, roasting, & toasting, while tannins & phytic acid decrease. Seeds contain all amino acids except lysine & offer significant tryptophan—great for bedtime! As a bonus, guava can replace apples in many recipes!

<u>NOTES</u>

Evelyn's "Apple" Roses $,V

Core 10 guavas. Purée 1 cup guava seeds (soaked 24 hrs, strained) & 1 cup ripe banana until fluffy. Pour ½ full into oiled muffin molds. Top w/ spiraled, thinly sliced guava (brushed w/ maple syrup). Bake 30-45 min at 350°F until caramelized.

Grilled Stuffed Guavas   Z

Halve 10 guavas. Scoop out seeds (1 cup). Soak 12 hrs in 2 cups water. Strain & pat dry. Toss in 1 tsp oil, toast 3 min, & grind finely in blender. Brush guava halves w/ oil; grill cut-side down 5 min. Stuff w/ queso fresco or feta. Drizzle 1 tsp honey over each & sprinkle w/ finely ground, toasted seeds.

Breakfast "Soup"   V

Halve 5 medium guavas. Scoop out ½ cup seeds. Soak seeds 12 hrs. Drain & pat dry. Toast in 1 tsp oil for 3 min, then grind finely in blender. Dice cored guavas & 1 avocado. Top w/ coconut milk, 1 tsp maple syrup, & toasted ground seeds.

Kumari's Guava Muffins

Halve 3 medium guavas. Scoop out seeds. Soak seeds 12 hrs. Strain. Purée guava & seeds finely until smooth, adding 1 tbsp+ water as needed. Mix 2 cups purée, 4 eggs, 2 tbsp maple syrup, & ¼ tsp salt. Pour into oiled muffin molds. Bake at 350°F for 30 min. Cool 10 min. Makes 10-12 muffins.

Guava Seed Yogurt   V

Soak seeds from 20 guavas (2 cups) 12 hrs. Drain & rinse. Simmer seeds in equal parts water 10 min. Cool slightly. Purée smooth. Blend again w/ 1 tbsp vegan yogurt. Pour in jar; cover lightly. Ferment at 95°F–113°F for 7-12 hrs. Purée 1 cup guava pulp simmered 5 min w/ ½ tbsp maple syrup for topping.

Appetizers, Snacks, & Sides

Pulp color varies—white, yellow, pink, orange, or red. Vit C content is up to 10x higher than citrus fruits. Fruits are considered ethnopharmaceutical—used in kitchen medicine for diarrhea, throat inflammation, & antibacterial activity. High in ascorbic acid, they aid iron absorption. Sprouted seeds have excellent prebiotic effects. Leaves & fruit can be pickled for on-demand folk healing.

NOTES

"Sun-dried" Guava — $,V

Halve 10 guavas. Deseed. Slice pulp into wedges (~4 cups). Dry 6 hrs at 170°F until leathery. Pack in quart jar w/ 2 tbsp dry mint & 1 dry guava leaf. Cover w/ oil & ½ tsp salt. Refrigerate. *Variation: Pickle (fridge). Cover fresh wedges & herbs in brine (1 cup ea: vinegar/water, 1 tbsp ea: salt/sugar).

Guava Salsa — Z,V

Halve 5 guavas. Scoop out seeds. Cube fruit pulp (~2 cups). Toss w/ ½ tbsp lime juice, ¼ tsp chili powder, a pinch of salt, ¼ cup chopped oregano, & 2 tbsp chopped cilantro. Serve w/ chips, as a side salad, or relish. *Variation: Soak, toast, & finely grind seeds as topping.

Guava Seed Sprouts — Z,V

Soak guava seeds 12 hrs. Drain & rinse. Repeat daily until sprouts are ¼–½ inch (3–7 days). Heat pan over medium. Sauté sprouts w/ a splash of soy sauce & ¼ cup diced onions for 2–3 min. Serve over salads, in wraps, or as a side.

Chutney — Z,V

Halve 3 medium white guavas. Scoop out seeds & soak 24 hrs. Strain & pat dry. Heat 1 tsp oil. Sauté 2 tbsp chopped young, tender guava leaves & soaked seeds. Add guava pulp, ½ cup grated coconut, ½ tsp ginger, 1 green medium-hot chili pepper, & pinch salt. Simmer 20 min. Cool. Purée smooth.

Leslie's Flat Bread — $,Z

Scoop seeds from 10 guavas; rinse & soak for 24 hrs. Strain, rinse, & purée 1 cup seeds w/ 2 eggs & 2 tbsp Parmesan cheese (or Kefalotyri). Add 1+ tbsp water as needed to purée. Ladle 2 tbsp batter onto medium-hot pan. Cook 3–5 min per side until crisp. Top w/ guava purée.

Drinks, Desserts, & Dips

Fruit, leaves, & seeds are considered nutraceuticals. Leaves contain the most phenolic compounds & are used for diabetes, diarrhea, cough, & as an antimicrobial, antiseptic, & antibiotic. Harvest leaves before fruiting season for max antioxidants. Chrysin glucoside & rutin (in fruit) offer anti-inflammatory benefits but, in large amounts, may contribute to photosensitivity.

Guava Ice Cream   V

Halve 5 medium guavas. Scoop out seeds. Dice & freeze pulp. Soak ½ cup seeds for 24 hrs. Strain, rinse, & simmer seeds in ½ cup water for 15 min. Purée seeds w/ water & 3 tbsp melted chocolate. Blend frozen guava pulp, ½ cup coconut cream & ½ cup banana. Form scoops. Top w/ chocolate sauce.

Sue-Ann's Guava Paste   V

Halve 10 medium guavas & scoop out seeds. Soak seeds 24 hrs. Strain. Purée pulp, seeds, ⅛ tsp salt, 1 tbsp coconut sugar, & 1 tsp citrus juice. Add 1+ tbsp water as needed. Simmer on low for 20 min, stirring. Pour into oiled 8 x 8" pan ½" thick. Chill 12 hrs. Delicious w/ queso fresco/feta (or tofu).

Tea for Cold & Flu $,V

Wash & chop 3 cups guava leaves. Dry at 95°F–113°F until brittle (6 hrs). Store in airtight container up to 6 months. Steep 1 cup dried leaves in 4 cups boiling water for 10 min. Strain. Dilute. Sweeten to taste. *Variation: Brew w/ equal parts dried guava fruit & toasted guava seeds (soaked 12 hrs).

Sue-Ann's Baked "Apples"   V

Halve 10 medium guavas. Core. Soak seeds (1 cup) for 24 hrs. Strain. Purée seeds w/ attached pulp, 1 cup water, 1 tbsp oil, 2 tbsp maple syrup, ½ tsp salt, & 3 tsp cinnamon. Slice guavas & toss in purée. Bake at 350°F for 30 min. *Variation: Cut off guava top, core, stuff w/ purée, & bake.

Guava "Tahini"   Z,V

Soak seeds from 20 medium guavas (2 cups) 24 hrs. Drain & pat dry. Toast seeds in 1 tbsp oil over medium heat, stirring, until browned (15 min). Blend toasted seeds w/ 1 tbsp olive oil, 2 garlic cloves, ½ tbsp cumin, & ½ tbsp lemon juice until smooth. Add 1+ tbsp water as needed to purée smooth.

Other Uses

Tender leaves are chewed for toothache in some regions. Leaves are traditionally applied to wounds to aid healing, including mouth ulcers (as a gargle or poultice). Some warm the leaves & wrap them on areas with rheumatic pain. Limbs are ideal for slow cooking in a smoker to infuse a mild, fruity flavor. The fruit is high in pectin & perfect for making jams.

NOTES 

____
____
____
____
____
____
____

Fiber Powder & Oil

Rinse 2 cups guava seeds. Soak 24 hrs. Rinse daily until sprouted (3+ days). Dry at 95°F–113°F 8hrs until crisp. Grind to powder. Simmer w/ 3 cups water 1–2 hrs, stirring. Skim off & transfer oil to clean jar. Place jar in boiling water; simmer 30 min to evaporate water. Strain. Store in fridge.

Guava Bark Tea $,V

Rinse guava inner bark/cambium. Cut into small pieces. Boil 1 tbsp bark in 1 cup water for 15 min. Strain. Sweeten & dilute to taste. Drink 1–2 cups daily for up to 2 weeks. Used in folk healing for gut health (e.g., for ulcers & diarrhea; astringent, antibacterial, & anti-inflammatory properties).

Guava Leaf Facial Toner

Wash 1 cup fresh guava leaves. Boil in 2 cups water for 10 min. Cool, strain, & store in a sterilized jar. Refrigerate up to 1 wk. Apply with a cotton cloth to clean skin. Patch test before use. Used in folk healing for rashes & skin disorders. Antioxidant & antibacterial properties.

Tilapia Feed

Soak guava seeds for 24 hrs, then strain. Dry at 170°F for 2 hrs or until crisp. Mix into regular feed, up to 30% of the diet. Suitable for tilapia, poultry, pigs, cows, goats, & sheep. Used as high-protein supplement.

Butterfly Host Plant

Guava is a host plant for the Guava Skipper & 20 other caterpillar species in Florida including moths. To protect eggs or larvae, prune guava after the caterpillars have matured or outside the breeding season, typically late winter or early spring, to avoid disrupting their life cycle.

Jackfruit
Artocarpus heterophyllus
Moraceae Family

ZONE/ SEASON	SIZE H*W	SUN/ SOIL
9-12/ May-Oct	50ft*50ft dwarf options	full-part/ well-draining

STAPLE CROP INFO
Balanced protein/carb seeds
Edible fruit, leaves, flowers & seeds
Seeds offer nutrition comparable to corn, rice, & wheat! A gluten-free flour: up to 85% starch, 15% protein . Considered one of the most promising solutions to sustainably feed the world. Largest tree fruit (e.g., 10-140lbs).

PROPAGATE/ PRUNE	PESTS/DISEASE	WATER/ WIND	LIFESPAN	MAX STAPLE YIELD
seed-spring/ open center every 3yrs	borers/ manganese deficiency	keep moist/ shelter-brittle	3+ yrs to fruit; lives 100+ yrs; fast growth rate	3k lbs seeds per acre; 30k lbs of fruit

STORYTELLING

Jackfruits are community pillars, reinforcing bonds through shared harvests & potluck meals. A perfect party food, especially for weddings! As the largest tree fruit, jackfruits are gifted as seedlings to newlyweds, symbolizing Eden-like food security. Tree-ripened fruit swells full like a pregnant belly carrying triplets, embodying a cross-cultural symbol of fertility. Extracting pods feels like midwifery! Greek philosophers admired this fruit eaten by sages, & the jackfruit trunk was likened to the axis mundi, connecting heaven & earth. Life is easy with abundant harvests. This heroic plant has saved entire communities from starvation—Sri Lanka used seeds as rice substitutes, turning famine into feast. For this reason, jackfruits are called "Rice Tree" by some, but since the flesh is a meat alternative, it is also nicknamed "Tree Mutton." Considered miraculous, jackfruit thrives even in drought. At peak production, a season's harvest can provide a year's worth of flour. Despite increasing pollution, breathe easy—jackfruit leaves purify the air!

HEALTH CAUTIONS	VARIETY & HEALTH	HEALTH FEATURES	20%+ DV NUTRITION	10%+ DV NUTRITION
Latex in sap; falling fruit hazard	Cochin = edible "rag"; rich in fiber	Ripe fruit=mild laxative	Vit A, C (ripe fruit) Magnesium (seed) Potassium unripe)	Fiber(seed, un/ripe) B6, iron (seed) Zinc, copper

Edible at all stages of ripeness.

FOOD FOREST PLANNING

- # to Plant/ Spacing: 3+/ plant full-sized 25ft apart
- Wildlife Info: May attract wild boars, flies, & beetles
- Native Companion (host): cowpea (35)- nitrogen
- Comparables (zone):Sacred lotus(5-11); Fox nut(7-10)
- Notable Varieties: Fruit weight average ranges: 2-30lbs
  - High Yield: Borneo Red, Black gold (200, 20lb) - Oct
  - Dwarf (8ft): Cochin & Cheena (5lb), June-Aug
  - Rich in seeds: J31 (25lb; 20% seed)- May

Breakfast, Lunch, & Dinner Entrees

Peak jackfruit season in Florida is spring-fall. Use coconut oil to remove sticky latex. To prepare unripe jackfruit, cut into disks. Slice off peel. Chop "meat" off core. Boil "meat" for 20 min. Drain. Pull out seeds. Shred "meat." Some bag unripe jackfruit after injecting w/ basting sauce, then bake at 350°F for 3 hrs—just like turkey! Others grill whole fruit on an open flame, then open & eat—no latex hassle!

NOTES

Wesley's Cacciatore Z,V

Simmer covered for 30 min: 6 cups shredded, unripe jackfruit (boiled for 20 min & drained) w/ 2 cups water, 4 cups marinara sauce, ½ cup each chopped mushrooms & olives, & 2 tbsp each chopped rosemary & oregano.

Ally's Pulled "Pork" V

Mix 3 cups shredded, unripe jackfruit (boiled for 20 min & drained) w/ ½ cup high-quality BBQ sauce (or Salsa Lizano), 1 tbsp Worcestershire, 1 tsp liquid smoke, 3 minced garlic cloves, & 1 sliced onion. Bake for 1 hr at 350°F, stirring often.

Mashed "Potato" Z,V

Purée until smooth 2 cups jackfruit seeds (boiled in husk for 30 min) w/ 2 cups unsalted broth of choice & 3 tbsp white miso paste (or nutritional yeast). Stir in 3 tbsp chopped chives/scallions. *Variation: Add 2 cups broth for soup.

Terry's & JC's Pot Roast Z,V

Dice 4 cups unripe jackfruit. De-seed. Let drain for 20 min to remove latex. Sear in Dutch oven on medium in 2 tbsp oil (4 min per side). Add ¼ cup mushrooms, 3 cups broth thickened w/ 1 cup puréed jackfruit seeds (boiled for 20 min), & ¼ cup Worcestershire. Roast for 50 min at 400°F.

Elana's Risotto "Spanakorizo" Z,V

In pan over medium heat, toast 3 cups coarsely grated jackfruit seeds (pre-boiled for 30 min & de-husked) in 3 tbsp oil. Add 2 cups chopped herbs of choice (e.g., thyme, chives, dill, Aibika). Gradually add 1 cup broth & 3 tbsp nutritional yeast. Simmer & stir until creamy.

Appetizers, Snacks, & Sides

Like an enormous raspberry or blackberry, jackfruit is composed of 100s-1,000s of flowers. We eat the fleshy petals & the seeds they enclose. Soak seeds overnight to reduce phytic acid. Harvest fruit when firm but before fully ripened on the tree. Store until soft & ripened. Ripe flavor is a cross between banana, mango, & melon. Edible at any size & ripeness.

<u>**NOTES**</u>

____
____
____
____
____
____

Pam's Chicken Salad   V

Mix 2½ cups boiled (20 min), drained, shredded, unripe jackfruit w/ ½ cup mayo or cashew cream (¼ cup soaked nuts, puréed w/ ¼ cup water). Add 2 tbsp chopped celery, 1 tsp salt, ½ tsp dried dill, & ½ tsp onion powder. Serve over greens.

Tortilla $,V

Purée 2 cups seeds (boiled for 20 min & strained) in 4 cups water. Use cheesecloth to strain out "milk" from pulp (reserve milk for drinks). Mix pulp w/ 1 tbsp oil. Form a ball & press into a thin tortilla shape. Cook on medium-hot pan until browned.

Sue-Ann's Roasted Seeds   Z,$,V

Boil 3 cups jackfruit seeds for 20 min. Drain. Toss in 2 tbsp oil & sprinkle w/ 2 tsp each: onion powder, garlic powder, & sea salt. Spread seeds in single layer on baking pan. Roast at 350°F for 20 min, stirring halfway. Crack off husk as you eat. *Variation: Boil in salt water like peanuts.

Emily's "Beef" Jerky $,V

Mix 4 cups strained, boiled (20 min) unripe jackfruit w/ 2 tbsp soy sauce, 1 tbsp molasses, 1 tbsp smoked paprika, & 1 tsp ground cumin. Shape into ¼" thick jerky sticks. Dry on oiled sheet at 250°F for 3 hrs. Leave in oven 2 hrs until leather-dry.

Jackfruit Flower Pickles   V

Pick 20 male jackfruit flowers. Slice into wedges. Boil for 5-7 min. Drain. Place in quart jar w/ brine (4 tbsp salt dissolved in 4 cups water). Add 1 tbsp each coriander & peppercorn, ¼ cup dill, & 3 chopped garlic cloves. Ferment for 1-10 days.

Drinks, Desserts, & Dips

Ripe pulp colors range from yellow to orange to pink. Dehydrated or freeze-dried jackfruit is delightful. Jackfruit is considered a medicinal food: fruits, seeds, leaves, & bark have been used in traditional healing for anticarcinogenic, antimicrobial, antifungal, anti-inflammatory, wound healing, & hypoglycemic effects. Celebrated in Ayurvedic medicine for immune benefits.

<u>NOTES</u>

Michele's Ice Cream   V

In high-speed blender, purée 2 cups frozen ripe jackfruit w/ 1 cup very cold coconut milk, ½ tbsp lime juice, & a pinch of salt. Serve immediately. Garnish w/ basil or mint sprigs.

Priya's Baked Jackfruit   V

Open ripe jackfruit. Separate seeds & fruit. Chop 2 cups fruit pods & place in a 2- to 3-quart casserole dish w/ 3 cups coconut milk, ¼ tsp cardamom powder, & ½ tsp salt. Boil 2 cups seeds for 15 min. Cool. Cut in half. Pop kernels out of husks. Chop. Add to dish. Bake at 350ºF for 1 hr. Top w/ mint.

Jackfruit Leaf Tea $,V

Wash 10 jackfruit leaves. Dry in oven (e.g., 170ºF for 1 hr) until brittle. For tea, steep 1 tsp crumbled leaves in 1 cup boiling water. Dilute to taste. Used as anti-inflammatory, anti-parasitic & digestive aid. *Variation: Brew w/ equal parts dried fruit & toasted/ground seeds (soaked 12 hrs).

Priya's "Tikkis"   Z

Slice unripe jackfruit into disks. Cut off rind. Remove "meat." Boil "meat" w/ seeds for 20 min. Strain & cool. Pull out seeds. Purée 1 cup seeds, ½ cup water, 2 eggs, 1 tsp salt, 1 tbsp oil, & 1 tsp cumin. Shred "meat." Press out liquid. Mix w/ purée. Form patties. Broil on oiled pan 20 min at 500ºF. Flip halfway.

James' Jackfruit Hummus   V

Purée 2 cups jackfruit seeds (boiled in husk 30 min) w/ 2 cups water, 2 tbsp oil, 3 garlic cloves, 2 tsp cumin, ½ tsp sea salt, 1 tbsp vinegar, & 2 tbsp nutritional yeast. Garnish w/ roasted garlic & a drizzle of oil. *Variation: For dinner rolls, purée 1 cup hummus & 2 eggs. Bake 35 min at 350ºF.

Other Uses

Jackfruit wood is ideal for construction & carving; it's resistant to termites & rot. Ground bark & leaves are used as an antimicrobial face & hand scrub. Latex sap serves as glue. The heartwood yields a yellow dye. All parts are useful, including rind, peel, & core (pectin).

NOTES

Jam Pectin $,V

Chop 3 cups jackfruit rind. Boil in 4 cups water for 1 hr until thickened. Strain & cool. Use 1–2 tbsp pectin in jam. Store in fridge for up to 1 wk. *Optional: Dry at 120°F for 6–8 hrs. Pulverize in blender. Store in airtight container for up to 1 yr. Use 1 tsp in jams.

Jackfruit Leaf Plates/ Wrappers

Use large/mature leaves (8–12") for plates or food wrappers. Rinse, then steam or boil for 1–2 min to soften. Leaves infuse mild, earthy flavor & trace nutrients. Provides a natural, eco-friendly alternative to disposable plates & plastic wraps.

Yellow Dye

Chip 2–3 lbs deep-colored jackfruit heartwood. Boil in stainless steel pot w/ 4–6 cups water for 2 hrs. Strain. Reduce liquid until thick & black (4 hrs). Add natural cloth to dye. Simmer, pound, & stir cloth in dye for 30 min. Cool dye, wring fabric, & hang to dry.

Glue/ Adhesive

Jackfruit sap (latex) is non-toxic & eco-friendly. Polysaccharides give strong binding properties. Collect 1–2 tbsp sap from tree, fruit, or leaves. Use in crafts, wood repairs, or bug traps. Press firmly to bond. Store in airtight container at room temp up to 2 wks.

Flute

Select 18" straight jackfruit limb, 1" in diameter. Hollow center using 3/8" to 1/2" drill bit (10–12" long). Carve 4–8 finger holes. Shape air hole & mouthpiece. Oil wood w/ non-toxic/food-safe oil (e.g., linseed). Jackfruit wood is ideal for flutes: durable, smooth, & resonant.

Katuk
Sauropus androgynus
Euphorbiaceae Family

ZONE/ SEASON	SIZE H*W	SUN/ SOIL
9-12/	9ft*2ft	65% sun/
all yr	keep 3ft tall	pH 6-6.5

STAPLE CROP INFO
Protein leaf

Edible shoots, fruit, flowers & leaves

Katuk leaf contains up to 30% protein. Thailand & Indonesia varieties have most protein. High concentrations of medicinal alkaloids & secondary metabolites. Ripe for pharmacological patents! Vast health benefits. Increasing demand. Profitable.

PROPAGATE/ PRUNE	PESTS/DISEASE	WATER/ WIND	LIFESPAN	MAX STAPLE YIELD
softwood cuttings/ ratoon late winter	aphids, mites/ root rot	brief flood- ok/ wind resilient	1 yr to harvest; lives 20+ yrs; fast growth rate	4k yrly lbs per acre/ 4k plants per acre

STORYTELLING

Katuk is called a "multi-vitamin leaf" for good reason. It's so nutrient-dense, many use it medicinally! Yet, herein lies a lesson: What's the difference between medicine & food? Dose & preparation. Katuk's history shows how diet fads can harm. Some weight loss fanatics juiced or powdered raw katuk in toxic doses ($1/3$-1 lb daily for months). Perennials survive by developing a chemical arsenal for protection. Traditional recipes cook katuk, making it a gentle staple. Learn the lessons of ancestors & time-tested recipes! Known as "sweet leaf," katuk tastes like fresh garden peas with a slightly nutty flavor. Shoots are used as tropical asparagus, & young green "peas" are crunchy like cucumber. A valued restaurant delicacy worldwide, katuk thrives in indoor hydroponic or aquaponic systems—pretty & delicious as a houseplant! For mass production, it's a well-behaved row crop requiring neither tilling nor weeding. It sends up suckers to fill in within 1-2 years.

HEALTH CAUTIONS	VARIETY & HEALTH	HEALTH FEATURES	20%+ DV NUTRITION	10%+ DV NUTRITION
Limit to $1/4$ cup raw per day: 580mg papaverine per 100g	Soil pH impacts medicinal level & nutrients	Boosts lactation clinically	Vit A, C (leaf) Folate, copper (leaf) Magnesium (leaf)	Protein (leaf) Calcium, iron (leaf) Zinc (leaf)

Tender leaves & young fruit sweetest.

FOOD FOREST PLANNING

- # to Plant/ Spacing: 20+/ plant 2ft apart
- Wildlife Info: Deer & rabbits may be attracted to leaves
- Native Companion (host): Oak(395), maple(171)
- Comparables (zone):Toona(6-11); Ora-pro-nobis(9-11)
- Notable Varieties: Leaf coloration varies
  - Variegated leaf: typically thicker; kale-like flavor
  - White fruit: cucumber-like when greenish
  - Pink fruit: sweeter cucumber flavor when greenish

Breakfast, Lunch, & Dinner Entrees

Peak katuk season in Florida is spring-fall. A delicious "spinach" & a key part of traditional SE Asian diets! Best cooked, as medicinal alkaloids degrade with heat. 1 cup raw katuk provides nearly 150mg of medicinal papaverine—a clinical dose. Consume no more than ¼ cup raw per day. Fermenting katuk can further enhance safety & health benefits. ***Each recipe makes several servings.

<u>**NOTES**</u>

Jay & Laura's Eggs in Purgatory   Z

Boil 6 cups washed, tender katuk leaves for 7 min. Drain. Simmer covered on medium-low for 3 min w/ 2 cups tomato sauce, 1 tbsp chopped chives, & 1 tbsp chopped basil. Crack 3–6 eggs into mix. Cover for 3–5 min, letting steam cook eggs sunny-side-up. Sprinkle w/ sea salt & chives.

Susan's Katuk Fritters   Z

Wilt & stir 10 cups washed, chopped katuk leaves in 1 cup water for 7 min over medium-high heat. Drain & squeeze dry. Mix w/ ½ cup chopped onions, ½ tsp salt, 2 chopped garlic cloves, 1 cup Parmesan, & 4 beaten eggs. Form patties. Bake on oiled pan at 350°F for 30 min, flipping halfway.

Spinach & Mushroom Stir-fry   Z,V

In 2 tbsp sesame oil, stir-fry 4 cups chopped katuk leaves, 1½ cups chopped button mushrooms, 2 tbsp chopped onion, a pinch of red pepper flakes, & 3 tbsp soy sauce/aminos. Cook over medium-high heat, stirring continuously for 7–10 min until leaves are tender.

Elana's Green Eggs & "Ham"   Z

In blender, purée 4 large eggs w/ ½ cup washed, very tender katuk leaves, a pinch of sea salt, & a pinch of black pepper. In 2 tbsp oil over medium-low heat, sauté for 5 min: ¼ cup king trumpet or oyster mushrooms (as "ham"). Add katuk-egg purée & scramble.

Priya's Spanakorizo   Z,V

Cut in half lengthwise & boil 3 green bananas for 15 min. Drain & cool. Peel. Grate/"rice" 2½ cups green banana. Boil 8 cups tender katuk leaves for 3 min. Drain & squeeze out liquid. Chop. Toss w/ "rice," 1 tbsp dried dill, ¼ cup olive oil, ½ cup feta, & zest & juice of 1 lemon.

Appetizers, Snacks, & Sides

Leaves taste similar to peas. 7g protein in ½ cup cooked leaves! Cultivated for centuries & enjoyed by millions worldwide. Avg. serving is 6 oz (1 cup) cooked katuk weekly. Mature leaves are higher in protein, Vit C, calcium, iron, zinc, & medicinal alkaloids than tender leaves. Avoid juicing or powdering raw leaves to prevent overconsumption of medicinal compounds.

NOTES

Elana's Pickled Peas   Z,V

Blanch 1 cup green, tender katuk peas for 3 min in 1 cup boiling water. Strain. Mix ½ tsp salt, ¼ cup water, ¼ cup vinegar, ½ tbsp maple syrup, 1–2 chopped, deseeded chili peppers, & 1 chopped garlic clove. Pour brine over peas in 12 oz/pint jar. Fully submerge. Store in fridge 2–3 days to infuse flavors.

Spinach Chips $,Z

Boil 4 cups washed, tender katuk leaves for 3 min. Drain & squeeze out liquid. Purée w/ 2 cups finely shredded Parmesan & 1 tbsp rosemary. Add 1+ tbsp water if needed to blend smoothly. Press thinly onto oiled or parchment-lined pan. Bake at 350°F for 30 min until crisp. Slice or break into wedges.

Spinach "Ohitashi"   Z,V

Blanch 5 cups tender katuk top shoots & leaves in boiling water for 3 min. Strain & squeeze dry. Chop. Whisk 1 tbsp miso, 1 tbsp mirin, 1 tbsp soy sauce in ¼ cup water. Pile katuk in center of bowl. Pour sauce over evenly. Top w/ slices of pickled ginger.

Katuk "Tabbouleh"   Z,V

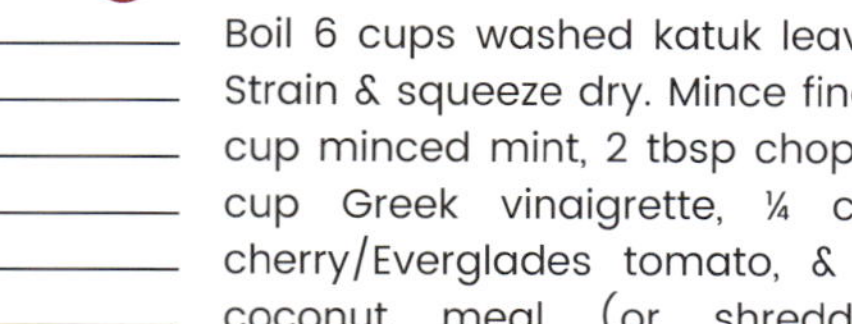

Boil 6 cups washed katuk leaves for 5 min. Strain & squeeze dry. Mince finely. Toss w/ ¼ cup minced mint, 2 tbsp chopped chives, ¼ cup Greek vinaigrette, ¼ cup chopped cherry/Everglades tomato, & ¼ cup fresh coconut meal (or shredded coconut, minced). Refrigerate 2–3 hrs. Serve chilled.

Stuffed Mushrooms   Z

Simmer covered 5 min, 4 cups katuk leaves in ¼ cup water. Drain & squeeze dry. Chop. Mix w/ 1 cup goat cheese. Remove cap & gills from 4 portobellos. Rinse. Stuff mushrooms w/ katuk-cheese mix. Top w/ 2 chopped garlic cloves. Bake at 400°F for 15 min. Drizzle w/ sweet balsamic vinegar.

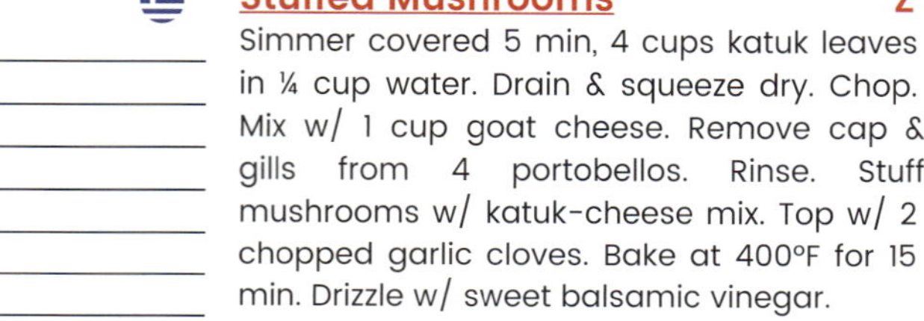

Drinks, Desserts, & Dips

Medicinal Phytometabolites: Katuk is used for cough, fever, ulcers, anemia, diabetes, lactation, uterotonic effects, insomnia, obesity, alopecia, erectile dysfunction, menopause symptoms, & osteomalacia. Isoflavonoids resemble estrogen, boosting prolactin & oxytocin, while anti-spasmodic papaverine dilates blood vessels & relaxes smooth muscles.

<u>NOTES</u>

Tina's Gremolata   Z,V

Boil 2 cups katuk leaves for 5 min. Strain & squeeze dry. Mince. Toss w/ 1 tbsp washed & minced mint. Finely grate 2 garlic cloves & zest of 1 lemon over katuk. Sprinkle w/ salt. Mash mixture w/ rolling pin or pestle. Stir. Use as garnish. *Variation: Simmer in 2 cups broth for soup.

Jessica's Mint Flan

Simmer 2 cups katuk leaves, covered, 5 min in ¼ cup water. Drain & squeeze dry. Purée w/ 1 cup banana, ½ tsp peppermint extract & 2 eggs. Steam in oiled mold lined w/ 2 tbsp maple syrup in microwave for 3 min or until center is firm. Cool 10 min in fridge. Demold & sprinkle w/ salt.

Katuk Tea   Z,$,V

Dry washed katuk leaves in oven on lowest setting. To make tea, brew 3g dried leaves (1 tsp) in 8 oz boiling water (1 cup). Strain, add splash of citrus, & sweeten to taste. Used in folk healing (e.g., cough, vasodilator, galactagogue). Limit to 2 cups daily for up to 2 wks.

Wendy's Green Goddess Pop   V

Boil 4 cups washed katuk leaves 3 min. Drain & squeeze dry. Purée until smooth: katuk, ¼ cup green mango, 1 cup ripe banana, 1 tbsp maple syrup, ½ tbsp sweet basil, & 2 tsp grated fresh ginger. Add 1+ tbsp water as needed for smooth texture. Press into popsicle molds & freeze 6 hrs.

Fruit Leather $,V

Blanch 5 cups katuk in boiling water 3 min. Strain. Purée with ½ cup banana, ½ cup ripe mango, 2 tbsp citrus juice, & ½ tsp cardamom seeds. Add 1+ tbsp water for smooth purée. Pour on parchment $\frac{1}{8}$" thick. Dehydrate at 140ºF for 6+ hrs until pliable. Roll.

Other Uses

Katuk is suitable as a houseplant, biofuel, feedstock, & for phytoremediation of heavy-metal-contaminated soil (avoid harvesting for food in contaminated soils as it absorbs heavy metals like lead & cadmium). Dried leaves are valued for pharmaceuticals. In the same plant family as chaya & cassava. The leaves yield a green dye, & the root has medicinal uses (e.g., as an antiseptic agent).

Children's Labryinth Hedge

Plant rooted cuttings or seedlings 1 ft apart in rows to form a labyrinth pattern. Katuk grows quickly &, with regular pruning, will form a dense hedge in 12–18 months. Prune regularly to shape walls & keep under 3 ft tall for children.

Stem Basket

Collect 16 katuk stems, each 18" long. Layer & cross 4 stems in a star shape to form spokes. From the center out, spiral-weave over-under to form a circular base. Continue upward to create walls. Basket will be 6" wide & 4" tall. Trim & tuck ends securely.

Natural Dye

In a stainless steel pot, simmer 2 cups chopped katuk leaves in 4 cups water for 1 hour. Cool & strain. Pre-soak natural fabric in high-protein milk (1-hour soak; air dry; repeat). Simmer fabric in katuk liquid for 1 hour to absorb color. Let cool, wring out, rinse, & air dry.

Katuk Cough Drop

Wash ¼ cup tender, raw katuk leaves & purée with 3 tbsp coconut oil & 2 tbsp honey until smooth. Pour into molds & freeze until firm. Once set, remove from molds & store in an airtight container in freezer. Use as a cough lozenge for soothing relief. Limit to 1 per 4 hrs.

Goat/ Cow Milk Enhancer

Lightly cook (steam or boil 3 min) katuk to reduce papaverine content. Chop & mix with regular feed. Give 1 cup cooked katuk leaves per goat per week to promote lactation, or feed ¼ cup raw per day.

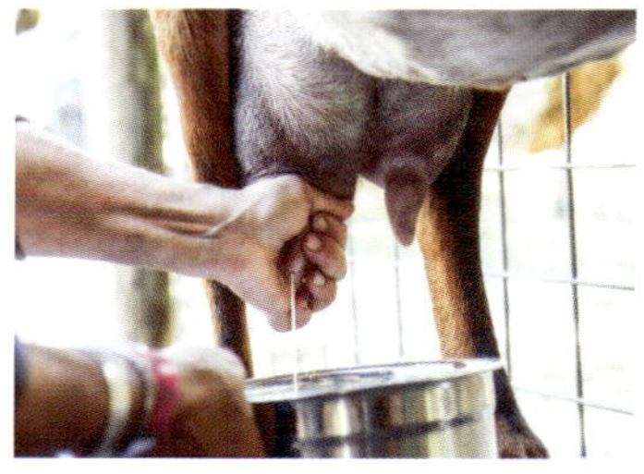

Mango

Mangifera indica
Anacardiaceae Family

ZONE/ SEASON	SIZE H*W	SUN/ SOIL
10-12/ May-Sept	82ft*82ft dwarf options	full-part/ well-draining

STAPLE CROP INFO

Balanced protein/carb & oil in seed
Edible leaves, fruit & seed

Mango seed is 6-13% protein, 70% carb, & up to 21% "butter"-rich in stearic & oleic acid. Mango seed flour is expected to help overcome food insecurity in years to come. The seed can be half of the fruit's weight (e.g., an average of 1/2 lb).

PROPAGATE/ PRUNE	PESTS/DISEASE	WATER/ WIND	LIFESPAN	MAX STAPLE YIELD
poly seed-spring/ shape post-harvest	mites, scale/ fungus	brief flood- ok/ Moderately resilient	2+ yrs to fruit; lives 300+ yrs; fast growth rate	20k lbs per acre; 80+ trees per acre

STORYTELLING

With a seed shaped like a heart & a taste sweeter than poetry, mangoes have symbolized love between star-crossed Romeos & Juliets. Some believe sharing a mango under a full moon ensures a long, happy romance. Known to 'sweeten the deal,' mangoes have been tools of diplomacy to solidify trade relations. This 'king of fruits' satisfies the masses with ample choices in size & color: yellow, orange, red, or green —all delicious. Packed with nutrients, mangoes have been part of Ayurvedic medicine for 4,000 years. Pulp, peel, seed, leaves, & bark are all used for protecting health. Even the timber offers protection: mango wood was historically used to build boats for surviving floods of mythic proportions. But what is a mango tree without the mango? Contemplating the austerity of a 'barren' mango tree is said to have aided Buddha's spiritual growth. Buddhist-level compassion comes in handy: Share your ripe mangoes! Not everyone is lucky enough to grow these treasured 'golden eggs.'

HEALTH CAUTIONS	VARIETY & HEALTH	HEALTH FEATURES	20%+ DV NUTRITION	10%+ DV NUTRITION
Urushiol/ allergen oil & pollen; wash off	Beta-carotene in orange fruit	Mangiferin in peel, leaves, bark	Vit C (ripe, unripe) Copper (ripe) Fiber (peel, fruit, seed)	Vit A, E, K, Folate (ripe) B6 (ripe, seed) Iron, Magnesium (unripe)

Soak & boil seed & then grind & dry for flour.

FOOD FOREST PLANNING

- # to Plant/ Spacing: 3+/ plant full-sized 25ft apart
- Wildlife Info: Butterfly host plant; attracts mammals
- Native Companion (host): Cowpea (35) - enrich soil
- Comparables (zone): Date (8-12), White Sapote (8-11)
- Notable Varieties:Polyembronic=true to seed, fruit in 2 yrs
  - Polyembryonic: Florigon, Nam Doc Mai, Okrung
  - Monoembryonic: Tommy Atkins, Keitt, Kent
  - Dwarf (6ft): Pickering, Honey Kiss, Cogshall, Carrie

Breakfast, Lunch, & Dinner Entrees

Peak mango season in Florida is summer-fall. Green mango has resistant starch & digestive enzymes—ideal at dinner to aid sleep. Fruit may contain allergenic sap; hot water removes it. Mango seed is an easy flour source. ***For flour: Dehusk, purée, soak 12 hrs, strain, & boil 50 min. Use as masa. Like corn, nixtamalization can be done (e.g., soak 12 hrs in 1g calcium hydroxide, 4 cups water & ½ cup seed).

Esther's Breakfast Donuts $,V

Whip 1 cup barely-ripe banana, 1 tbsp melted chocolate & 3 tbsp full-fat coconut flour. Chill batter 30 min. Dice 2 cups firm ripe mango. Use ice cream scooper to form batter ball. Poke cubed mango in center, wipe batter closed, & release onto oiled pan. Spritz with oil. Bake 30 min at 350ºF.

Tostada Z,$,V

After dehusking, puréeing, soaking & boiling, strain mango seed purée through cloth. Form balls with ice cream scooper & place on oiled pan. Cover with parchment & press with plate to form thin disk. Bake at 350ºF for 30 min. Top with veggies or mango. *NOTE: 1 mango seed yields ¼–⅓ cup ground flour.

Wesley's Mango "Purin"

Purée 2 cups ripe mango pulp with 3 tsp coconut cream & 3 eggs. Pour into oiled muffin molds. Bake 35 min at 350ºF or until puffed & golden. Serve drizzled with 1 cup mango purée mixed with 1 tbsp coconut cream. Garnish with mint. *Variation: Microwave 3–5 min or until firm.

Seven's Mango Breakfast Bar $,V

Purée 6 cups ripe mango pulp & 2 cups coconut flour. Add 1+ tbsp water if needed. Fold in ¼ cup chia seeds & let sit 10 min to absorb moisture. Pour mix into oiled 8"x8" pan. Bake at 350ºF for 50 min or until firm. Let cool, then drizzle with honey & crushed pistachios. Slice into squares.

Mango Seed Soup "Trahana" Z,V

Add 1 cup ground, soaked & boiled mango seed to 2 cups salted vegetable broth. Simmer 20 min, stirring often. Turn off heat & allow to cool slightly. Gently stir in ½ cup full-fat yogurt of choice & salt & pepper to taste. Top with parsley.

Appetizers, Snacks, & Sides

120 days from flower to fruit. Heavy crops occur every few years. Mangoes are harvested in 3 stages: immature (no shoulder), half-mature (shoulder), & fully mature (shoulder beyond stem). As fruit ripens, Vit C decreases & sugars increase. Ripe fruit phytochemicals have anti-inflammatory effects on chronic disorders (e.g., bowel). Green mango & green papaya are used interchangeably in many recipes.

<u>NOTES</u>

Sue-Ann's Mango Pickles Z,V

Stir 2 tbsp salt in 1 qt water. Blanch 3 green mangoes, peel & cut into wedges. Place in quart jar. Add 1 cinnamon stick, 5 cloves & 1 grape or oak leaf. Cover with brine, 1" above mangoes but 2" from rim. Keep submerged with weight. Cover & ferment 3+ days. Refrigerate.

Cecilia's Mango Salsa V

Toss 2 cups diced ripe mango with 1 cup grated green mango, ¼ cup chopped red onion, 2 tbsp chopped herbs (e.g., culantro, cilantro, or longevity spinach), 2 minced garlic cloves, ½ tbsp minced jalapeño & ¼ tsp sea salt.

Tanja's Green Mango Salad V

Slice or grate 5 cups green mango & ½ cup ripe mango into thin strips. Purée ½ cup soaked nuts into sauce with 2 tbsp soy sauce, 2 tbsp lime juice, 2 tbsp honey & 5 garlic cloves. Garnish with nuts. *Variation: 1. Use recipe with green papaya/mix in. 2. Spiralize mango into noodles.

Priya's Chips & Spice Z,$,V

Boil 5 green mangoes for 30 sec to remove sap. Rinse & peel. Dehydrate peel in oven or dehydrator at 135°F–170°F until crisp. Use as anti-inflammatory digestive aid & all-purpose flavor enhancer. *Variation: 1. Grind chips into spice, "amchoor." 2. Steep 1 tsp in 1 cup water for tea.

Elana's Mango Smoothie Z,V

Purée 1 cup nut yogurt, 2 cups mango purée, 1–2 tbsp honey, ½ cup nut milk & 1 tbsp mango blossom water (steep 1 cup washed mango blossoms in 2 cups boiling water). *Variation: Replace blossom water with $1/8$ tsp ground cardamom.

Drinks, Desserts, & Dips

Young leaves, still rose or bronze, & mango blossoms can be blanched to make them safely edible. When harvesting mango leaves, ensure they are organic, vibrant green, free of yellowing, pest damage, mold, or fungal growth, & have a firm texture without wilting. As a hack, freeze whole, washed mangoes, thaw for 1 min in microwave, peel the top, & scoop out semi-frozen pulp as sorbet.

NOTES

Ken's Mango Tiramisu   V

Purée 2 cups ripe mango & 1 cup coconut cream. Simmer 3 min, then cool. Halve 5 mini semi-ripe bananas & spray with oil. Broil/toast for 5–10 min. Sprinkle with 2 tsp instant coffee. Cool. Dust plate with cocoa powder. Layer 3x: 3 halved bananas & ⅔ cup purée. Dust with cocoa powder.

Cecilia's Mango Pie   V

Blend 1 cup ripe bananas & 1 cup coconut flour. Form crust in an 8" oiled pie pan. Bake at 350°F for 15 min. Cool completely. Add 1 cup chilled coconut cream. Peel & thinly slice 6 mangoes. Arrange tightly in a spiral from center. Refrigerate 4 hrs. Serve very cold.

Carolyn's Chutney   V

Mix 2 cups diced green mango pulp with 1 tsp salt. Let "sweat" 30 min. Squeeze out moisture. Mix with ½ tsp ground turmeric, ¼ tsp ground ginger, ¾ tsp pepper & 2 tbsp light maple syrup. *Variation: Replace syrup with 3 tbsp puréed banana & ½ tsp apple cider vinegar. Anti-inflammatory.

James' Ice Cream   V

In a high-speed blender, purée 2 cups frozen mango purée, ½ cup frozen ripe banana, 1 cup coconut cream & 1 tbsp chia seeds. Blend until smooth. Serve immediately & garnish with fresh herbs.

James' Morning Elixir   V

Purée 1 cup peeled green mango pulp, ½ cup blanched greens (e.g., boiled chaya, longevity spinach, aibika; or ½ tbsp moringa powder), ½" peeled fresh ginger & 1–2 cups water. Considered helpful for optimal liver function. *Variation: Use herbs for greens & add ½ cup ripe banana for salad dressing.

Other Uses

Mango trees host the red-banded hairstreak butterfly. Mango seed butter shows commercial promise as a functional food ingredient & cosmetic, substituting for coconut, cocoa, & shea butter. Mango belongs to the poison ivy family—don't burn the wood (smoke harms lungs). SE Asian "races" are poly-embryonic, true to seed, & disease resistant. Green mango is high in pectin, aiding jam setting.

NOTES

Whittled Carving

Open wet mango shell with a sharp knife to extract kernel. Dry kernel at 95°F for 1–2 wks until hardened. Sand smooth. Use whittling tools/Dremel for designs. Seal finished carving with oil (e.g., mango butter).

Mango Butter

Open 25 seeds. Grate/purée kernel to a paste (add water as needed). In a stainless steel pot, simmer 1–2 hrs until oil rises. Cool. Scoop off solid butter (2 cups). Reheat & strain. Solid at room temp. High saturated fat—ideal for hair & skin (comedogenic scale 2; non-drying).

Mango Vinegar

Place mango peels & seeds from 2–3 mangoes in a jar. Fill with water, leaving space at top. Cover with cloth & secure with rubber band. Stir daily for 2–4 wks until fermented. Strain, then let sit another 2 wks before use.

Mango "Flower" on a Stick $,V

Select a firm, ripe mango. With a sharp knife, slice off bottom of stem end. Cut into seed. Push skewer into seed. Cut peel off. Starting at base, make 4 slices & flare "petals." Rotate & make 4 more slices higher between petals. Repeat to top. Sprinkle with ground nutmeg. Dry 6hrs at 170°F until leathery.

Butterfly Host

Allow mango tree leaf litter to accumulate underneath. Red-banded hairstreaks lay eggs near decaying leaves, with larvae active in spring & fall. Prune tree in winter to avoid disturbing eggs or larvae.

Money Tree

Pachira glabra
Malvaceae Family

ZONE/ SEASON	SIZE H*W	SUN/ SOIL
9-12/ yr-round	50ft*50ft keep 8ft	70+ sun/ poor - ok

STAPLE CROP INFO

Balanced carb/protein & oil in seed
Edible leaves, flower & nut
Seeds up to 16% protein, 25% carb, & 40-50% fat - 52% oleic acid. $7 million ornamental agricultural export in Taiwan. Feng shui houseplant - an aesthetic of prosperity. Untapped U.S. potential as a food, bonsai, biodiesel, & soap-oil.

PROPAGATE/ PRUNE	PESTS/DISEASE	WATER/ WIND	LIFESPAN	MAX STAPLE YIELD
seed-spring/ summer-shape	aphids, mites/ root rot, fungus	brief flood - ok/ wind resilient	4+ yrs to fruit; lives 30+ yrs; fast growth rate	500lbs nuts per acre; 200 trees per acre;

STORYTELLING

According to legend, a special tree bestows 5 blessings: good luck, peace of mind, wealth, health, & long life. Locals called it the "Money Tree," using it to ensure sustenance & inspire ambition. Business ventures may be uncertain, but with this tree, food is always on the table. Able to withstand hurricane winds, flooding, & drought, it provides nourishment no matter what! Known as French peanut & Malabar chestnut for its seeds, which resemble chestnuts in shape & sweet flavor. With multiple harvests year-round, essential nutrients "rain from the sky," replacing inflated grocery costs. Growing it is as good as having money! Often given at New Year's, the tree serves as a gift-economy lesson: after health, friends & family are our greatest assets. Strong communities take care of each other. This tree teaches a vital lesson in financial literacy: a penny saved is a penny earned. Free food from this tree prevents costly disease.

HEALTH CAUTIONS	VARIETY & HEALTH	HEALTH FEATURES	20%+ DV NUTRITION	10%+ DV NUTRITION
CPFAs - soak overnight, roast at 30 min, 375+F	Location matters - bioaccumulates heavy metals	Not classified as a tree nut; bark is medicinal	Magnesium (seed) Vit A (leaf) Fiber (seed)	Iron & Zinc (seed) Vit C (flower, leaf) Potassium (seeds)

Edible when pod opens on its own. Roast.

FOOD FOREST PLANNING

- # to Plant/ Spacing: 5+trees per person/ 15ft apart
- Wildlife Info: Night pollination: limit light pollution
- Native Companion (host): Greenbrier (18)
- Comparables (zone): Cashew (9-12); Chestnut (4-8)
- Notable Varieties: N/A - Mistaken for other species
    o *P. aquatica* (9-11): stamens white base/crimson tip
    o *P. insignis* (9-12): Red petals; crimson base stamen
    o *Bombax ceiba* (10-12): Bright red, cup-shape flower

Breakfast, Lunch, & Dinner Entrees

Peak season for *Pachira glabra* in Florida is spring-fall. An ideal candidate for sustainable agriculture. ***Traditional preparation methods (e.g., soak 12 hrs & roast 30 min at 375ºF) maximize health benefits. To make a wheat flour substitute: Soak seeds for 12 hrs. Strain. Dehusk. Roast for 30 min at 375ºF. Cool. Grind. Store in freezer.

NOTES

"Escargot" Z,$,V

Boil 1 cup *P. glabra* seeds for 5 min. Let cool. Strain, rinse, & peel husks. Toss with 1 tbsp olive oil, 1 tbsp minced garlic, & 1 tbsp chopped rosemary. Sprinkle with salt & roast in a mini muffin pan or escargot mold at 375ºF for 30 min, until sizzling. Sprinkle with sea salt & serve warm.

Picadillo Z,V

Soak 2 cups *P. glabra* seeds overnight. Strain & de-husk. Roast at 375ºF for 30 min, stirring often, until fragrant & golden brown. Mince. Sauté 10 min on high with ¼ cup mushrooms, ¼ cup onions, 2 tsp ground cumin, ¼ tsp salt, & ½ cup rinsed, chopped green papaya (¼").

Chestnut Stir-Fry Z,V

Soak 1 cup *P. glabra* seeds 12hrs. Strain & de-husk. Roast 30 min at 375ºF, stirring often. Chop. Boil 2 cups chopped very young *P. glabra* leaves 12 min. Drain. Stir-fry seeds & leaves in 1 tbsp oil, 1 tbsp garlic & ginger, & 2 tbsp soy sauce for 5 min. Add splash of vinegar & toss.

Elana's "Mac & Cheese" V

Soak 3 cups *P. glabra* seeds overnight. Strain & de-husk. Roast at 375ºF for 30 min, stirring often. Divide seeds in 2. Cut 1 set in half. Purée the other set with 2 cups water, 3 tbsp nutritional yeast, ¼ tsp salt, 2 tbsp onion, 3 garlic cloves, & ¼ tsp turmeric. Toss purée over halved seeds.

"Bean" Puree with Greens Z,V

Soak 2 cups *P. glabra* seeds overnight. Strain & de-husk. Roast at 375ºF for 30 min with 3 garlic cloves & 1 halved onion until fragrant & golden brown. Purée with 2 cups salted broth. Top with tender, young *P. glabra* leaves boiled 5 min, strained, & chopped. Sprinkle with salt & olive oil.

Appetizers, Snacks, & Sides

A staple for centuries across continents & cultures, *Pachira glabra* has been eaten by indigenous tribes, ancient civilizations, & modern societies alike. Listed by the UN as one of the most important yet underrated trees, it offers edible leaves & flowers, often cooked as vegetables. Raw Malabar chestnuts can be stored in the fridge for several months, helping prevent aflatoxin contamination.

NOTES

Vivian's Roasted "Chestnuts" Z,$,V

Soak 2 cups *Pachira glabra* seeds overnight. Strain. Cut an "X" in the husk. Roast in a cast iron pan over an open flame or in oven at 375°F for 30 min, stirring often, until fragrant, golden brown, & soft. Sprinkle with sea salt. Peel off husk & eat warm. *Variation: Skewer de-husked nuts as kebabs.

Pickled "Chestnuts" Z,V

Soak 2 cups *P. glabra* seeds 12 hrs. Strain & de-husk. Roast at 375°F for 30 min, stirring often. Dissolve 2 tbsp salt & 1 tbsp honey in 2 cups water. Add 2 cups vinegar (5% acidity). Place roasted seeds in 2 qt jars. Top with brine, leaving 2" from top. Add 2 garlic cloves & 1 chili pepper. Store in fridge.

Ginger Tea Cake Z,$,V

Soak 1 cup *P. glabra* seeds overnight. Strain & de-husk. Roast at 375°F for 30 min, stirring often. Purée until smooth with ¼ tsp salt, 1 tbsp grated ginger, 1 tbsp maple syrup, 2 large eggs, & ½ cup water. Add 1+ tbsp water if needed. Pour into oiled glass mold. "Steam" in microwave 3-5 min or until firm.

"Chestnut" Soup V

Soak 2 cups *P. glabra* seeds overnight. Strain & de-husk. Roast at 375°F for 30 min with 3 garlic cloves & 1 halved onion. Chop 3 seeds. Purée remaining seeds, onion, & garlic with 3 cups broth, 2 tsp rosemary, 1 tbsp lemon juice, & ½ tsp salt. Pour into 3 bowls. Garnish with chopped "chestnuts."

Chestnut Stuffing

Soak 4 cups *P. glabra* seeds overnight. Strain & de-husk. Roast at 375°F for 30 min with 4 garlic cloves & 1 chopped onion, stirring often. Coarsely chop & toss with ½ cup chopped sage leaves & 4 beaten eggs. Bake in an oiled pan at 350°F for 30 min.

Drinks, Desserts, & Dips

Malabar chestnut is considered a substitute for, & alternative to, cashews' toxic industry, with the potential to contribute to global food security & sovereignty. For mass, commercial-scale production (e.g., flour), GC-MS, HPLC, & NMR spectroscopy can test for CPFAs (e.g., sterculic/malvalic acid). Fortunately, CPFAs are highly unstable, decomposing readily through heat, oxidation, & acid.

Herbed "Cheese" — Z,V

Soak 2 cups *P. glabra* seeds overnight. Strain, de-husk, & rinse. Roast at 375°F for 30 min, stirring often. Purée with ¼ tsp salt, 2½ tbsp lemon juice, & 2 cups water. Strain. Mix with 2 tbsp fresh chopped chives. Wrap tightly in cheesecloth & refrigerate for 4 hrs.

Vivian's Hot "Chocolate" — V

Soak 1 cup *P. glabra* seeds overnight. Strain & dehusk. Roast at 375°F for 30 min, stirring often. Purée until smooth with 2 cups water, 1 tbsp maple syrup, 1 tbsp cocoa, ⅛ tsp cinnamon, & ¼ tsp sea salt. Serve warm in mugs.

Chestnut Tea — $,V

Wash 1 cup *P. glabra* young leaves & flowers in very hot water. In an oven at the lowest temp (e.g., 170°F), dry the leaves & flowers until brittle (1 hr). Crumble. Steep 1 tbsp in 2 cups boiling water for 5-7 min. Strain. Serve warm or iced. Considered anti-inflammatory & immune-boosting.

Nut Butter — Z,V

Soak 2 cups *P. glabra* seeds overnight. Strain, de-husk, & rinse. Roast at 375°F for 30 min, stirring often. Purée with ¼ tsp salt, ½ tsp vanilla bean powder, 1 tbsp dark maple syrup, & ½ cup water. Scrape sides & reblend as needed. Add 1 tbsp extra water if needed. Store up to 2 weeks in the fridge.

"Tahini" — Z,V

Soak *P. glabra* seeds overnight. Strain, de-husk, & rinse. Roast at 375°F for 30 min, stirring often. Purée ⅓ cup roasted seeds with ⅓ cup water, 1 tbsp citrus juice, 1 tsp soy sauce, & 1 garlic clove. Add 1+ tbsp water if needed to purée. Store up to 2 weeks in the fridge.

Other Uses

A resilient indoor bonsai/houseplant, the braided trunks of the money tree symbolize how intertwined lives & comforts bring stability. Pet-safe & air-detoxifying, it removes indoor ethyl benzene & formaldehyde. Leaves are used as compresses to aid wound healing—supported by research! Terpenoids in the bark help with headaches & detox.

Cordage

Harvest bark strips (1-2" wide, 12-18" long) from pruned limbs & branches to avoid harming the tree. Soak in water for 24 hrs to soften. Pull apart into thin strips, then twist or braid tightly to form cordage. Ideal for small crafts, bracelets, or tying bundles.

Cold Compress

Tear 6 washed *P. glabra* leaves. Steep in 2 cups boiling water for 20 min, covered. Strain liquid & cool in fridge. Soak cloth/bandage in infusion. Apply to minor burns (incl. sun), insect bites, rashes, or eczema for 15 min. Used in folk healing for burning, itchiness, & inflammation.

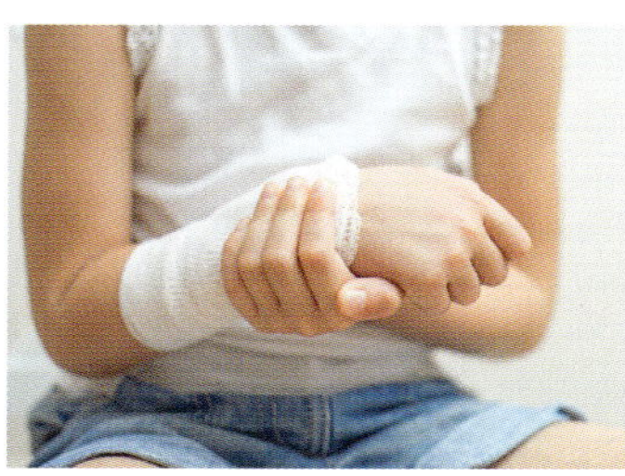

Bonsai

Plant 2-3 seeds in a shallow pot (4-6" deep) with bonsai soil (akadama, pumice, & lava rock mix). Place near a south-facing window. Trim taproot after 2-3 months. Prune in spring, water lightly weekly by misting leaves, & fertilize monthly. Braid stems.

Homemade Soap

Extract 1 cup oil from 20–30 *P. glabra* kernels using a masticating juicer. Wear gloves and goggles & work in a ventilated area for safety. Slowly stir ¼ cup lye into 1 cup water (never reverse). Combine with oil, stirring until thick. Pour into mold & harden for 48 hrs. Cure for 4–6 weeks.

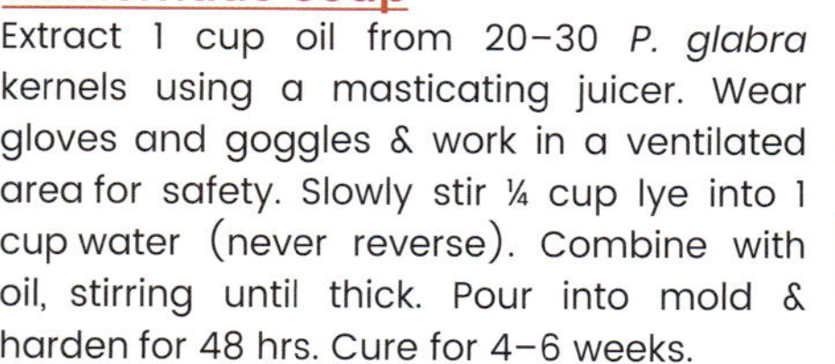

Poultice

Wash & boil 5-6 fresh, healthy *P. glabra* leaves for 20 sec. Drain & cool. Crush/blend into a paste. Apply to minor wounds, cuts, or scrapes. Leave for 30-60 min, then rinse. Repeat 2-3 times daily for anti-inflammatory & antimicrobial benefits.

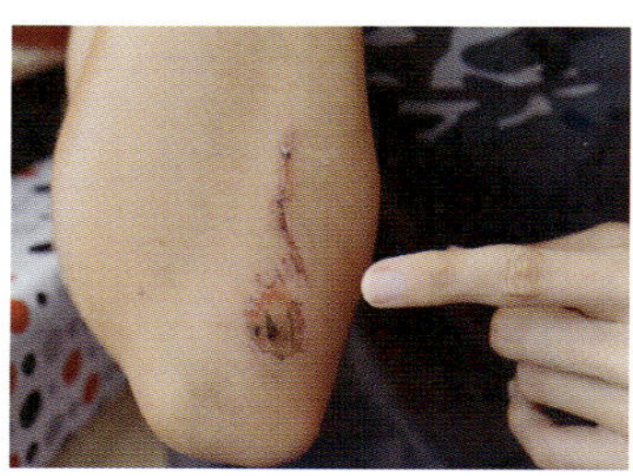

Moringa
Moringa oleifera
Moringaceae Family

ZONE/ SEASON	SIZE H*W	SUN/ SOIL
9-12/ yr-round	35ft*20ft Pollard to 4ft	full/ poor - ok

STAPLE CROP INFO
Balanced protein in leaf & oil in seed
Edible leaves & seed
Dried leaves have more protein than eggs. 9 times more protein than yoghurt. Pods contains around 20+% protein. Mature seeds are 40+% oil (76% PUFA). Tallest brassica vegetable - towers over cousins like kale, & arugala.

PROPAGATE/ PRUNE	PESTS/DISEASE	WATER/ WIND	LIFESPAN	MAX STAPLE YIELD
seed-spring/ winter-pollard	leaf-eaters/ canker, rot	drought tolerant/ shelter from wind	1 yrs to fruit; lives 40+ yrs; fast growth rate	800lbs oil per acre; 2k lbs dry leaf per acre

STORYTELLING
Villagers tell of moringa-fed warriors with almost superhuman strength, who needed very little sleep, never fell sick, & had quick-healing wounds. Moringa is seen as an anomaly of nature—evolutionarily rare, it's considered a "superfood" & nutritional powerhouse that "moves like an arrow" in the body to drive out "bad energy." A top-10 plant to end world hunger, it's called the 'Miracle Tree,' 'Mother's Best Friend,' & a panacea. Moringa is added to children's snacks to combat malnutrition. Egyptians, Romans, & Greeks consumed moringa & buried their dead with it. As a symbol of healing & rejuvenation, moringa regrows leaves even more prolifically when cut down, like a happy 'Giving Tree.' Thriving in poor, dry soils where hunger is common, moringa offers hope in despair. The desert story of Exodus (15:22-27) is believed to reference moringa: "And the Lord showed him a tree, & he threw it into the water, & the water became sweet." Moringa seeds purify water worldwide!

HEALTH CAUTIONS	VARIETY & HEALTH	HEALTH FEATURES	20%+ DV NUTRITION	10%+ DV NUTRITION
Root & flower abortifacient; leaf goitrogens	Soil nitrogen promotes leaf/pod protein content	Leaf used for blood sugar/ pressure	Iron, Calcium (leaf) Magnesium, B2, 6 (leaf) Vit A (seeds)	Potassium, B1, B3 (leaf) Zinc, Folate (pod) Vit C, B5 (pod)

Edible leaf, pod, & flowers at all stages.

FOOD FOREST PLANNING

- # to Plant/ Spacing: 10+/ 10ft apart for pods; 3ft for leaf
- Wildlife Info: Cross-pollination for yield - attract bees
- Native Companion (host): Violet (19) - prevent erosion
- Comparables (zone): Winged bean (8-12); Agati (9-12)
- Notable Varieties: N/A - genus consists of 14 species
  - *M. stenopetala* (9-12): Slower-growing; longer lived
  - *M. peregrina* (10-12): Ornamental leaf; quality oil
  - *M. drouhardii* (10-12): Bottle-shape; fast-growth

Breakfast, Lunch, & Dinner Entrees

A child dies from hunger-related diseases every 5 seconds. Moringa can help combat this. Peak moringa season in Florida is spring-fall. Powdered moringa leaves are nutrient powerhouses: 100g of dry leaf provides 7x more vitamin C than oranges, 10x more vitamin A than carrots, 17x more calcium than milk, 15x more potassium than bananas, & 25x more iron than spinach. Sulfur-rich leaves.

NOTES

Kathleen's Green "Beans"   Z,V

Harvest 4 cups pods <6" long & ⅓" thick (easy to snap). Cut off ends & chop. Boil for 10 min. Add ½ cup moringa flowers & leaves after 7 min. Strain. Sauté for 3 min: 2 tbsp oil, flowers/leaves, ½ tsp salt, ½ tsp each: minced garlic & rosemary. *Variation: Coat in cream of mushroom & crispy onions.

Tanja's "Spinach" Stew   V

Sauté 1 diced onion, 2 cups diced green papaya, & 5 chopped garlic cloves in 1 tbsp oil. In a pot, boil 2 cups chopped green banana/plantain for 15 min. When 3 min remain, add 6 cups chopped moringa leaves. Strain. Simmer all ingredients for 20 min in 8 cups salted broth of choice.

Lisa's Egg Rolls "Tamagoyaki"   Z

Beat 3 eggs with 1 tsp soy sauce. Pour ½ in oiled pan. Coat evenly. Cover. When half-cooked, top edge with a thin line of ¼ cup cooked moringa leaves (1 cup raw, boiled 3 min, strained). Roll up, starting with greens. Push to edge. Re-oil pan. Create second layer of egg to wrap roll. Cool & slice.

Saag "Paneer"   Z,V

Blanch 8 cups moringa leaves for 5 min. Strain. Sauté leaves for 3 min in 2 tbsp oil with 2 tsp garam masala. Cool slightly, then purée in ¼ cup broth of choice. Stir in ¼ cup yogurt & top with cubes of toasted tofu.

Spinach Pie   Z,V

Purée 1½ cups ripe banana with 1½ cups coconut flour. Press 2 cups thinly in oiled 8" pie dish. Poke with fork. Bake 15 min at 350ºF. Boil 8 cups moringa leaves for 3 min. Strain & squeeze dry. Purée coarsely with 1½ cups ricotta & 3 eggs. Pour into crust. Add top crust "H" (1 cup). Bake 45 min at 350ºF.

Appetizers, Snacks, & Sides

Research shows boiled, dried, & powdered moringa leaves provide 3x more bioavailable iron than raw leaves. One tbsp of blanched, powdered moringa helps kids under 3 meet their DV: 14% protein, 40% calcium, 23% iron, & 100% vitamin A. Moringa leaves contain BITC (shown to induce cancer cell death in studies).

<u>NOTES</u>

April's Pesto   Z,V

Boil 3 cups moringa leaves for 3 min. Strain & squeeze out liquid. Purée until smooth with 2 cloves garlic, 3 tbsp Parmesan (or nutritional) cheese, ½ tsp salt, ¼ cup high-fat nuts, & 1 tbsp vinegar or citrus juice. Add 1 tbsp water at a time as needed to purée. Serve with crackers.

Fortified Tortilla   Z,$,V

Deshell 1 cup moringa seeds. Purée coarsely. Soak 12 hrs. Strain. Boil 35 min. Strain. Purée with ½ cup blanched moringa leaves (2 cups raw, boiled 3 min, strained), ½ tsp salt, & 3 eggs until smooth. Pour rounds onto griddle. Cook each side for 3-5 min on medium-high heat.

Sprouts & Crackers   Z,$,V

In a covered dish, cover 2 cups moringa seeds with 5 cups water. Soak 12-24 hrs. Drain, rinse, & strain daily for 7-10 days until sprouted. Stir-fry or roast at 375°F for 30 min in 1 tbsp oil & 1 tbsp soy sauce/aminos. *Variation: Purée sprouts coarsely, press thin rounds & dry crisp at 95°F 24 hrs (sellable).

Refrigerator Pickles   V

Stir 1½ cups vinegar, 1½ cups water, & 1½ tbsp salt until integrated. Boil 7 min 4 cups young, green moringa pods (cut into 3" lengths, ⅓" thick, with ends removed, snap easily). Strain. Add pods, 2 chopped garlic cloves, & 2 dill sprigs to quart jar. Submerge with brine. Let infuse in refrigerator for 2 weeks.

Moringa "Lathera"   Z,V

Boil 4 cups moringa leaves (de-stemmed) for 3 min. Strain. Purée 1 tbsp oil, 2 tbsp Cuban oregano, ¼ cup onion, & ¼ cup tomato. Toss with moringa. Simmer for 2 min until infused.

Drinks, Desserts, & Dips

When young, moringa pods are used as a remedy for digestive problems (47% fiber). Dried seed oil resembles olive oil in fatty acids, & roasting the seeds increases the bioavailability of calcium, zinc, & iron. To make "milk": Deshell 1 cup dried seeds, purée coarsely, soak for 12 hrs, & strain. Boil in 3 cups fresh water for 35 min. Strain. Purée with 2½ cups water, 2 tsp honey, & ¼ tsp salt.

NOTES

Angela's Chocolate Bites $,V

Boil 3 cups moringa for 1 min. Strain. Dry & pulverize in high-speed blender. Measure ¼ cup powder. Melt 1 cup high-quality dark chocolate (70%+ cocoa). Mix in moringa powder. Pour into molds or dollop on parchment. Sprinkle with sea salt. High in iron. Boost absorption: Pair with Vit C fruit.

Salsa "Verde" V

Boil 2 cups moringa leaves for 5 min. Strain. Broil for 10 min until charred: ½ cup diced green mango or 3 green tomatillos, ¼ cup onions, & 2 mild green chili peppers. Purée all ingredients with ½ tsp salt & 3 tbsp coconut cream.

Michelle's Tea Latte V

Whisk 1 tsp moringa powder with 2 tbsp hot water. Froth 1 cup milk of choice (e.g., moringa seed). Pour milk over moringa mixture in a circular motion. For a heart, drizzle milk foam in a dot & drag a toothpick downward to shape.

"Nut" Butter Z,V

Deshell 4 cups moringa seeds. Purée coarsely. Soak overnight. Strain. Boil for 35 min in 8 cups water. Strain. In a high-speed blender, purée with 2 tsp honey & ¼ tsp salt, adding 1 tbsp water as needed until smooth. Store in an airtight jar; refrigerate for up to 1 week.

Infused Honey "Electuary" Z,$,V

Boil 3 cups moringa for 1 min. Strain. Dry at 120°F for 4 hrs or until crisp. Pulverize in a high-speed blender. Place ¼ cup powder in a glass jar. Add 1 cup raw honey. Stir well to combine. Add 2 tbsp to ½ cup fresh citrus juice & 1 cup water for an iron boost.

Other Uses

Seedlings make suitable houseplants when small. Outdoors, moringa acts as a carbon sink, reportedly assimilating CO_2 20x faster than general vegetation. For animal feed, harvest leaves every 75 days. The seed oil can be processed into biodiesel or used in skin creams, hair oils, & soaps. Dried leaf powder is used in oil for massage/cramping. Seed & leaf powder purify water ("flocculation").

Fodder Fencing & Bricks

Chop 4 cups fresh moringa leaves & 2 cups stems. Mix with 2 tbsp molasses for binding. Compress into 4"x3"x2" bricks. Sun-dry for 2-3 days. Suitable for cattle, goats, sheep, & chickens. Rooted 3-5 ft stem cuttings are favored as living fencing & supplemental feed. Repels bugs.

Blue Dye

Select a small limb. Remove bark. Chip inner cambium. Boil 1 cup wood in 4 cups water for 1 hr, stirring occasionally. Strain. Add 2 tbsp vinegar to intensify color. Let sit for 24 hrs, then use the blue liquid as dye.

Purified "Sweetened" Water

Deshell seeds. Grind kernels into powder. Pour 1 cup powder into 4 cups water. Mix fast (2 min), then slowly (10 min) clockwise & counter-clockwise. Let rest for 2 hrs until particles settle. Pour off top water into a glass jar. Place in direct afternoon sun for 3 hrs. Use like a charcoal filter.

Moringa Oil

Deshell & air-dry 4 cups moringa seeds. Feed seeds into a masticating juicer or cold press. Collect the extracted oil. Strain oil through fine mesh or muslin cloth to remove impurities. Store oil in an airtight glass jar in a cool, dark place. Yields about 1 cup oil.

Bark Rope

Strip moringa bark from a small, pruned branch. Peel bark into long, thin fibers. Twist two fibers tightly together, adding more as needed to reach desired length. Tie ends securely. Use twine for light tasks like making bracelets, staking plants, or crafting.

Mulberry

Morus spp.
Moraceae Family

ZONE/ SEASON	SIZE H*W	SUN/ SOIL
5-11/ Mar-June	30ft*30ft dwarf options	full-part/ pH 6.5–7.5

STAPLE CROP INFO

Protein in leaves & oil in seeds
Edible fruit, leaves & seed
Leaves are rich in easy-to-digest protein (up to 35% dried). Fresh fruits average 5% seeds, and mulberry seeds are up to 35% oil. This oil is rich in polyunsaturated fatty acids (PUFA); an omega-3, linoleic acid source.

PROPAGATE/ PRUNE	PESTS/DISEASE	WATER/ WIND	LIFESPAN	MAX STAPLE YIELD
half-ripe cuttings/ shape young	nematodes/ fungus	brief flood- ok/ wind-tolerant	3+ yrs to fruit; lives 100+ yrs; fast growth rate	6+k lbs fruit, 65lbs oil; 20k leaf lbs per acre

STORYTELLING

In a world where self-care is often overlooked, the nursery rhyme "Here We Go Round the Mulberry Bush" passes down more than just a tune—it teaches the practical wisdom of tending to our well-being. Every line in the song aligns with mulberry plant uses. At the heart of self-care is nutritious food, & mulberry is a treasure trove of nutrients & antioxidants, appealing to 80% of the world who rely on traditional medicine. Beyond health benefits, mulberries symbolize protection, faith, & patience in Judaic & Christian scripture (2 Samuel 5:23-24, 1 Chronicles 14:14-15). This spiritual significance inspires the use of mulberry paper for prayers, mulberry cuttings for living fences, mulberry wood carvings as talismans for newborn cribs, & mulberry coffins for final rest. Mulberry not only protects people but also the planet—sinking carbon, removing air pollution, bioremediating soil, absorbing heavy metals, & reducing erosion. As climate change debates unfold, one thing is certain: clean air & soil are essential elements of self-care.

HEALTH CAUTIONS	VARIETY & HEALTH	HEALTH FEATURES	20%+ DV NUTRITION	10%+ DV NUTRITION
Pollen allergen; latex sap; unripe fruit - toxic	Anthocyanins (black/purple)	Leaves have antidiabetic effect	Vit C (fruit, leaf) Vit K (fruit) Iron, Calcium (leaf)	Iron, Potassium (fruit) Zinc (dry leaf) Vit E (seed)

Fruit are edible when ripe but color varies.

FOOD FOREST PLANNING

- # to Plant/ Spacing: 5+/plant 15ft apart, east–west row
- Wildlife Info: Hosts 12 caterpillar; *M. alba* - invasive risk
- Native Companion (host): Goldenrod (82)
- Comparables (zones): Blackberry/ Rasberry (5-12)
- Notable Varieties: Hybridizes. *M. ruba* = dioecious native
  o *M. nigra*: Prefers less humidity (e.g., Everbearing)
  o *M. alba*: Protein leaf (e.g., FL Giant, Thai, Shangri La)
  o *M. macroura*: Long fruit (e.g., Pakistan, Skinner)

Breakfast, Lunch, & Dinner Entrees

In Florida, peak mulberry fruiting is spring-summer. Subspecies & cultivars influence the nutritional value of mulberry leaves. *Morus alba* cultivars offer the highest protein content, especially in mid-spring. The leaves are an easily digestible & inexpensive protein source—comparable to soybeans! Seeds are highly nutritious & can be strained, dried, & toasted as a tasty topping for salads or yogurt.

<u>NOTES</u>

Breakfast Tart $,V

Purée 1½ cups ripe banana with 1½ cups coconut. Form crust with 2 cups in 8" pan. Bake 15 min at 350ºF. Mix 5½ cups mashed, strained mulberries with ½ cup just-ripe, puréed banana, 3 tbsp maple syrup, 2 tbsp nut butter, & ¼ tsp salt. Pour in crust. Form 2" crust rim with 1 cup. Bake 35 min at 350ºF.

Breakfast Tamales $,V

Purée 1 cup ripe banana, ⅔ cup coconut flour, ½ tsp cinnamon, & ¼ tsp salt to form batter. Let thicken for 10 min. Wash 2½ cups mulberries. Strain. Boil 3 min 20 large mulberry leaves. Strain & pat dry. Spread ¼ cup batter per leaf. Add 2 tbsp mulberries. Fold leaf burrito-style. Steam for 30 min.

Niquelle's Mulberry Stir-Fry Z,V

Boil 2 cups young, chopped, de-ribbed mulberry leaves in salted water for 3 min. Drain. In a bowl, combine leaves with 1 tbsp crushed garlic, 2 tbsp chopped onion, 1 tbsp oil, & 1 tbsp miso mixed with ¼ cup water. Stir-fry on low for 7-10 min until fragrant & softened. Top with ¼ cup dried mulberries.

Mulberry Breakfast Casserole

Preheat oven to 375ºF. Boil 60 mulberry leaves 5 mins; pat dry. Mash 5 cups white mulberries with 1 tbsp maple syrup. Mix 2 cups ricotta, 2 eggs, & 1 cup mozzarella. In a greased 8x11" pan, layer 20 leaves, 1 cup cheese mix, & 1 cup mash. Repeat twice. Top with mozzarella. Bake for 45 mins.

Rebecca's Spinach Lasagna Z,V

Boil 60 large mulberry leaves for 3 min. Drain & pat dry. Mix 2 cups crumbled feta, 2 eggs, & 1 tbsp minced oregano. In an oiled 8x8" pan, layer 3 times: 20 mulberry leaves, feta mixture, & chunky mushroom marinara. Top with 1 cup Parmesan. Bake at 375ºF for 45 min.

Appetizers, Snacks, & Sides

Mulberry leaves & fruit are functional foods. Prune in late winter (basal suckers, vertical shoots) to encourage a large berry harvest or simply cut limbs at harvest to collect leaves & berries. Cuttings can serve as windbreak fences or be used to grow oyster & shiitake mushrooms. Logs should be 5" thick & 4 ft long. Fruit can be red, green, white, purple, or black.

Elana's Mulberry Cold Soup V

Purée & strain 3 cups mulberries. Microwave 1 medium green banana (7 min), peel. Grate, soak, & rinse 1 cup green papaya. Purée until smooth: mulberries, cooked green banana, soaked papaya, 3 tbsp olive oil, 2 tbsp lemon juice, & 1 tsp salt. Chill for 2 hrs. Serve cold.

Fruit Sausages $,V

Cut 10 rosemary stems (8"); skewer 5 dried mulberries on each. Boil 10 mulberry leaves for 3 min; pat dry. Roll 1 leaf tightly around each skewer. Simmer 2 cups mulberry purée for 10 min until thick. Paint purée layers on skewers. Hang at 95°F–113°F for 24 hrs or until no longer sticky.

Mulberry Leaf "Kimchi" Z,V

Massage 2 tbsp pickling salt on 7 cups torn mulberry leaves for 5 min. Rest 2 hrs. Rinse. Mix with 2 tbsp each: crushed garlic, ginger, mulberry fruit, & ¼ cup chili flakes. Pack leaves & liquid in quart jar. Cover with brine (4 cups water & 1 tbsp salt), leaving 2" from rim. Ferment 3+ days, stirring daily.

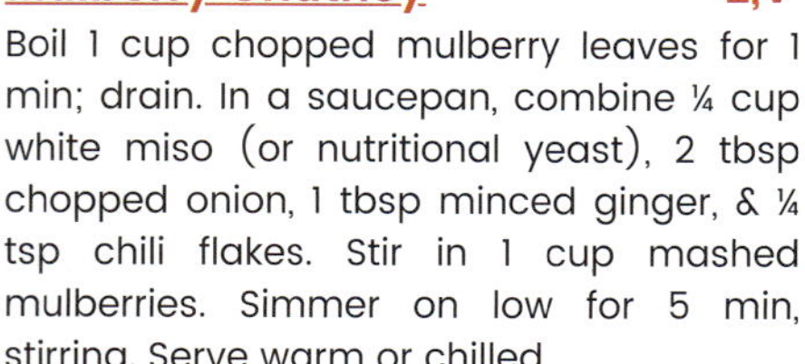

Mulberry Chutney Z,V

Boil 1 cup chopped mulberry leaves for 1 min; drain. In a saucepan, combine ¼ cup white miso (or nutritional yeast), 2 tbsp chopped onion, 1 tbsp minced ginger, & ¼ tsp chili flakes. Stir in 1 cup mashed mulberries. Simmer on low for 5 min, stirring. Serve warm or chilled.

Sweet Dolmades V

Boil 20 mulberry leaves for 3 min; pat dry. Peel & grate 1 cup green banana. Boil for 5 min; strain. Mix banana "rice" with ½ cup dried mulberries, 2 tbsp chopped nuts, 1 tsp cinnamon, & ½ tsp lemon zest. Fill leaves with 1 tbsp mix; roll tightly. Steam for 30 min. Serve warm or chilled.

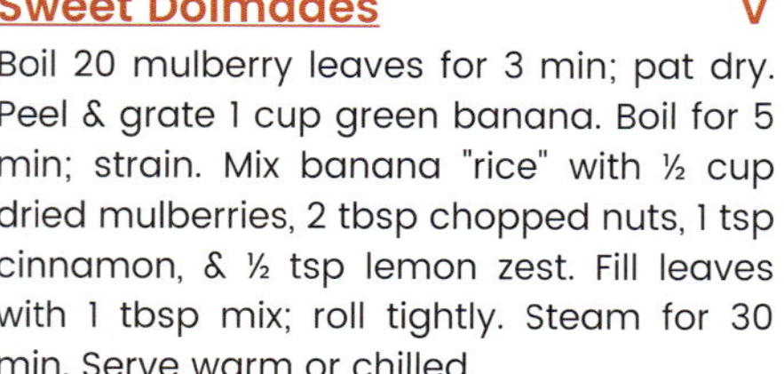

Drinks, Desserts, & Dips

All parts of *Morus alba*—fruits, leaves, twigs, bark, & roots—have been used in Traditional Chinese Medicine (TCM) for over 3,000 years. It's also featured in Ayurveda, the British Pharmacopoeia, & "Foodomics." Leaves are considered antidiabetic, antimicrobial, anticancer, anthelmintic, immunomodulatory, hypocholesterolemic, nephroprotective, & hepatoprotective.

NOTES

Mulberry Curd

Purée & strain 3 cups mulberries. On medium-low, stir strained purée with 2 tbsp maple syrup, 2 tbsp coconut oil, 2 tbsp lemon juice, & a pinch of salt. Slowly whisk a small amount of the warm purée into 4 whisked eggs, then mix eggs into the saucepan. Stir for 8–10 min until thickened.

Mulberry Tea $,V

Wash 5 cups mulberry leaves. Flavor varies (*M. alba* = mild; *M. nigra* & *M. rubra* = robust). Dry at 95°F–120°F for 6 hrs or until brittle. Crumble. Store airtight up to 6 mo. Steep 1 tsp in 1 cup boiling water 5 min. Called "Immortal Mountain Wizard Tea." *Variation: Add equal parts dry mulberry fruit.

Mulberry Juice   V

Blend 3 cups washed mulberries, 1 cup water, 1–2 tsp rosemary, 2 tsp lemon juice, & 2 tbsp maple syrup. Strain through cloth. For fermentation, transfer to sterilized jar, cover loosely, & ferment for 3–5 days until bubbly. Refrigerate. Save pulp as jam substitute; refrigerate for up to 5 days.

Mulberry Energy Balls $,V

Purée 1 cup dried mulberries, 1½ tbsp finely ground, dried mulberry leaves, 1 tbsp maple syrup, ½ tbsp melted coconut oil, & ¼ tsp salt into sticky dough. Refrigerate for 30 min. Form 12–16 balls & roll in toasted coconut. Store airtight for 1 week or freeze for 1 month.

"Baklava" Breakfast Bites $,V

Boil 25 mulberry leaves 5 min; pat dry. Mix 2 cups minced nuts, 1 tsp cinnamon, 1 tbsp oil, & ⅛ tsp salt. Layer leaves & nuts in oiled 8x8" pan (5 layers). Brush oil on top. Slice diamonds. Bake 1 hr at 325°F. Simmer 2 cups mulberry purée & 2 tbsp maple syrup for 10 min. Pour syrup over baklava. Chill for 12 hrs.

Other Uses

Mulberry wood uses match self-care lines in "Here We Go Round the Mulberry Bush"—combs ("comb our hair"), toothbrushes ("brush our teeth"), caterpillar leaf fodder for silk clothes ("put on our clothes"), & bark for soap ("wash our face"). For soap, boil bark in 1 cup water for 10 min to release saponins. For prayer "paper," dry leaves in cloth under a plate in microwave (15-sec bursts).

NOTES

Hair Comb

Harvest a straight mulberry branch, 6" long & 1" thick. Remove bark; sand smooth with 100-220 grit. Mark teeth ~⅛" apart; carve 1" deep with fine saw. Sand teeth smooth. Apply natural oil (e.g., coconut); cure for 24 hrs. Test for smoothness & durability. Reapply oil as needed.

Toothbrushes

Harvest 6" long, 1" thick young mulberry twigs. Blanch in boiling water for 5 mins. Remove bark from one tip; gently pound to fray fibers. Dry at 170°F for 4 hrs. Store in an airtight container. Mulberry has anti-microbial properties to promote tooth & gum health.

Leaf Protein Concentrate

Rinse 2 cups mulberry leaves. Blend with ½ cup water. Strain juice through fine cloth. Boil juice for 5–10 mins until curds form. Strain curds; press gently. Dry at 95°F for 4 hrs. Grind. Store airtight. Use ¼ tsp daily. Encapsulate or add to bread & soup for immunity & liver health.

Watercolor Paint

Freeze 1 cup mulberries in a glass container. Thaw at room temp to release juices. Strain through fine mesh sieve or cheesecloth to separate liquid from pulp. Use strained liquid as natural watercolor pigment for eco-friendly painting.

Butterfly & Animal Enclosure

Plant mulberry cuttings 3 ft apart. Espalier limbs at alternating heights of 1 ft & 3 ft, 2 ft & 4 ft. Secure espaliered limbs to neighboring trunks, creating a tight, secure perimeter. This provides an animal enclosure & nutritious leaf fodder. Also hosts the red admiral butterfly & others!

OAK

Quercus spp.
Fagaceae Family

ZONE/ SEASON	SIZE H*W	SUN/ SOIL
3-11/ Sept-Dec	60ft*60ft dwarf options	full-part/ poor - ok

STAPLE CROP INFO

Balanced protein/carb & oil in seed
Edible leaves, seed & fruit
Mature acorns are up to 9% protein, 50% starch & 30% oil. A pound of acorns are up to 1265 calories. Better nutrition than cereals. Acorn oil compares with olive oil in flavor but is less likely to spoil during harvest.

PROPAGATE/ PRUNE	PESTS/DISEASE	WATER/ WIND	LIFESPAN	MAX STAPLE YIELD
seed-autumn/ winter-crown	acorn weevil/ wilt, canker, rot	brief flood- ok/ wind break	3+ yrs to fruit; lives 300+ yrs; fast growth rate	6+k lbs per acre; 2k lbs per tree

STORYTELLING

We can rocket to the moon & beyond but can't leach tannins from acorns? Of course we can! The real question is: Why don't we? Oaks aren't just wartime assets—acorns are as nutritious & productive as cereal grains without the ecological toll. Oaks are keystone species, supporting entire ecosystems, including humans. Acorns ripen all at once, are easy to collect, & once made up 50% of our ancestral diet, allowing us to live in harmony with nature. They nourished us as bread, coffee, & cookies, providing food sovereignty. Oaks are cultural pillars—the Latin word for 'oak' & 'strength' are the same. By blocking lightning strikes, they've come to symbolize military prowess, religious devotion, & political resilience. Cultured societies gathered under 'Gospel Oaks' for biblical readings, while revolutionaries met beneath "Liberty Oaks" to plot change. Such pivotal experiences led to the belief that heaven-bound souls have oaks growing from their pure hearts in cemeteries. Let's restore oaks to their rightful place, reviving their power to nourish us, sustain ecosystems, & create a butterfly garden paradise!

HEALTH CAUTIONS	VARIETY & HEALTH	HEALTH FEATURES	20%+ DV NUTRITION	10%+ DV NUTRITION
Tannic acid - leach acorns if bitter	"White"-low tannin; "red"-high oil Big cap-high tannin	Rich phytosterols high phenolics high-oleic oil	Vit A, E manganese copper	Protein, carbs magnesium potassium

Edible when acorns are ripe & tan-brown.

FOOD FOREST PLANNING

- # to Plant/ Spacing: 3+; full-sized 40ft apart/ 3ft-dwarf
- Wildlife Info: Hosts 395 caterpillar species
- Native Companion (host): Black/raspberry (93)
- Comparables: Keystones-maple, elm, pine
- Notable Varieties: Hybridizes
  - Versatility: *Q. geminata* (zones 7-10) fruit in 20 yrs
  - Dwarf (1-3ft): *Q. minima* (zones 7-10) fruit in 3 yrs
  - Edible Raw: *Q. michauxii* (zones 5-9) fruit in 20 yrs

Breakfast, Lunch, & Dinner Entrees

Peak acorn season is fall. Acorns from all oak species are edible. Traditional songs speak of tree "grains" (oak orchards). ***Leach tannins by puréeing 1 cup shelled acorns with 4 cups water. For first soak, add 1 tsp baking soda per quart. Rinse & change water daily for 5+ days until bitterness is gone. For faster leach, boil for 15 min, changing water (e.g., 5x), adding acorns to hot water.

NOTES 

Acorn Pancakes

____
____
____
____
____
____
____

Purée 1 cup leached, dry acorn flour with 2 eggs & ½ cup high-protein milk. Add more milk if batter is too thick. Pour 2 tbsp at a time onto a medium-hot, oiled skillet or waffle griddle. Cook 2–3 mins per side or until golden. Serve with maple syrup. Yields 6 small pancakes or 4 waffles.

Acorn Omelette "Migas"   Z

____
____
____
____
____
____
____

Heat 1 tbsp oil in a skillet over medium heat. Sauté 1½ cups leached coarse acorn meal with 1 tbsp minced garlic & 2 tbsp chopped onion until caramelized. Beat 3 eggs, pour into skillet, cover & cook 5–10 mins until set. Top with 1 tbsp fresh herbs. Serves 2–3.

Acorn Noodles   Z,$,V

____
____
____
____
____
____
____

Purée 1 cup leached acorn meal, 2 cups water, & 2 tsp agar agar until smooth. Simmer on low for 5 mins, stirring. Spread thinly on a non-stick surface. Chill for 1–3 hrs until firm. Cut into noodles. Top with 2 tbsp soy sauce mixed with 1 tsp vinegar & chopped green onions.

Acorn Porridge   V

____
____
____
____
____
____
____

Mix 1 cup leached acorn meal with 3 cups water in a medium-hot saucepan. Cook on medium heat for 10 mins, stirring until thickened. Add 1 tbsp chopped nuts, a pinch of salt, & 1 tsp cinnamon. Drizzle with maple syrup & milk of choice. Serves 2. *Variation: Top with stewed seasonal fruit.

Acorn & Herb Stew   V

____
____
____
____
____
____

Purée & simmer 1 cup leached acorn meal in 4 cups broth with 2 tbsp olive oil, 2 tbsp minced oregano, & 1 tbsp minced thyme on medium heat for 20 mins, stirring often. Cool. Stir in ½ cup plain yogurt of choice. Top with fresh oregano. Serves 2–3.

Appetizers, Snacks, & Sides

A typical person can collect 50 lbs (average year) to 300 lbs (mast year/every 2-3 years) of acorns per year from an oak at its peak. A life-giving gift, acorn "tree grains" are far less polluted by pesticides & heavy metals. Cold leaching preserves gluten-like starches & amino acids. Acorn meal substitutes for cornmeal & can replace chickpeas, nuts, peanuts, & olives in dishes.

NOTES

Acorn Bread/ "Pan'Ispeli" — Z,$

Mix 3 cups leached acorn flour with 2½ cups hot water, 4 eggs, 2 tbsp oil, 2 tbsp minced rosemary, & 1 cup grated Parmesan until a thick but pourable dough forms. Pour into an oiled 9x5" loaf pan. Bake at 350°F for 1 hr or until firm. Cool. Slice. Toast. *Variation: Fold in chopped nuts or dried fruit.

Boiled Acorns — Z,V

Boil 1 cup acorns in shell in 5 cups water for 30 mins. Strain. Cool. Halve with a serrated knife. Pop out kernels & rub off skin. Taste for bitterness. Repeat boiling (up to 5x) with fresh water until not bitter. For flavor, boil final time in 2 cups water, 2 tsp allspice, 1 tbsp orange peel, & ½ tsp salt for 30 mins.

Acorn "Tofu" — Z,V

Mix 1 cup leached acorn flour with 5 cups water. Simmer on medium for 10 mins, stirring until thick & uniform. Pour into an 8x8" parchment-lined dish. Refrigerate overnight. Slice with serrated knife. Top with 3 tbsp soy sauce, 2 tsp sesame oil, 1 tbsp toasted sesame seeds, & 2 green onions.

Acorn Soup — V

Sauté 2 cups leached, coarse acorn meal (rice-like texture) with 1 cup chopped mushrooms & 1 tbsp minced garlic in 1 tbsp oil until fragrant. Add 4 cups high-protein salted broth. Simmer on medium heat for 10 mins. Top with chopped chives.

Pickled Acorns — Z,V

Boil 1 cup acorns in 5 cups water for 30 mins. Halve, remove kernels & rub off skins. Repeat boiling up to 5x if bitter. Strain. Simmer 1 cup fresh water, 1 cup vinegar, 1 tbsp salt, 1 tbsp peppercorns, 2 tbsp maple syrup, & 2 bay leaves for 5 mins. Pour brine over acorns in jar. Infuse in fridge 2 weeks.

Drinks, Desserts, & Dips

Research highlights the anti-inflammatory benefits of acorns as a functional food for preventing chronic diseases. Knowledge of wild foods is disappearing, while wild food products now fetch high prices in exclusive dining experiences. Acorn meal sells for $16–$30 per lb.

Acorn Coffee/ Tea $,V

Roast 1 cup leached, coarsely ground dry acorn meal at 350ºF for 10–15 mins, stirring often, until dark & fragrant. Grind to a fine powder. Store in an airtight container in the fridge. To brew as coffee, use 1½ tbsp acorn meal per 1 cup water. Add ½ tsp cinnamon or ¼ tsp cocoa for enriched flavor.

Acorn Syrup   V

Simmer 1 cup leached acorn flour with 7 cups water for 2 hrs. Add ⅔ cup pineapple juice; simmer on low for 1 hr more. Strain. Simmer strained liquid on low for 2 hrs until thickened. Cool & store in a sterilized jar in the fridge.

Acorn Cookies $,V

Mix 1 cup leached, wet acorn meal, 2 tbsp maple syrup (or Kuromitsu), ½ cup puréed ripe banana, 1 tbsp sesame oil, 1 tsp citrus zest, & ⅛ tsp salt until smooth. Add 1+ tbsp water as needed. Roll into a log in parchment. Refrigerate for 1 hr. Slice into ¼" thick disks. Bake at 350ºF for 30 mins.

Acorn Pudding   V

Simmer 1 cup leached acorn flour, 1 tsp vanilla extract, ¼ cup cocoa powder, ⅛ tsp salt, 2 tbsp maple syrup, & 3 cups water for 20 mins or until thickened. Cool. Mix with 2 tbsp coconut cream until smooth. Pour into serving dishes & refrigerate for 2 hrs before serving.

Elana's Acorn "Cheese"   Z,V

Simmer 1 cup leached, wet acorn flour with 3 cups water for 10 mins. Cool slightly. Blend with 1 tbsp vegan yogurt. Ferment at 113ºF for 7 hrs. Gently strain through cloth by hanging in the fridge for 4 hrs above a bowl. Form balls. Roll in 3 tbsp dried herbs & refrigerate for 12 hrs. Consume within 5–7 days.

Other Uses

Oak forests are among our best carbon capture technologies, producing "grains" exponentially & ethically. In contrast, annual agriculture drives species extinction & topsoil loss. Agriculture occupies 44% of habitable land—imagine if it were full of oaks, central to the planet's biology! For quick ID: White oak leaves have rounded lobes; red oak leaves have pointed lobes. Larger acorn caps = more tannins.

<u>NOTES</u> 

Fodder

Turkey, deer, & pigs (including wild boar) have tannin-binding salivary proteins & can consume raw acorns in high doses. Acorns can comprise 50–75% of their diets from 6 months of age.

Traditional Medicine

Harvest mature oak leaves in early fall. Dry in shade. Steep 1 tbsp dried leaves in 1 cup boiling water for 10 mins. Use as a wash for wounds to reduce inflammation, backed by research on tannins & polyphenols in oak species that promote healing.

Shiitake Mushroom Logs/ Charcoal

Cut oak logs (4–6 inches in diameter, 3–4 ft long) in late winter/early spring. Store in a shaded, moist area. Drill holes, insert mushroom spawn plugs, & seal with wax. Harvest shiitakes in 6–12 months. Spent logs make excellent charcoal. Partially burn wood, cover with sand, & smolder for 24 hrs.

Ink

Collect 10 oak galls, crush, & boil in 2 cups water with 2 rusty nails for 1 hr. Strain. Reboil for 15–20 mins to thicken. Refrigerate. U.S. Constitution, Declaration of Independence, Leonardo da Vinci's drawings, & Bach's music were all created with gall ink.

Hairstreak Butterfly Host

Oak trees support butterflies like hairstreaks & duskywings by hosting caterpillars. Avoid pesticides. Prune in late winter to prevent disturbing cocoons or feeding cycles. Remove only dead or crowded branches to maintain tree health. Plant native species & keep leaf litter for habitat.

Papaya
Carica papaya
Caricaceae Family

ZONE/ SEASON	SIZE H*W	SUN/ SOIL
9-12/ yr-round	10ft*3ft dwarf options	full-part/ poor - ok

STAPLE CROP INFO
Protein & oil in seed
Edible leaves, flower, fruit & seed
Papaya is one of the most widely cultivated crops in the world. Fruits weigh up to 10lbs. A low calorie but nutrient-dense fruit. The seeds are 26% fat (oil is similar to olive oil), 25% protein & 29% fiber.

PROPAGATE/ PRUNE	PESTS/DISEASE	WATER/ WIND	LIFESPAN	MAX STAPLE YIELD
seed-spring/ winter-cut to 4ft	papaya wasp/ fungus, rot, PRSV	drought tolerant/ shelter from wind	1 yr to fruit; lives up to 5 yrs; fast growth rate	50k lbs fruit per acre; 5k lbs seeds per acre

STORYTELLING
Looks can be deceiving. Papaya resembles a tree but is actually a giant medicinal herb. All parts, but especially the leaves, are revered by herbalists. Referred to as "fruit of angels" & "feel well" thanks to the nutritional & healing uses of roots, leaves, peel, latex, flower, fruit, & seeds. Comes in a rainbow of flavors & colors, including yellow, orange, or red flesh varieties. This plant is the answer for those wondering how they can grow food quickly & easily for their family. Several varieties generously produce from seed within one year. By enriching both health & income, papaya brings salvation for those avoiding the inflated cost of groceries. Dating back to ancient Mayan & Aztec cultures, papaya is believed to promote prosperity. By strengthening the stomach & aiding digestion, the immune system can prosper & thrive. Nicknamed "tree of health" & "fruit of long life." Clustered fruit is compared to a mother's bosom full of milk. Ripe papaya helps wean babies around the world.

HEALTH CAUTIONS	VARIETY & HEALTH	HEALTH FEATURES	20%+ DV NUTRITION	10%+ DV NUTRITION
Allergens: pollen, latex. Avoid unripe if pregnant.	Lycopene (red fruit) β-carotene (yellow fruit)	Papain aids digestion; seeds antiparasitic	Vit C (un/ ripe) Vit A (ripe) Protein, fiber (seeds)	Folate, copper (ripe) Potassium (un/ripe) Magnesium (ripe)

Edible at all stages of ripeness & sizes.

FOOD FOREST PLANNING

- # to Plant/ Spacing: 5+/ plant 7ft apart
- Wildlife Info: Caterpillar host, now considered native
- Native Companion (host): Dune sunflower (58)
- Comparables (zone): Paw Paw (5-8); fig (6-10)
- Notable Varieties: Hermaphroditic types
  - Maradol: Large, sweet (e.g., Maradol Red)
  - Mexican: Robust (e.g., Tainung, Red & Yellow Lady)
  - Hawaiian: Melon-like (e.g., Solo, Sunrise, Sunset)

Breakfast, Lunch, & Dinner Entrees

Peak papaya season in Florida is summer-fall. Replace zucchini & cucumber with green papaya or carrot with semi-ripe papaya! Solo papaya is among the most popular in Florida. Green papaya offers health benefits. Soak or boil to reduce papain, an enzyme that reportedly breaks down cancer cell walls, aids protein digestion, but may stimulate uterine contractions.

<u>**NOTES**</u>

Kacie's "Lasagna"   Z,V

Peel & thinly slice 2 green papayas using a mandoline. Boil 5 min & drain. In an oiled 8"x8" casserole dish, layer 4x: Papaya, 1 tbsp oil, ⅓ tbsp Italian seasoning, ¼ cup diced onion, ⅓ cup almond flour (or nutritional yeast) & ⅓ cup chunky marinara. Bake at 375°F for 45 min. *Dry "lasagna" is sellable.

Nicole's Veggie Cakes   Z

Peel, deseed & grate 2 cups green papaya. Squeeze dry with towel. In a large bowl, toss with 2 beaten eggs, 2 tbsp chopped herbs, 3 tbsp coconut flour, ¾ cup Parmesan & ½ tsp salt. Spoon 12 dollops onto an oiled pan. Bake at 400°F for 30 min, flipping at 15 min, until browned.

Michelle's & Elana's Ramen $,V

Pick 3 zucchini-sized papayas. Cut off ends & peel. Deseed & spiralize or grate into long strips. Rinse. Simmer 5 min (or until softened) in 5 cups broth with 5 tbsp brown miso. Top with chives. *Variation: Simmer in marinara, Italian-style. NOTE: Dry "noodles" are sellable.

Ana's Green Papaya Soup   V

Halve 2 green papayas lengthwise. Deseed. Roast cut-side down at 400°F for 50 min or until tender. Sauté 1 Granny Smith apple with ½ yellow onion & 8 basil (or sage) leaves. Puree until smooth: roasted papaya pulp, sautéed mix, 1½ tsp salt, 2½ cups broth & 2½ cups water. Garnish with basil.

Green Papaya Spiral   Z

Whip 1 cup each: coconut flour & ripe banana. Press into oiled 8" pie pan. Bake at 350°F for 15 min. Fill with ½ cup ricotta mixed with 1 egg. Peel & thinly slice 3 semi-ripe papayas using a mandoline. Rinse. Spiral in crust. Brush with oil & ⅛ tsp salt. Bake 30 min at 350°F.

Appetizers, Snacks, & Sides

Papaya is known as a "nutraceutical," a term combining 'nutrition' & 'pharmaceutical,' due to its believed health benefits & disease prevention (e.g., cleansing intestines). The plant is also linked to anti-cancer & anti-tumor research. In some cultures, papaya leaves are used as spinach. Older leaves contain carpaine (which lowers blood pressure), so younger leaves are recommended.

NOTES

Carly's Coleslaw   Z,V

Grate 2 green/semi-ripe papayas (3 cups). Rinse & strain. Drizzle with your favorite coleslaw dressing or whisk together 3 tbsp oil, 1 tbsp vinegar & 1 tbsp honey. Add salt/pepper to taste. *Variation: Mix in 2 tbsp each (minced): Cuban oregano, basil, sprouted pumpkin seeds & dried fruit.

Sue-Ann's Pickled Papaya   Z,V

Massage 4 cups grated, rinsed green papaya with 1 tsp salt. Rest 5 min. Rinse. Put in quart jar. Mix 1 cup vinegar, 3 tbsp coconut sugar, 2 tbsp peppercorns & 1 cup water. Pour over papaya. Refrigerate 24hrs. *Variation: Add 2 tbsp chili paste & 1 lemongrass stalk for an Asian twist.

Elana's Curry   Z,V

Dice 4 cups green papaya (½" cubes). Boil 3 min. Strain. In a pan on medium-high, simmer covered for 30 min: 1½ cups coconut milk, ½ tbsp each: minced ginger & turmeric, 1 tsp cracked pepper, 2 curry leaves (optional), 1 tsp salt, ½ cup water & diced papaya.

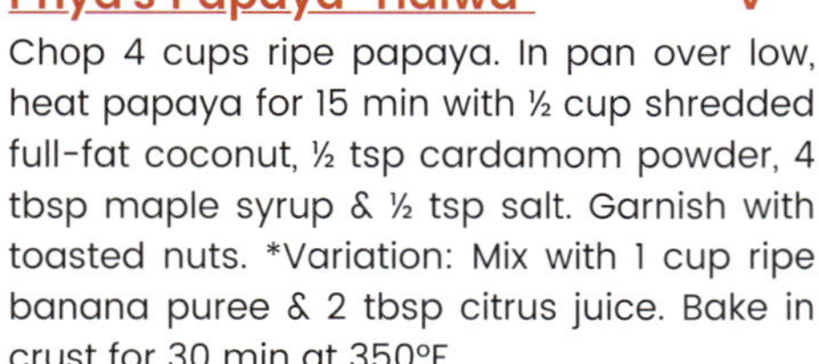

Priya's Papaya "Halwa"   V

Chop 4 cups ripe papaya. In pan over low, heat papaya for 15 min with ½ cup shredded full-fat coconut, ½ tsp cardamom powder, 4 tbsp maple syrup & ½ tsp salt. Garnish with toasted nuts. *Variation: Mix with 1 cup ripe banana puree & 2 tbsp citrus juice. Bake in crust for 30 min at 350ºF.

Papaya Leaf "Horta"   Z,V

Wash 4 cups young, tender papaya leaves & 1 cup male flowers. Remove hard leaf ribs. Chop & sprinkle with salt; massage. Let rest 30 min. Rinse. Boil for 10 min. Drain. Sauté for 10 min with 1 tbsp oil & 1 tbsp citrus juice. Drizzle with 1 tsp honey. *Variation: Serve with yogurt.

Drinks, Desserts, & Dips

Papaya seeds are reportedly rich in BITC, which research shows can have cancer cell-killing effects. Like most seeds, soaking overnight removes phytic acid & tannins, improving nutritional quality. Consume in moderation—excessive intake may temporarily lower sperm count (spermatozoa contraceptive). Some researchers are calling for pharmaceutical patents for this male contraceptive.

NOTES

Red Lady Marinara   Z,V

Sauté 5 min in 3 tbsp oil: 1½ cups minced red onion, 2 tsp paprika & 1½ tbsp basil. Add 4 cups pureed ripe, red-pulp papaya, 1 cup broth, 3 tbsp balsamic vinegar & 2 tsp salt. Simmer for 20 min. Store in quart jar. *NOTE: (1) Great on green papaya "noodles"! (2) Pumpkin substitutes well!

Britten & Robyn's Tea $,V

Wash, soak overnight & rinse ½ cup black papaya seeds, 2 cups diced ripe papaya, 2 young papaya leaves & ⅓ cup male flowers. Dry in oven at 170ºF or lower for 4+ hrs. Grind in blender. Brew 1 tsp tea in 1 cup boiling water. *NOTE: Used in folk healing (for diabetes, detox & obesity).

Michelle & Britten's Smoothie   V

Purée 2 cups ripe papaya, 1 cup coconut milk, 1 cup water, 1" turmeric root, 1 tbsp pepper (or papaya seeds) & 1 tbsp honey. Drink fresh or ferment covered overnight. *NOTE: Believed to have anti-aging effects.

Tony's Green Papaya Dip   Z,V

Chop 3 cups green papaya (peeled, deseeded). Blanch for 7 min with 1 cup cashews. Strain & purée with 2 cloves garlic, 1 tbsp dried onion, 3 tbsp nutritional yeast, 1-2 tsp salt, 1 tbsp vinegar or citrus juice & 3 cups broth.

Spice Cookies $,V

Purée 1 cup ground black papaya seeds (soaked overnight, drained, rinsed), 2 tsp cinnamon, 3 dates (soaked, pitted), 1 tsp citrus zest & ⅔ cup ripe banana. Fold in 2 tbsp mini chocolate chips. Form drop cookies & press flat onto a parchment-lined sheet. Bake for 25 min at 325ºF.

Other Uses

Folk healers suggest yearly "Papaya Therapy"—eat papaya daily for 2 wks to boost immunity & cleanse intestines. Healthy intestines absorb vitamins & minerals efficiently, especially B12. In some cultures, dried papaya leaves are used as a meat tenderizing wrap & smoked for calming effects (e.g., rolled like a cigar or crumbled in a cigarette). For first-aid, papaya sap soothes insect bites & stings.

NOTES

Sue-Ann's Healing Caviar   Z

Mix 1 tbsp mature (black) papaya seeds with 1 tsp honey & a pinch of salt. Eat plain or on buttered crackers as "caviar" topped with citrus zest or chives. Consume for a max of 10 days straight. Used as an antimicrobial, anti-parasitic/anthelmintic & digestive health support. 29% fiber.

Robyn's Pepper Substitute

Soak mature/black papaya seeds overnight. Rinse & rub off any fruit or gel coating. Dry in oven or dehydrator on lowest setting until thoroughly shriveled. Grind in a pepper grinder or pulverize in a blender. Excellent in salad dressings.

Face/ Skin Mask

Powdered leaf contains papain. Collect 3 large papaya leaves. Dry completely. Pulverize in a blender. Mix 1 tbsp papaya powder with 2 tbsp aloe vera gel. Apply for 20 min. Rinse. Supports wound healing/skin whitening. *Variation: Boil leaf 3 min. Cut holes (eyes/mouth). Use as a face mask.

Wesley's Stem Straw

Papaya stems are hollow. Cut 8" segments of papaya leaf stem. Soak in warm water & vinegar (1:3 ratio) for 10 min to clean & leach latex. Rinse. Dehydrate in bulk: 150°F for 30 min, then 95°F for 6-12 hrs or until dry.

Sphinx Moth Host Plant

Papaya hosts several caterpillars, including the sphinx moth. White, hollow, cotton-like cocoons may be found on papaya leaves. These cocoons aren't the moth's; they are wasp pupae that prey on sphinx moth caterpillars.

Pigeon Pea

Cajanus cajan
Fabaceae Family

ZONE/ SEASON	SIZE H*W	SUN/ SOIL
9-12/ Nov-Feb	12ft*6ft dwarf options	full-part/ poor - ok

STAPLE CROP INFO

Balanced protein/carb in seed
Edible leaves, flowers & seed
Pigeon peas offer 18-22% protein! 10g per 1/2 cup. 48-53% starch (green pea-dry pea). One of our oldest food crops. Yet, still "a perfect" 21st-century cash crop. Resilient to climate change; drought-tolerant & nitrogen fixing grain-legume!

PROPAGATE/ PRUNE	PESTS/DISEASE	WATER/ WIND	LIFESPAN	MAX STAPLE YIELD
seed-spring/ summer-shape	scale, pod suckers/ root rot	drought tolerant/ wind break	6+ months to fruit; lives up to 6 yrs; fast growth rate	8k lbs (green pod) & 3k lbs (dry pea) per acre

STORYTELLING

Like little marbles, legume seeds like peas & beans have historically inspired gameplay & creativity. Pigeon pea—also called Congo bean—is special for its resilience. Pigeon pea seeds found in Egyptian tombs highlight the symbolic & nutritional value & proven shelf life! History also tells of children worldwide carrying dried beans in pockets & pouches, collecting them little by little. As a result, beans like these symbolize resourcefulness. The Greek proverb, "bean by bean, you fill the bag," emphasizes persistence & consistency—reminding us that progress, no matter how slow, leads to greater achievements. However, all seeds, including beans, are plant embryos protected by their mother plants—imbued with anti-nutrients. In fact, 20% of food poisoning cases are linked to undercooked beans, which is why tribal shamans traditionally prepared the community's beans. Soaking, fermenting, & cooking helped shamans "cure" diseases "magically" through medicinal phenolic compounds.

HEALTH CAUTIONS	VARIETY & HEALTH	HEALTH FEATURES	20%+ DV NUTRITION	10%+ DV NUTRITION
Ants may inhabit dried pods	Dry/ mature pea higher in minerals	Leaves & flowers used in Traditional Chinese Medicine	Magnesium, Zinc (dry) Vit C, B6 (green) Copper, Iron, B1 (dry)	Calcium(dry, leaf) Vit C (soft pod) B2, 3, Selenium (dry)

FOOD FOREST PLANNING

- # to Plant/ Spacing: 30-50/ plant 3ft apart
- Wildlife Info: Caterpillar host (e.g., Io moth)
- Native Companion (host): Pine (191)
- Comparables (zone): Mesquite (6-11); Tamarind (10-12)
- Notable Varieties: Dwarf = ICP 7035
  - High-Yield: Hawaiian hybrid = 2+lbs peas per plant
  - Nematode Resistant: Norman & FL81d
  - Long-Lived: BRS Mandarim (Brazilian variety)

Pea is edible at all stages when cooked.

Breakfast, Lunch, & Dinner Entrees

In Florida, peak pigeon pea season is fall-winter. Soak dry beans for 12 hrs (add a pinch of baking soda to reduce anti-nutrients). Rinse & strain. Boil in fresh water for 60 min. Don't add salt when boiling—beans may not soften. Green pods are easier to prepare (13 min cook time), easier to digest, & have fewer anti-nutrients than dried peas. However, mature peas may contain more calcium & magnesium.

NOTES

"Meatloaf"   Z

In a high-speed blender, purée 2 cups cooked mature pigeon peas with 1 cup water, ½ cup Parmesan cheese, 4 eggs, 2 tsp salt & 2 tbsp sage (or blanched pigeon pea leaves, basil, or curry leaf). Pour into a loaf pan. Streak top with ketchup. Bake at 375°F for 1 hr or until firm.

Nicole's "Rice" & Beans   Z,V

Boil 2 large green bananas, cutting off ends & slitting lengthwise, for 20 min. Strain. Peel. Grate into "rice." Purée ¼ cup annatto seeds with ¼ cup water, 1 tsp salt & ½ tbsp apple cider vinegar. Drizzle over "rice." Shell 2 cups green pigeon pea pods. Boil for 13 min. Strain. Toss into "rice." Top with oregano.

Kathleen's "Burgers"   V

Soak 2 cups dry pigeon peas 12hrs. Drain. Boil 30 min. Drain. Pat dry with towel. Mix in 2 tbsp white vinegar & 1 tsp tempeh starter. Roll in a banana leaf or fill a circular glass dish. Cover lightly. Ferment 36-48 hrs at 95°F. Slice. Grill, bake, or steam with 1 tbsp soy sauce. *Variation: Roll as "hot dogs."

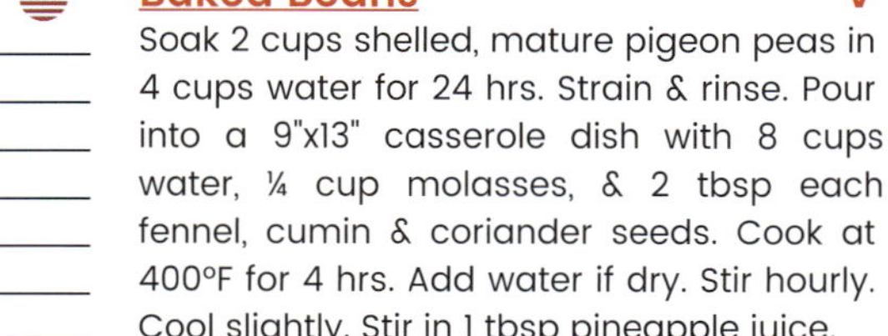

Baked Beans   V

Soak 2 cups shelled, mature pigeon peas in 4 cups water for 24 hrs. Strain & rinse. Pour into a 9"x13" casserole dish with 8 cups water, ¼ cup molasses, & 2 tbsp each fennel, cumin & coriander seeds. Cook at 400°F for 4 hrs. Add water if dry. Stir hourly. Cool slightly. Stir in 1 tbsp pineapple juice.

"Falafel"   Z,$

Coarsely mash 2 cups boiled, strained pigeon peas with 2 eggs, 1 tsp ground cumin, 2 tsp fennel, 1 tsp salt & 2 tbsp minced mixed herbs (e.g., blanched pigeon pea leaves). Add 1+ tbsp coconut flour if too wet. Form balls. Lightly oil & salt. Bake for 30 min at 350°F on an oiled pan.

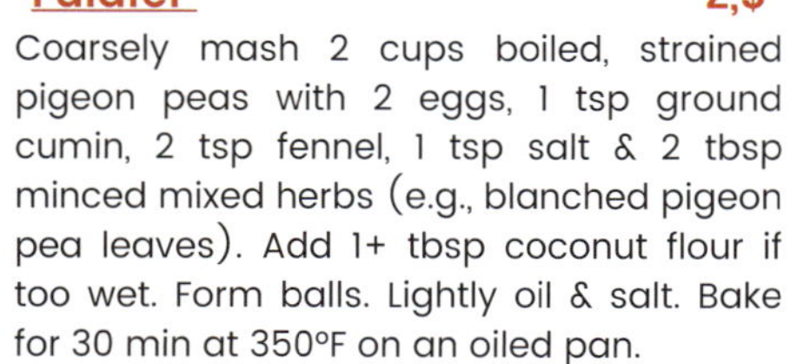

Appetizers, Snacks, & Sides

Pigeon peas are nutritionally comparable to soy. Beyond tofu, experiments with miso & natto are worth exploring! Even pigeon pea leaves & flowers are highly nutritious & used medicinally in tea for antimicrobial, anti-inflammatory, & antioxidant properties. The beans have research-backed benefits for antidiabetic effects, sickle cell anemia management, & potential anticancer properties.

<u>NOTES</u>

Lisa's Bean's & Greens   V

Soak 2 cups shelled, mature pigeon peas in 4 cups water for 12 hrs. Strain & rinse. Boil in 8 cups water for 50 min. When 5 min remain, add 2 cups chopped pigeon pea leaves. Strain. In a pot, sauté 2 tbsp diced onions, 1 tsp salt & 1 cup diced red pepper in 2 tbsp oil. Mix with cooked greens & beans.

Brielle's Tortillas   Z,$

In a high-speed blender, purée 1 cup boiled/mature pigeon peas with ½ tsp salt, ½ tbsp oil & 2 eggs until smooth. Use a crêpe dipping plate or pour onto a griddle. Cook for 5 min per side. Cool. *Variation: (1) Feed plain puréed peas to sourdough. (2) Add 2 tbsp pigeon pea leaves to tortilla purée.

Pigeon Pea Tofu   Z,V

Simmer, stirring for 10 min: 8 cups pigeon pea milk (recipe in drinks). Turn off heat. With a slotted spoon, stir in coagulant (e.g., ¼ cup vinegar, 2 tsp nigari, or 1½ tsp calcium sulfate). Rest for 15 min. Strain curds with cloth. Refrigerate in square mold 4hrs. *Option: Mix "whey" with 1 tbsp miso for soup.

Amy's "Edamame"   Z,V

Trim ends off 2 cups green, plump pigeon pea pods. Bring water to a boil & cook pods for 13 min. Drain. Toss with sea salt. Serve warm. Peel & eat 'edamame'-style.

Molly's Casserole "Strata"   Z,V

Wash, chop & boil 5 cups pigeon pea leaves for 5 min. Strain. Keep liquid as tea. Toss wilted greens (2 cups) with 1 cup ricotta cheese & ½ cup Romano cheese (or 1½ cups tofu mixed with 2 tbsp nutritional yeast), 1 tsp minced garlic & ½ tsp salt. Bake at 350°F for 20 min in an oiled casserole dish.

Drinks, Desserts, & Dips

Blue zone centenarians average ½ cup of beans daily. Pigeon pea offers a perennial source! It's one of the most significant pulse crops for food & feed security in dry months & areas. No irrigation needed—a rain-fed agricultural gem. Pigeon pea is a key protein source due to its low-cost production compared to traditional cereal crops. Ground, dried beans can be used as a flour substitute.

NOTES

Brownie Pie "Torta Tenerina" $

Purée 2 cups boiled/mature pigeon peas with 3 tbsp cocoa powder, 4 eggs, 3 tbsp maple syrup, 2 tbsp nut butter & 1 tsp salt. Bake in an oiled 9" pie pan for 1 hr or until firm. *Variation: Add dried fruit & nuts for a holiday "fruit cake."

Milk & "Egg Nog"/ "Rompope"

Purée 4 cups boiled beans & 8 cups water. Strain w/ cloth over bowl. Rest 1 hr. Save top milk. (Bottom starch/meal in cloth works as flour.) Add ½ tsp salt, 2 tbsp maple syrup & ¼ tsp vanilla to milk. *Eggnog: Simmer milk in pot. Stir ½ cup hot milk into 2 beaten eggs. Add to pot. Stir 5 mins. Top w/ nutmeg.

Kumari's Tea Cake "Yokan" Z,V

Purée 1 cup boiled/strained pigeon peas, ¼ tsp salt, 1 tsp vanilla & 3 tbsp maple syrup. Simmer 1 tsp agar (or gelatin) in 2 cups water, stirring until dissolved (5 mins). Stir in purée. Simmer 1 more min, stirring. Spread in dish or mold. Refrigerate 2 hrs or until set.

Kumari's Whoopie Pie $,V

Blend 1 cup boiled/mature beans, 1 tbsp oil, 2 eggs & 1 tbsp maple syrup. Add 1+ tbsp water if needed. On a griddle, dry fry 1 tbsp rounds for 5 mins per side (or bake 30 mins at 350°F). Sandwich with 1 tbsp purée of: ¾ cup boiled/mature beans, 3 soaked dates & ¼ cup melted chocolate.

Tea/ Herbed "Coffee" $,V

Dry 1 cup soaked/boiled mature pigeon peas with 2 tbsp each: washed & chopped pigeon pea leaves & flowers at 170°F until brittle. Roast beans at 350°F for 5 mins until fragrant. Grind all in blender. To brew: Steep 1 tsp in 1 cup water for 5 mins. Strain, dilute & sweeten to taste. Use for cough.

Other Uses

Pigeon pea is known as a "biological plow" due to its deep taproots. Plant along slopes to prevent erosion—avoid pruning to encourage deep rooting. Shriveled seeds serve as animal feed (e.g., chickens, fish). Pruning & mulching ("chop & drop") stems & leaves enrich soil, provide excellent mushroom substrate & craft material. Stems can be woven into baskets or shredded for toothbrushes.

<u>NOTES</u>

Basket-Making

Harvest 25 stems, each 4 ft long. Use fresh stems for pliability. Arrange 4 stems in a 2x2 "X" spoke pattern. Weave additional stems over & under to form the base. Continue spiraling upward to shape an 8-10" wide basket. Sun-dry until firm.

Broom

Harvest 50 thin, flexible pigeon pea stems (⅛-¼" thick, 2 ft long) & a sturdy 4-ft central limb (1" thick) for the handle. Bundle stems & tightly secure to one end of the limb with strong twine, 6" from the bottom. Hang to dry for 2 wks.

Mushroom Substrate

Chop 3½ cups leaves & stems coarsely. Simmer in 170ºF water bath for 1 hr. Drain & cool. Sterilize 1-liter jar & lid in 350ºF oven for 15 mins. Poke 2 holes in lid. Add 60g spawn to stems & leaves in jar. Cover lid holes with micropore tape. Store in cool, dark place. To fruit, wet cloth (not lid) in indirect light.

Fodder

Leaves & shriveled, insect-damaged pigeon peas serve as animal fodder. Soak peas in water for 24 hrs to improve digestibility & release nutrients. Rich in protein & fiber for cattle, goats & poultry. Can replace up to ¼ of feed, reducing costs.

Io Moth - Host Plant

The moth flashes hindwings with eye spots that mimic an owl's to startle predators. Wear gloves when handling pigeon pea plants from late spring to fall, as stinging caterpillars are active.

Pumpkin

Cucurbita moschata
Cucurbitaceae Family

ZONE/ SEASON	SIZE H*W	SUN/ SOIL
4-11/ Oct-Dec	25ft*2ft compact options	full sun/ pH 6.5

STAPLE CROP INFO

Protein & oil in seed
Edible leaves, stem, fruit & seed
The seeds offer 25-35% protein & 25-55% oil rich in unsaturated oleic & linoleic acids. Omega-3 & 6 rich. Cultivated since pre-historic times. Pumpkins are considered a health gold mine due medicinal & nutritional features.

PROPAGATE/ PRUNE	PESTS/DISEASE	WATER/ WIND	LIFESPAN	MAX STAPLE YIELD
seed-summer/ winter-cut back	beetles/ blight, mosaic virus	keep moist/ untrellised = wind tolerant	4 mo to fruit; lives up to 5 yrs; fast growth rate	20k lbs fruit/1k lb seed per acre; 5 fruit per plant

STORYTELLING

Cinderella's carriage was a pumpkin for a reason! This crop symbolizes transformation—turning dreams into reality. Early settlers believed pumpkins ensured the fruition of the American dream by aiding self-sufficiency. Adopted into Thanksgiving, Halloween, All Saints' Day, & Day of the Dead celebrations, pumpkin painting & carving reflect cultural rituals of nourishment & protection. Seminole pumpkin, our hardy native landrace, thrives on neglect. Yet, enthusiasts cross-pollinate male & female flowers from different varieties to grow pumpkins weighing over a ton! Considered a marvel of the vegetable world, some cultures use pumpkins as floating vessels & even host giant pumpkin water races. Nearly all parts of the plant are edible—flesh, shell, seeds, leaves, & flowers. Thanks to this abundance, pumpkins have been cultivated since prehistoric times. No one goes hungry with a pumpkin patch mound—provided there are pollinators. Native insects like eastern bumblebees ensure large harvests. Yay for Florida ground bees!

HEALTH CAUTIONS	VARIETY & HEALTH	HEALTH FEATURES	20%+ DV NUTRITION	10%+ DV NUTRITION
Stem hairs; limit seeds to 1/4 cup daily (bezoars)	Nitrogen-rich soil promotes seed tryptophan	Phytoestrogen (seeds) β-carotene (pulp)	Magnesium (seed) Vit A, Copper (pulp) Vit E, Iron, Zinc (seed)	Iron, B6 (pulp, leaf) Potassium (pulp) Vit C, Folate (flower)

FOOD FOREST PLANNING

- # to Plant/ Spacing: 4+; 4ft apart along trellis
- Wildlife Info: Use mulch mounds to reduce pests
- Native Companion (host): Pine (171), Sunflower (58)
- Comparables (zone): Seeded Breadfruit (10-12); Peach Palm (10-12)
- Notable Varieties: Cross-pollinate
  - FL Native: Seminole pumpkins = 6-12 lb gourds
  - Large Fruits: Calabaza = 5-50lb gourds
  - Compact Vine (10ft): Waltham = 3-8 lbs gourds

Edible fruit at all stages, colors & sizes.

Breakfast, Lunch, & Dinner Entrees

Peak pumpkin season is fall. All parts of the pumpkin plant are edible, including protein-rich seeds, ripe & unripe fruit, & nutritious greens. Pumpkin offers wide nutritional benefits & diverse uses. Pairing pumpkin flesh with fats like coconut milk or pumpkin seeds enhances carotenoid absorption. ***For flour: Soak seeds 12 hrs. Dry & grind finely in blender. Store in freezer (high fat).

NOTES

Pumpkin Seed Pizza Crust   Z,$

Scoop out 1 cup pumpkin seeds & fibers. Soak 12 hrs. Drain. Purée with 1 cup water, ¼ tsp salt, 1 tbsp Italian seasoning, ½ tsp smoked paprika & 3 eggs. Pour into oiled 9" cast iron. Spread ½-inch thick. Lightly spritz with oil. Bake 30 mins at 350ºF. Top with favorites. Rebake 15 mins at 350ºF.

Elana's Breakfast Brittle   Z,$,V

Roast halved pumpkin & seeds (soaked 12 hrs, strained) 1 hr at 350ºF. Coarsely chop 3 cups seeds. Mix with purée: 1 cup roasted pumpkin, ½ cup ripe banana, 2 tbsp coconut sugar, 3 tsp pumpkin pie spice & ¼ tsp salt. Spread ½" thick on parchment. Dry 4+ hrs at 170ºF until leathery. Cool. Slice.

Breakfast Soup   V

Simmer 2 cups 1" diced pumpkin, 1 cup coconut milk, 1 cup water, ¼ tsp salt, 1 tsp grated ginger & 2 lemongrass blades. When pumpkin is fork-tender (15 mins), remove lemongrass. Ladle soup into bowls. Drizzle with honey to taste. *Variation: Spiralize pumpkin "noodles." Simmer gently 1 min.

Elana's Soup   V

Halve a pumpkin. Remove seeds. Soak 12 hrs. Strain. Spread seeds & place pumpkin halves cut-side down on a pan. Roast 30 min (seeds), 1 hr (pumpkin) at 350ºF. Purée 2 cups roasted seeds with 5 cups water, 2 tsp cinnamon, 1 tsp salt & 2 tbsp honey until smooth. Add 3 cups pumpkin. Purée again.

Pumpkin Leaf Pinwheels   Z,$

Halve a pumpkin. Scrape out seeds, soak 12 hrs & strain. Roast seeds & pumpkin halves (cut-side down) at 350ºF for 1 hr. Purée 1 cup pulp, ⅓ cup seeds, ¼ tsp salt & 2 eggs. Spread 2 tbsp purée on a pumpkin leaf (8 leaves pre-boiled 3 mins). Roll burrito-style. Bake 30 mins at 350ºF. Cool, slice & toast.

Appetizers, Snacks, & Sides

Soaking, boiling, or roasting pumpkin seeds enhances nutrition & digestibility. Rich in magnesium & tryptophan, they're ideal for dinner to aid sleep. High in zinc, they support immune function—making them a perfect travel snack! In Chinese medicine, seeds are used as an antidepressant, to expel parasites, & to support liver function. Both seed & fruit exhibit cytotoxic properties against tumor cells.

NOTES

Stuffed Flowers   Z,V

Wash & pat dry 12 male pumpkin flowers & 1 cup minced pumpkin leaves & stalks. Sauté leaves & stalks with 1 tbsp minced garlic & ¼ tsp salt until wilted. Toss with ⅓ cup goat cheese. Stuff each flower ¾ full & gently pinch closed. Lightly spritz with oil & sprinkle with salt. Roast 10 mins at 400°F.

James' Pumpkin Seeds   Z,$,V

Scrape out 2 cups pumpkin seeds (fibers mixed in). Soak 12 hrs, strain & pat dry. Spread on an oiled pan. Lightly spritz with oil & sprinkle with ½ tsp salt. Roast at 350°F for 30-45 mins or until browned. *Variation: Unseasoned roasted seeds can be ground & brewed as coffee or pressed for oil.

Elana's Tofu   Z,V

Soak 3 cups pumpkin seeds 12 hrs. Strain & rinse. Purée with 6 cups very warm water. Strain with cloth & collect milk. Let starch settle 20 mins. Pour top milk into a pan. Stirring, heat to 160°F-180°F. Curdle with 2 tbsp lemon juice. Cool. Strain with cloth & press out liquid. Form block & chill 4 hrs.

Pumpkin Chutney   Z,V

Toast 2 cups pumpkin seeds in 1 tbsp oil with 5 curry leaves (or 2 garlic cloves), 3 tbsp minced onion, 2 chili peppers & 1 tsp salt. Add 2½ cups water & simmer 2 mins. Stir in ¼ cup tamarind purée. Purée until smooth. Serve as a dip with crackers or veggies, or as a sandwich spread.

Wesley's Pickle/ "Pitas"   Z,$,V

Slice 3 cups green, tiny pumpkins. Boil 1 min. Drain. Place in quart jar. Cover with brine: 1 cup water, 1 cup vinegar, ½ cup honey, 1 tbsp salt, 1 tbsp peppercorns, & 1 tbsp mustard seeds. Refrigerate 1 week. *For "pickle pitas": Wrap each pickle in boiled green banana "dough." Bake 30 mins at 350°F (sellable).

Drinks, Desserts, & Dips

Carotenoids in pumpkin act as antioxidants & may reduce risk of certain diseases (e.g., cardiovascular disease & cancer). Pumpkin is one of the most underutilized medicinal plants, historically valued as an anti-inflammatory, antioxidant, antiviral, & antidiabetic. In Chinese medicine, seeds are used as an antidepressant. A mix of 2 cups pumpkin purée & 1 cup melted chocolate makes great fudge—chill 1 hr.

NOTES

Kerrie's Jam & Pie $,V

Roast halved pumpkin 1 hr at 350ºF. Purée 3 cups pulp, 1 cup ripe banana, 3 tsp pumpkin pie spice, 2 tbsp citrus juice, 3 tbsp maple syrup & ½ tsp salt. Chill as jam. *For 8" pie: Bake jam 50 mins at 350ºF in crust (e.g., of 1 cup ea: puréed ripe banana/pumpkin seed flour; pre-baked 15 min). Chill 4 hrs.

Molly's Mayo/ Sour Cream   Z,V

Soak 1 cup pumpkin seeds (with husk) 12 hrs. Strain & rinse. Simmer in 1 cup boiling water for 3 mins. Cool. Purée seeds & water until smooth with ½ tbsp apple cider vinegar, ¼ tsp mustard powder, 2 tbsp nutritional yeast, ½ tsp onion powder & ¼ tsp salt. Add 1 tbsp water to thin, if needed.

Jan & Jenn's "Ketchup"   Z,V

Roast halved, de-seeded pumpkin face down 1 hr at 350ºF. Purée 1½ cups pulp, 2 tbsp apple cider vinegar, 1 tbsp maple syrup, ½ tsp salt, & 1 tsp smoked paprika. Add 1+ tbsp water if needed. Refrigerate. * For Asian dressing: Add 2 tbsp each: sesame oil, soy sauce & ginger.

Seed Butter & Cookies   Z,$,V

Soak 2 cups pumpkin seeds 12 hrs. Strain. Boil in fresh water for 2 mins. Strain. Purée with 2 tbsp maple syrup, ½ tsp salt & 2 tsp cinnamon. Add 1+ tbsp water as needed. Refrigerate. *Variation: Purée 1 cup seed butter, 2 eggs & 3 dates. Flatten drop cookies. Bake 20 mins at 350ºF (sellable).

Lisa's Pumpkin Tea $,V

Wash & roast a halved, deseeded pumpkin for 1 hr at 350ºF. Julienne the roasted peel into thin, short slices. Dehydrate at 150ºF-170ºF until fully dry (4+ hrs). To serve tea, pour 1 cup boiling water over 1 tbsp dried pumpkin. Steep 10 mins. Strain. Antioxidant-rich. Supports immune system.

Other Uses

Pumpkin oil from cold pressing is greenish, while hot-pressed oil is dark red & more fluorescent under UV light. Cold-pressed oil is used for edible & medicinal purposes, while lower-grade hot-pressed oil serves as burning oil. Organic pumpkins contain higher levels of β-carotene & vitamin E.

<u>NOTES</u>

Face Mask

Roast a pumpkin (seeds removed), open-face down at 350°F for 1 hr. Scoop out ¼ cup pulp & mash. Apply to clean skin for 15 mins, then rinse. Rich in vitamins A, E & C, beta-carotene, zinc & AHAs. Believed to reduce skin damage.

Anti-Parasitic

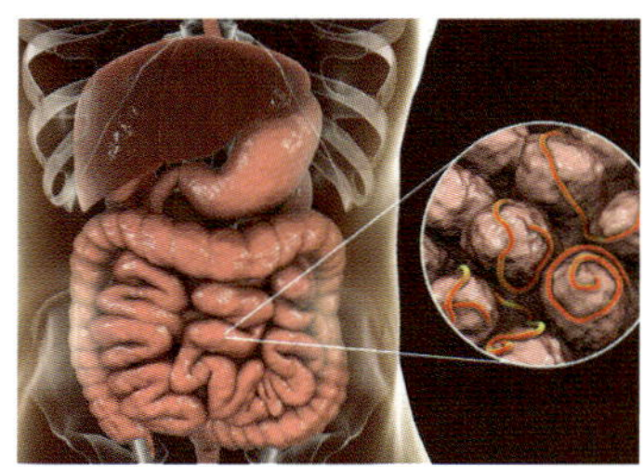

Soak seeds for 12-24 hrs, then roast at 170°F for 4+ hrs until dry. Cucurbitacin in the seeds paralyzes parasites, aiding natural expulsion. Consume up to 4 tbsp pre-soaked & lightly roasted, unshelled pumpkin seeds daily.

Mood Boosting Oil

Soak seeds for 12-24 hrs, then roast at 170°F for 4+ hrs until dry. Use a masticating juicer to extract oil. Consume 1-2 tsp daily. Tryptophan & serotonin in pumpkin seeds (576 mg per 100g) support sleep quality & improve mood.

Long-Lasting Pumpkin Carving

Lightly scar rind by scraping surface with a small knife to create shallow designs. Avoid deep carving to prevent decay. Apply a thin layer of coconut oil to reduce moisture loss & mold. Optional: Dust with activated charcoal to accentuate carving. Lasts weeks.

Bumblebee Attractor

Bumblebees help create large harvests in crops like pumpkins by "buzz pollinating," vibrating flowers with their wings to release pollen. Plant native wildflowers like dune sunflowers & goldenrod near your pumpkin patch to attract them. Avoid pesticides.

Sweet Potato

Ipomoea batatas
Convolvulaceae Family

ZONE/ SEASON	SIZE H*W	SUN/ SOIL
8-12/	10ft*1ft	50%+ sun/
Oct-Dec	compact options	loose

STAPLE CROP INFO

Pure starch tuber/ root
Edible leaves & root
Tubers are 60-70% starch! A top 5 food to feed the world! Edible leaves, stems, & root. Green tops outyield other veggies. Great for small yards in beds or as a houseplant. This one plant can provides over 90% of daily nutrients people need.

PROPAGATE/ PRUNE	PESTS/DISEASE	WATER/ WIND	LIFESPAN	MAX STAPLE YIELD
15" slips-spring/ winter-divide	white fly, weevils/ fungus	brief flood- ok/ wind tolerant	4 mo to fruit; lives up to 5 yrs; fast growth rate	25k lbs per acre; 5+ tubers per slip

STORYTELLING

In some tribal customs, gifting sweet potatoes symbolizes a peace offering & an attempt at conflict resolution. Flood, war, & drought-proof, sweet potatoes are the ultimate insurance policy—they even thrive in poor soil! Given their life-saving nutrition, many cultures honor mythical sweet potato deities. A delicious superfood & staple crop, they're best grown in raised beds or mounds to avoid destructive tilling. Like Joseph's coat of many colors, sweet potatoes come in various hues. The purple variety, rich in antioxidants, once made up 70% of the Okinawan diet. Consuming such nutrient-dense food is believed to contribute to living over 100 years disease-free. In Florida, year-round harvests mean unlimited goodness! Sweet potatoes are the ultimate comfort food in a society facing an onslaught of chronic disease. Called "potent" in the fight against cancer, they also make excellent food forest ground cover.

HEALTH CAUTIONS	VARIETY & HEALTH	HEALTH FEATURES	20%+ DV NUTRITION	10%+ DV NUTRITION
Mannitol in tuber. $\frac{1}{2}$ cup ok for IBS	Anthocyanin (purple) β-carotene (orange)	22% DV tryptophan; low FODMAP	Vit A, B6, C (leaf, root) Fiber (peel) Manganese (root)	Potassium (root) Vit K, B2, Folate (greens) Iron & Calcium (greens)

Low nitrogen & sandy soil for large tubers.

FOOD FOREST PLANNING

- # to Plant/ Spacing: 10+/plant 3ft apart (e.g., 30ft² bed)
- Wildlife Info: Self-fertile but native pollinators help yields
- Native Companion (host): Live oak (395) - leaf litter
- Comparables (zone): Malanga (8-11); Sago palm (9-12)
- Notable Varieties: Tuber color varies; 50+ varieties
  - Purple: Molokai, Stokes Purple, Okinawan
  - Orange/Red: Tainung #64, Covington (compact)
  - White/Yellow: Bonita, Satsuma-imo (compact)

Breakfast, Lunch, & Dinner Entrees

Peak sweet potato season is fall-winter. After harvest, cure sweet potatoes at 85°F & 90-95% humidity for 4-8 days. Don't refrigerate raw tubers—off flavors develop. Instead, freeze cooked sweet potatoes. Blanch leaves (5 min) & boil halved tubers (12-15 min until tender) to remove soil toxins & anti-nutrients (e.g., oxalic acid). This method preserves Vit A & optimizes tryptophan to aid sleep.

NOTES

Sweet Potato "Torte" Z

Divide into 3 parts to layer 3 levels in an 8" oiled pie pan: ⅛" slices of 3 medium sweet potatoes, 1 cup grated Parmesan & 1 cup chopped, lightly sautéed mixed greens (e.g., sweet potato greens). Sprinkle each layer with smoked paprika, olive oil & lemon juice. Bake 50 mins at 350°F. Cool & slice.

Ana's Pancake "Chorreadas" Z

Cook sweet potato (bake poked, 50 mins at 425°F or microwave 5-7 mins). Peel. Purée 1 cup with 2 eggs & ¼ tsp salt. Spoon onto oiled pan as small cakes. Cook on medium-high for 3 mins each side, or bake 30 mins at 350°F. Top with coconut cream & herbs. Crispy exterior, creamy interior.

Alissa's "Buddha Bowl" Z,V

Boil 3 cups chopped sweet potato leaves for 2 min. Strain. Stir-fry with 1 tbsp soy sauce, 1 tbsp sesame oil & ¼ cup chopped high-protein sprouts (e.g., mung, moringa, or pigeon pea). Stuff into 2 sweet potatoes (boiled 16 min). Drizzle with pineapple/citrus juice.

Sue-Ann's Casserole & Pie Z,V

Mix 3 cups boiled, peeled sweet potatoes, 2 tbsp coconut cream, ½ cup ripe mango puree, 3 tsp cinnamon & 1 tsp salt. Bake 25 min in oiled 8-inch pie dish. Top with shredded coconut & toast 5 min. *For pie: Add 6 beaten eggs. Pour over pineapple/cherry rings in pan. Bake 50 min. Turn over.

Kacie's Balls & Mug Muffin Z,$

Mash 2 boiled, peeled sweet potatoes with 1 tsp salt, 2 eggs & ½ cup sweet potato greens sautéed in 1 tsp oil. Whip with 1+ tbsp coconut meal & form into 1-tbsp balls. Bake at 400°F for 30 min or until browned. *Variation: Mix purée without flour & microwave 2+ min in 2 mugs.

Appetizers, Snacks, & Sides

Blue Zone centenarians average 2½ cups of starchy veggies (like sweet potatoes) each day. Raw sweet potatoes contain oxalic acid—pair with calcium-rich foods to reduce absorption. Compared to raw carrots, they have about half the oxalic acid. Soak, blanch, or boil to lower oxalate content. Offering different sweet potato types (orange, purple, or white) introduces kids to diverse flavors & nutrients.

Nancy's Firecracker Salad   V

Wash & peel 2 cups multi-colored sweet potatoes. Grate, soak 10 min, rinse & drain. Mix with 2 tbsp sliced cherry tomatoes & 1 tbsp chopped chives. Top with dressing of 2 tbsp olive oil, 1 tbsp citrus juice & ¼ tsp fennel seeds. *Variation: Spiralize as noodles, toss in oil & salt, bake 10 min at 400ºF.

George's Pickled Sweet Potato   V

Cut 3 cups washed, peeled sweet potatoes into sticks. Boil 1 min. Drain. Place in quart jar with 3 sprigs rosemary & 1 tbsp peppercorns. Simmer 2 cups apple cider vinegar, 2 cups water & 2 tbsp sea salt until dissolved. Let cool. Pour over sweet potatoes. Refrigerate 2 wks to infuse flavors.

Lis' Purple "Jello"   Z,V

Purée 2 cups boiled, peeled purple sweet potato, 2 tbsp maple syrup, 3 cups coconut milk & 1 tbsp chia seeds. In a pot, simmer ½ cup water & 1 tsp agar powder, stirring, for 3 min. Stir purée into agar. Simmer 3 more min. Pour into mold. Refrigerate 4 hrs. *For cold soup, drizzle coconut milk over 'jello'.

Rebecca's Toast & Chips   V

Slice 2 washed sweet potatoes ⅓" thick. Rub with oil & salt. Broil 15 min on oven rack until browned & tender. (Or grill/toast). Top with piped "icing" of: 1 boiled, peeled sweet potato puréed with ¼ cup melted chocolate. *Variation (chips): Slice $^1/_{16}$" thick. Bake 10 min at 400ºF. Use purée as dip.

Robyn's "Spanakopita"   Z

Boil 5 cups chopped sweet potato leaves & stems for 3 min. Drain. Mix with ¼ tsp salt, ½ cup feta, ½ tsp garlic powder, 1 tbsp lemon juice & 2 beaten eggs. Toss peels of 5 boiled, halved sweet potatoes in oil & salt. Layer half in 8" pan. Add greens. Top with remaining peels (light side up). Bake 25 min at 375ºF.

Drinks, Desserts, & Dips

For pies, baking or microwaving removes moisture, helping the pie "set" faster. Vit A —in orange sweet potatoes—is crucial for immune function & cell growth, & is fat-soluble. Pair with healthy fats for absorption. For antioxidant-rich tea: Boil sweet potato leaves & stems 20 sec. Dry until brittle, grind in blender & steep 1 tsp in 1 cup boiling water for 5 min.

NOTES

Wesley's "Soda" Float V

Wash 2 sweet potatoes. Peel & dice. Juice using a masticating juicer or high-speed blender, then strain. Dilute with equal parts carbonated water. Top with a scoop of frozen coconut cream & drizzle with maple syrup. *Variation: Use boiled sweet potato, puréed with nut milk. Top with sweet cream.

Vanessa's "Empanadas" $,V

Boil 3 halved sweet potatoes for 16 min. Peel. Cut peels into circles. Brush both sides with maple syrup. Mash sweet potatoes with 1 tbsp oil, 1 tsp salt, 2 tsp cinnamon & 1 tbsp maple syrup. Spoon mash onto center of peels (dark side up). Fold over & press to seal. Sprinkle with salt. Broil 10 min.

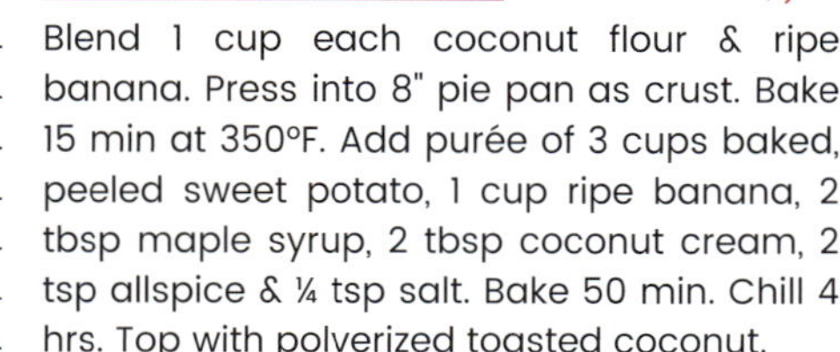

Wesley's Purple Puffs Z,$,V

In a food processor, whip 4 cups boiled, peeled purple sweet potato with 2 cups ripe banana, 1 tbsp fennel seeds, 1 tsp salt & 2 tsp cinnamon. Chill 30 min. Form into 1-tbsp balls. Spritz with oil & sprinkle with a pinch of salt. Bake at 350°F for 30 min or until firm.

Ken & Adrienne's Pie $,V

Blend 1 cup each coconut flour & ripe banana. Press into 8" pie pan as crust. Bake 15 min at 350°F. Add purée of 3 cups baked, peeled sweet potato, 1 cup ripe banana, 2 tbsp maple syrup, 2 tbsp coconut cream, 2 tsp allspice & ¼ tsp salt. Bake 50 min. Chill 4 hrs. Top with polverized toasted coconut.

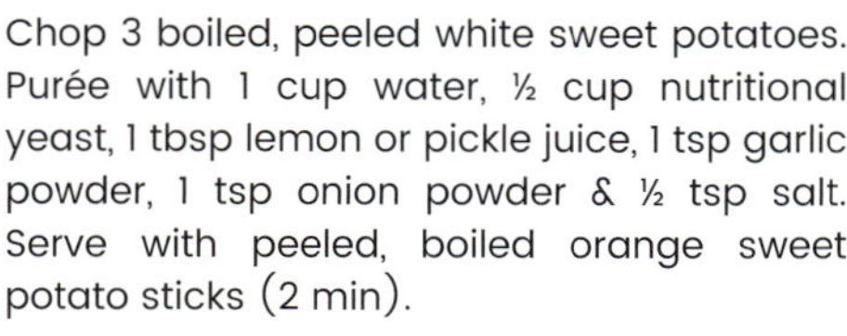

Kerrie's "Hummus" V

Chop 3 boiled, peeled white sweet potatoes. Purée with 1 cup water, ½ cup nutritional yeast, 1 tbsp lemon or pickle juice, 1 tsp garlic powder, 1 tsp onion powder & ½ tsp salt. Serve with peeled, boiled orange sweet potato sticks (2 min).

Other Uses

Sweet potatoes make great houseplants & endless craft material. The purple discard water from boiling can be used as dye. Dehydrated & powdered sweet potato roots serve as natural food coloring. End pieces can be carved into stamps, using their color as "ink." Sweet potato is a top potential NASA "space crop" due to its nutrition, water efficiency, rapid growth, abundance & shelf life.

<u>NOTES</u>

Heart Leaf Confetti

Harvest heart-shaped sweet potato leaves early in the morning when fresh & firm. Rinse gently in cool water & pat dry. Place leaves between 2 sheets of paper & iron on low heat until dry & flat. Use at Valentine's/ Mother's Day parties or weddings.*Optional: Leaves can be used for tea.

Dye & Watercolor Pigment

Boil 3 peeled, chopped sweet potatoes for 1 hour. Strain & soak fabric 2+ hrs while liquid is hot. Orange variety = yellow to brown dye. Purple variety = lavender to deep purple dye. Red variety = pink to red dye. pH-sensitive: vinegar shifts color to pink tones. Dehydrate & pulverize for food dye/watercolor paint.

Mukimono - Veggie Carving

Peel a sweet potato & slice into 1"-thick rounds. Use a small paring knife to carve petals, making shallow cuts around the edges to shape each round into a simple flower. Soak in water with a splash of vinegar to prevent browning. Serve as an edible garnish or decoration.

Space Food/ Transgenic Crop

Replicate NASA's food studies. Use a hydroponic system to root "slips" in vermiculite-filled vinyl pots, with drip irrigation tubes providing a water-based nutrient solution. This method mimics NASA's zero-gravity experiments (e.g., Use Beauregard, Covington, or Satsuma-imo).

Stamps

Cut a sweet potato in half. Carve a simple design on the flat side. Dip the stamp in a vinegar-water solution (1 tbsp vinegar per 1 cup water) to aid pigment transfer to paper. Stamp bleeds pigment for 5-10 uses before fading. Cut a fresh layer to renew or dip in powdered sweet potato "paint" or charcoal.

Tropical Almond

Terminalia catappa
Combretaceae Family

ZONE/ SEASON	SIZE H*W	SUN/ SOIL
10-12/	90ft*70ft	75%+/
Aug-Dec	prune to 10ft	pH 6-8

STAPLE CROP INFO

Protein & oil in seed
Edible leaves, fruit & seed
Up to 36.9% protein & 31.05% oil which is rich in oleic, linoleic & palmitic acid. Profitable. The nuts retail $36 per lb in supermarkets (e.g., Port Vila). Tropical Almond (TA) can replace diseased citrus farms where fertilizers caused soil salinity.

PROPAGATE/ PRUNE	PESTS/DISEASE	WATER/ WIND	LIFESPAN	MAX STAPLE YIELD
seed-spring/ winter-shape	beetles, thrips/ leaf spot	saline-ok/ provide wind break	3+ yrs to fruit; lives 300+ yrs; fast growth rate	440+ lbs per acre; 11-22lbs nuts per tree

STORYTELLING

California almonds supply 80% of the world's demand, making them one of the most valuable nuts globally. However, they require a gallon of water per almond & contribute to mass bee deaths due to pesticides. As sustainability debates unfold, Florida's tropical almonds (TA) offer a resilient alternative with similar nutrition, taste, & market potential. This crop could integrate into the multi-billion-dollar almond industry, thriving with pest, drought, & saline resistance. Organic almond farming can boost reforestation efforts, aligning with the almond's symbolic link to wisdom. Historically planted in monastic gardens, almond trees stand tall in barren, desertified landscapes. For this reason, almond trees are likened to the endurance of the human spirit. As deforestation spreads & Florida's heat intensifies, planting fast-growing shade trees like tropical almonds offers relief. Almonds, one of the 'choice products of the land' (Gen. 43:11), could become a valuable Florida commercial crop. As a bonus, their vibrant red & orange fall foliage adds seasonal charm.

HEALTH CAUTIONS	VARIETY & HEALTH	HEALTH FEATURES	20%+ DV NUTRITION	10%+ DV NUTRITION
Several look-alikes; ants may inhabit	Minerals in nuts depend on soil.	Rich in fiber (nut skins, leaves)	Calcium, Magnesium (nut) Phosphorus (nuts) Vit C (fruit, leaf)	Zinc (nut) Vit B1,3,6,9 (nut) ß-carotene (fruit)

FOOD FOREST PLANNING

- # to Plant/ Spacing: 4+/ plant 30 feet apart
- Wildlife Info: Avoid planting near shoreline/ wetland
- Native Companion (host): Passionfruit (7)
- Comparables (zone): Almond(6-9), Sacha Inchi(10-12)
- Notable Varieties: N/A - confused for other species
  - *T. littoralis*: Smaller, thicker leaves
  - *T. glabrata*: Narrower, pointed, glossy leaves
  - *Fagraea crenulata*: Tubular flowers, not edible

Mature fruits/nuts fall to the ground.

Breakfast, Lunch, & Dinner Entrees

In Florida, peak TA season is fall. A rich resource! Blue Zone centenarians eat about ¼ cup nuts daily. To shell, strike pointed apex with hammer on firm surface. Soaking for 12 hrs improves digestibility. Roasting enhances protein bioavailability. Relished by children worldwide as a forage snack, TA provide more protein than peanuts, lentils & chickpeas. The oil is similar to sunflower oil.

NOTES

Nana's Breakfast Canoli's   Z,$

Purée 1 cup almonds (soaked 12 hrs), 2 eggs, ¼ tsp salt & 1 tbsp maple syrup. Pour 12 2-tbsp rounds on parchment. Bake 18 min at 350°F. Remove paper. Roll tubes. Toast seam down 5-10 min. Pipe in 1 tbsp purée chilled 1 hr: 1 tbsp almond butter, ¾ cup ripe banana & 1 tbsp coconut flour.

James' Half-Moon Pies   Z,$,V

Blend 1 cup almond flour, 1 tbsp psyllium husk powder, 1 tbsp lemon juice & ¼ tsp salt. Add ¼+ cup hot water as needed until ball forms. Rest 10 min. Form 2 tbsp balls. Press 4" circles. Fill with ½ tbsp almond butter. Top with banana slices (or jam). Fold in half & crimp with fork. Toast until crisp.

"Dango" Moon Balls   Z,V

Simmer 4 min: 1 tsp agar powder in 1 cup hot tea (e.g., lemongrass). Purée 1 cup almonds (soaked 12hrs, strained) in 1 cup water. Add & simmer with agar 2 min. Cool 5 min. Form balls in mold. Chill 4hrs. *Optional: Add 2 tsp veggie powder for color. Top with mix of 2 tbsp honey, 1 tsp soy/aminos & 1 tsp vinegar.

Rebecca's Muffins $

In a blender, pulse 2 cups frozen almonds into fine flour (1-sec bursts, scraping sides). Purée flour, 1 cup overripe banana, 2 eggs, 2 tbsp maple syrup, 1 tbsp coconut cream & 2 tsp vanilla. Add 1+ tbsp water if needed. Pour into 6 oiled muffin molds. Top each with 3 almonds. Bake at 350°F for 30 min. Cool.

"Pilaf"   Z,V

Soak 3 cups almonds in 6 cups water for 12 hrs. Strain, rinse & chop/grate in food processor. Simmer on low in 1 cup water & 1½ cups chunky marinara, covered, for 20 min. Sauté 1 tbsp chopped oregano, ½ tsp turmeric & ½ cup sliced mushrooms in 1 tbsp oil. Mix into "pilaf."

Appetizers, Snacks, & Sides

Leaves are a valued Ayurvedic herb for anti-inflammatory, antifungal (e.g., *Candida* spp), antibacterial, & hepatoprotective properties. Rich in polyphenols. Young leaves have fine hairs—boiling removes. The nuts, rich in heart-healthy fats, make a nutritious snack for blood sugar management. *For Parmesan substitute: Mix 1 cup grated, salted nuts with ½ cup nutritional yeast.

Almond Soup   V

Peel & chop 1 cup green banana. Boil 15 min with 2 cups almonds. Drain. Purée with 4 cups water, 2 tsp salt, ½ tbsp vinegar, 2 roasted garlic cloves & 2 tbsp nutritional yeast until smooth. Garnish with toasted almond slices.

Raw/ Roasted Nuts   Z,$,V

De-flesh fresh tropical almonds: Rub pulp into water & keep as "juice." Dry husks in oven at low temp (e.g., 170°F) for 4 hrs. Hit dry husk with hammer on pointed apex to open. Soak kernels 12 hrs. Strain. Dry at 170°F for 2 hrs. Roast at 350°F for 5 min, stirring once, until golden & aromatic.

Stir-fried Bitter Greens   Z,V

Boil 3 cups very young, chopped tropical almond leaves for 12 min. Strain & rinse. Stir-fry with 2 cloves chopped garlic, 1 tbsp chopped, peeled ginger, 1 tbsp oil & 1 tbsp soy sauce/aminos. Add 3 tbsp water, cover & simmer on low for 10 min. Spritz with citrus juice.

Elana's Crackers   Z,$,V

Soak 1 cup almonds 12 hrs. Strain. Purée with 1 cup fresh water. Strain with cloth. Use liquid as "milk." Blend: pulp, ¼ tsp salt, 2 tbsp fresh herbs & 2 tbsp oil. Press $1/8$" thick between 2 parchment sheets. Bake 5 min at 350°F. Remove top parchment. Cut squares & poke holes. Bake 10 min at 350°F. Flip. Bake 15 min.

Kerrie's "Feta"   Z,V

Soak 1 cup almonds for 12 hrs in 3 cups water. Strain. Peel off husk. Purée with 1 cup water. Strain with cloth. Keep liquid as "milk." Mix pulp with 1 tbsp nutritional yeast, 2 tsp vinegar & ½ tsp salt. Press in parchment-lined cupcake molds. Fold parchment to cover. Bake at 400°F for 20 min.

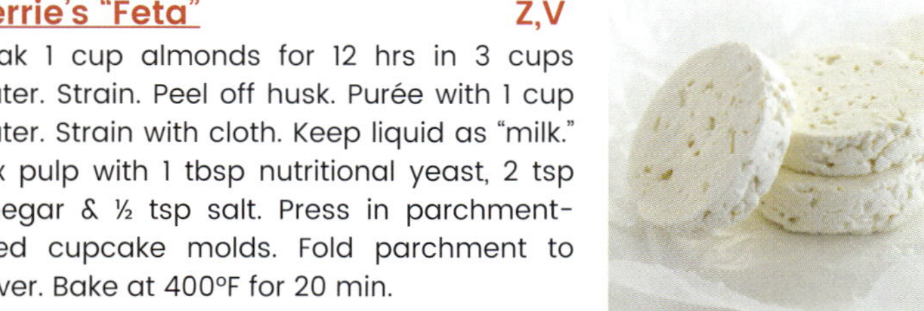

Drinks, Desserts, & Dips

When ripe, tropical almond fruit changes from green to yellow, reddish-purple, or brown. The fresh fruit has an acidic taste & may fruit multiple times per year. Fruit & kernel size vary. Research compares the nut endocarp to a vegetable. For consistent nut size, mass propagation is recommended using root or multinode, semi-hardwood cuttings.

NOTES 

Kerrie's "Jordan" Almonds   Z,$,V

Purée ½ ripe banana with ¼ tsp veggie/fruit powder (e.g., blue butterfly pea). Skewer 1 cup roasted almonds with toothpicks. Dip almonds in purée, coating evenly. Dry at 145ºF for 8 hrs or until no longer tacky. Store in an airtight container.

Churros $

Purée 1 cup almond butter, 1 egg, ½ cup ripe banana, 1 tbsp maple syrup, 2 tsp cinnamon & ¼ tsp salt. Add 1+ tbsp water as needed to purée. Chill 20 min. Pipe churros with star tip on oiled pan. Sprinkle with cinnamon & spritz with oil. Bake 30-45 min at 375ºF or until crispy.

Leaf Tea $,V

Wash & dry mature red leaves at 160ºF for 2 hrs in a single layer. Crumble. To brew: Steep 1 tsp leaves per cup boiling water for 5–10 min. Strain & dilute to taste. Believed to aid liver health. *Variation: Rub fruit pulp off 20 tropical almond nuts in 1 cup water. Add "juice" to tea.

Wesley's Nut Butter/Cookies   Z,$,V

Roast 2 cups almonds 5 min at 350ºF. While warm, blend in food processor in bursts, scraping sides, until almonds release oils & form butter. Store in fridge. *For cookies, mix: 1 cup almond butter, 3 tbsp coconut flour, 1 cup ripe banana. Form drop cookies & flatten. Bake 12-15 min at 350ºF (sellable).

Niquelle's Milk & Yogurt

Soak 2 cups almonds for 12 hrs. Drain. Purée with 5 cups hot water, 2 tbsp honey, 1 tsp cinnamon & ¼ tsp salt. Strain with cheesecloth. Serve chilled. Use pulp for crackers, "cheese" or flour. *Variation: Purée 3 cups almond milk with 1 tbsp vegan yogurt. Ferment 7 hrs in glass jar at 113ºF.

Other Uses

Considered a legume tree, its timber yields reach 215–286 ft³/ac/yr. A general-purpose hardwood, it's ideal for intercropping during the first 2–3 years or longer with aggressive pruning to allow light. Saplings coppice strongly, & the main leader can be cut to encourage a 'pagoda' shape. A vital part of desert cultural heritage & ecology.

NOTES

Skin & Hair Oil

Lightly roast nuts to release oils. Use a masticating juicer or press to extract oil. Strain through fine cloth. Store in dark, sealed jars to preserve nutrients (vit A & E). High saponification. Useful for cooking, skin & hair health & biodiesel. Yield 50%+ oil.

Canoe & Furniture Hardwood

Harvest wood in late fall. Cut logs to desired size, then air-dry for several months in shade with good airflow to prevent cracking. Highly water-resistant. Used for canoes, drums, interior building & fuelwood.

Biogas Fuel

Collect dried leaves, chop finely & place in an airtight container/biogas digester. Add water. Ferment anaerobically for several weeks. Capture gas for cooking or heating. Provides a sustainable energy source. If fermentation stalls, ensure proper airtight sealing & warmer temps (85–100°F).

Aquaponic Treatment

Place 1 mature leaf per 10 gallons of water or for every 2–3 fish. Leaves release humic acids, flavonoids & tannins, reducing pH, treating bacterial & fungal infections, promoting healing & supporting fish breeding. Replace every 2–3 weeks. Monitor pH to ensure safe conditions.

Black Dye

Boil 2–3 handfuls of bark, fruit &/or leaves per gallon of water for 1 hr to release pigment. High tannin content. Mordant optional. Leftover liquid can be reused as fertilizer or in fish tanks, making it eco-friendly!

Appendix A

COMMONLY CELEBRATED AMERICAN HOLIDAYS AND CLASSIC DISHES

HOLIDAY	CLASSIC DISHES WITH PAGE NUMBERS FOR FOOD FOREST RECIPE SUBSTITUTES
Birthday Parties	Cake/cupcakes (23); ice cream (23, 53, 58, 68); sandwiches (38); chips (62, 107); punch (28, 108)
Valentine's Day, Mother's Day, Weddings, Baby Showers, Brunch	Chocolate desserts (18, 46, 78); muffins (51); mousse/pudding (43); tarts (48); red desserts (48, 82); bread sculpture (36); Jordan almonds (113); fruit salads (36); pasta (21, 93)
St. Patrick's, Easter, Passover	Roasted meat (56); deviled eggs (17); dyed eggs (27); potato salad (22); matzo ball soup (21); potato wedges (22); green desserts (16, 47, 63); hot cross (76)
Fourth of July, Memorial Day, Labor Day, Father's Day, Cinco de Mayo, Superbowl	Hot dogs/burgers (96); jello (28); shredded meat (56); potato salad (22); skewers (38, 66); chicken salad (57); marshmallow (23); salsa/ slaw (67, 92, 107); whoopie pie (98); baked beans (96); dips (58, 108)
Halloween/Day of the Dead	Pumpkin pie (103); candied apple (38); churros (113); candied pumpkin (103); tamales (81); hot chocolate (73); pinwheels (27, 101); eggs in purgatory (61)
Thanksgiving	Stuffing (72); mashed potatoes (56); cranberry sauce (23); pumpkin pie (103); sweet potato casserole (106); casserole (31, 32, 76)
Christmas, Hanukkah	Roasted meat (56); gingerbread (37, 72); mashed potatoes (56); green beans (76); fruitcake (98); latkes (21); jelly donut (66); hot chocolate (73); sugar plum (42); baked "apples" (53); roasted "chestnuts" (57, 72); eggnog (98)
New Year's Day	Hoppin' John (97); cooked greens (32); caviar (94); wine/champagne (28); Bundt cakes/ring shapes (41, 46); deviled eggs (17); moon-themed (111)

Appendix B

EASY-TO-MEMORIZE UNIVERSAL RECIPES

TYPE	RECIPE RATIO (BLUE ZONE-INSPIRED)	NOTES
Ferment in Salt Brine	■ **4 cups water** (boiled, filtered, distilled) ■ **3 tablespoons** non-iodized salt Folk way: Shred vegetable, sprinkle with salt, let rest, brush off excess salt and squish to release juices, stuff into a jar and submerge under juices. Cover with brine. Used in traditional vegetable fermenting in Ikaria, Greece, and Okinawa, Japan.	Simmer the water and salt to integrate. Cool before pouring onto vegetables. Ferment 1-4 weeks at room temperature. Ensure all content stays submerged. Skim off foam as it forms. 3–5% salt brine and creates an inhospitable environment for harmful bacteria, while allowing beneficial lactic acid bacteria (if fermenting) to thrive.
Pickle in Vinegar	■ **1 cup water** ■ **1 cup vinegar** (5% acidity) ■ **1 tablespoon salt** (non-iodized) ■ **1 tablespoon honey** Found in Nicoya, Costa Rica, recipes.	Optional Add-Ins: Add a few slices of onion, garlic, or spices like mustard seeds, dill, or peppercorns for added depth of flavor.
Vinaigrette/ Hot Sauce	Blend and pour mix into a saucepan. Simmer over low heat for 5-10 min to enhance flavors and slightly thicken. ■ **¾ cup oil/fat** ■ **¼ cup vinegar or acidic fruit juice** ■ **2 tbsp herbs (e.g., hot chilies)** ■ **1 tsp salt** Common in Ikaria, Greece.	Ripe banana can be a substitute for oil at a 1:1 ratio. Puree all ingredients and use immediately. Oil can also be replaced by avocado, high oil nuts/seeds, or coconut cream.
Sourdough Bread	Feed the starter once daily if kept at room temperature or once weekly if stored in the fridge. Use a ratio of: ■ **1 part starter,** ■ **1 part puree (e.g. green banana)** ■ **1 part water** Fermented seeds, starches and more are universal to all blue zones.	For a standard gluten-free bread loaf, a typical recipe might include: ■ 3 cups fermented puree (e.g., green banana, sweet potato) ■ 3 tbsp psyllium husk powder ■ 1 to 2 cups water (adjust) ■ 2 tsp salt ■ 2 tbsp If puree is unfermented, add 1 packet (2¼ tsp) active dry yeast or 1 tbsp instant yeast

TYPE	RECIPE RATIO (BLUE ZONE-INSPIRED)	NOTES
Easy Flatbread	**■ 1 cup starchy puree** **■ 2 eggs** **■ ¼ tsp salt** **For vegan flatbread or low-starch foods (like coconut)**: whip 1 cup flour, ¼ tsp salt, 1 tbsp psyllium husk powder, 1 tbsp vinegar, 1-2 cups hot water in a food processor until a ball forms. (optional: Add 1-2 eggs). Form small balls, flatten and cook on griddle. *Add psyllium and water gradually until a ball forms. Limit servings of psyllium (fiber). Flat breads are universal in blue zones.	To make puree: Cook the starchy bean, nut, seed or vegetable until soft. Then puree in a blender with eggs and salt. Add 1 tbsp water at a time if needed until smooth. This batter can be cooked in any shape: muffin, bagel, rolls, or tamales. Alternatively, pour 2 tbsp at a time on a medium-hot griddle as flatbread/pancakes. Thin with water or milk to make pourable. For crepes, thin batter with ½ cup high-protein, full fat milk. Makes 6 flat breads.
Tea and Broth	**■ 1 tsp dried or 1 tbsp fresh content** **■ 1 cup boiling water** Teas are universal in all blue zones.	To make a soup broth, choose more savory herbs. For breakfast tea, you can add fresh or dried fruits. For a more robust tea, add roasted nuts and seeds.
Vegetable-Scrap Soup	**Fill pot ¾ with vegetables, cover vegetables with water, submerging under at least 2" of water. Simmer with lid 1-2 hours. Add water as needed.** Vegetable soups are universal in all blue zones.	Most blue zones make a daily soup with whatever produce is in season. Nuts, beans, vegetables and spices can all go into the same pot and simmer. Most make this first thing and enjoy it all day. In Japan soup is classic at breakfast.
Blanching Greens and High-Alkaloid Foods	**Use 4 cups water + 1 tbsp lemon juice/vinegar per 2 cups greens. Blanch in boiling water or steam above for 2-3 min. Drain.** Cooked greens are universal in all blue zones.	Blanching aids digestion by breaking down anti-nutrients like oxalates/alkaloids and making vitamins more bioavailable.
Drying Fruits and Veggies	Place dried fruits in a dehydrator at **160°F for 30 minutes** to pasteurize then lower to **135°F for 6 hours to dry**. Or simply use an oven's lowest temperature (typically 170°F) for 3-6 hrs. Dried fruits are universal in all blue zones.	Wash fruits and vegetables to remove surface contaminates. Cut into even slices or pieces for consistent drying. For vegetables, including leafy greens, blanch in boiling water 2 min before drying. Fruit should feel leathery and pliable; veggies will be crisp.

TYPE	RECIPE RATIO (BLUE ZONE-INSPIRED)	NOTES
Salad Template	■ **Cooked greens** (Base): 3 cups ■ **Crunchy** (Texture): 1 cup ■ **Soft** (Creamy Element): ½ cup (e.g., avocado, cheese, roasted sweet potato) ■ **Fat/Acid** (Dressing/Flavor): 3 tbsp fat and 1 tbsp acid ■ **Protein** (Satiating Element): ¾ cup (e.g., tofu, beans, eggs, nuts, sprouts) Cooked "salads" are universal in all blue zones.	**Example Salad Combination:** ■ **Greens:** Cooked chaya ■ **Crunchy:** Green papaya grated ■ **Soft:** Roasted sweet potato ■ **Fat/Acid:** Avocado + citrus juice ■ **Protein:** Boiled pigeon pea
Pesto Template	■ **Fat** (Creaminess): ½ cup ■ **Acid** (Brightness): 2 tbsp ■ **Aromatic** (Flavor): 3 cups ■ **Accent Flavor (Depth):** 2 tbsp ■ **Protein** (Umami): ½ cup ■ ½ tsp salt ■ ¼ tsp black pepper or red pepper Herbal purees are universal in all blue zones.	Example Recipe ■ **Fat:** ½ cup avocado ■ **Acid:** 1 tbsp green mango grated ■ **Aromatic:** 3 cups moringa ■ **Accent Flavor:** 4 garlic cloves ■ **Protein:** ⅓ cup almonds ■ ½ teaspoon salt ■ ¼ teaspoon black pepper
Healthy Cookies/ Pie Crust	■ **1 cup high-fat nuts** (soak 12 hrs, strain) ■ **1 cup high-sugar dried fruit** (rehydrated in hot water if rigid) ■ **¼ tsp salt** **Optional:** For softer cookies, add 1 egg. Press crust in 8" pie dish. Blind bake the crust at 350°F, 15 min to eat immediately. Ripe fruits and high-fat nuts are considered desserts in blue zones.	Any protein-oil or oil nut would work for a cookie recipe. The high fat is what makes this a dessert. If the fruit is dried, first soak in hot water to rehydrate to make blending easier. Use a food processor to mix ingredients thoroughly. Roll out and cut shapes or drop spoonfuls on an oiled cookie sheet. An 8" pie needs 4-5 cups of filling; 2 cups of crust. If baking for long-term storage, dry at 170°F 3-6 hrs.
Fermenting Nuts/Seeds Milk as Yogurt	For yogurt: Whisk 2 tbsp vegan yogurt in 4 cups warm milk (110–115°F). Pour into round container. Cover lightly. Ferment at 110°F, 7 hrs until thickened. Chill 4 hrs. Fermenting nuts, beans and seeds is universal in all blue zones.	To make nut milk, simmer 2 cup soaked nuts, seeds, or beans 15 min in 5 cups water. Sweeten to taste. Typical flavoring is 2 tsp sweetener and ¼ tsp salt.

TYPE	RECIPE RATIO (BLUE ZONE-INSPIRED)	NOTES
Tofu/ "farmer" cheese (ricotta) and "jello"	■ **8 cups high-protein milk** ■ **¼ cup vinegar or lemon juice** Cheese and tofu have similar creation processes—coagulated proteins. Some cultures use beans, nuts, or seeds to make milk/yogurt. Other cultures use animal milks. This process is universal in all blue zones. NOTE: Agar is a vegan option used to set and solidify foods (as with gelatin) and can make a "tofu" or "cheese-like" product.	**Easy-to-Find Coagulants:** ■ **Lemon Juice (or Vinegar):** Mild tangy flavor; ricotta-like tofu. Crumbly texture ■ **Nigari (Magnesium Chloride** Traditional Japanese coagulant; firm tofu; rich in minerals. Requires precise measuring; slower curd set ■ **Calcium Sulfate** Ideal for traditional firm tofu; neutral flavor; adds calcium; may be grainy texture if not mixed well ■ Non-Coagulate Solidifier: Agar Firm Set: 1 tsp per cup liquid Soft Set: ½ -¾ tsp per cup liquid Jam Set: ⅓ tsp per cup of liquid

Appendix C
BLUE ZONE DESIGN EXAMPLES

CULTURAL IMPACTS ON DIET	ECO-TYPE
Mealtime folktales, storytelling & poetry songs help younger generations know the value & origins of food.	Fire-prone. Acidic, compacted soil.

HEALTHY HABITS	TOP FOOD
Multicultural homes. Food prep skill seen as wisdom.	40% -/+ flat bread

LAYER EXAMPLES

Canopy: Oak
Subcanopy: Honey mesquite
Shrub: Bay laurel, myrtle, cocoplum
Herbaceous: Rose, Job's tears, rosemary
Vine: Grape
Groundcover: Oregano, basil
Fungal: Porcini
Tuber: Garlic
Aquatic: Watercress
Livestock: Goat, wild boar, snails

MINDSET

Land stewardship

FOOD AS MEDICINE

Sourdough starter kept for generations. Sourdough ferments use native yeast for bread-making.

DINING TRENDS

Paper-thin flatbread is often presented with a variety of toppings: fresh herbs, roasted veggies, cheese, pesto, tapenade, and purées (think pizza).

FOOD PREP

Hearty vegetable soup is made daily with whatever is in season. Decorative bread sculptures are for holiday celebrations.

DESIGN INSPIRATION

- Symmetrical & geometrical shapes
- Tidy rows for mass harvest
- Bread labyrinths
- Pruned edible hedges

STYLE ELEMENTS

Topiary. Statues. Outdoor bread ovens. Espalier.

YEARLY PLANNING

Latin liturgical cycle

NICOYA, COSTA RICA

CULTURAL IMPACTS ON DIET	ECO-TYPE
Gardening reflects a trust in divine blessings & provides a free form of health insurance.	Wet/dry seasonal extremes. Salt in soil.

HEALTHY HABITS	TOP FOOD
Drink hardwater with calcium & magnesium.	30%-/+ beans

LAYER EXAMPLES

Canopy: Coconut
Subcanopy: Mango, avocado, annona
Shrub: Pigeon pea, chaya, prickly pear cactus
Herbaceous: Banana, papaya
Vine: Chayote, dragonfruit, inca peanut
Groundcover: Pumpkin, marigold, pineapple
Fungal: Lactarius indigo
Tuber: Cassava
Aquatic: Taro
Livestock: Chicken, rabbit

MINDSET

Physical chores strengthen

FOOD AS MEDICINE

Plants & fruits are juiced for folk healing. Ancestral artifacts placed among medicinal & sacred plants.

DINING TRENDS

A variety of sweet fruits served at breakfast. Most eat a large breakfast, medium lunch & tiny dinner. Tamales offer "meals to go."

FOOD PREP

Tortillas & beans served with picadillo "hash" (chopped, stir-fried veggies). Fermented hot sauce prevents gassiness.

DESIGN INSPIRATION

- Agroforestry
- Slash & burn milpas
- Companion planting
- Bean jungle tunnels
- 4ft wide mow paths with swales

STYLE ELEMENTS

Intercropping. Spiny plant perimeter to protect home.

YEARLY PLANNING

Lunar calendar

OKINAWA, JAPAN

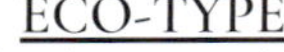

<u>CULTURAL IMPACTS ON DIET</u>	<u>ECO-TYPE</u>
Edible "paradise" gardens valued as high art. Zen riddles & ancient manuals (Saku-teiki) guide design.	Humid subtropical. Flood prone. High winds.

<u>HEALTHY HABITS</u>	<u>TOP FOOD</u>
7 daily servings of veggies. 2 daily flavonoid servings.	60% + purple sweet potato

<u>LAYER EXAMPLES</u>

Canopy: Elm, coconut
Subcanopy: Mulberry, toon
Shrub: Pigeon pea, chaya
Herbaceous: Camellia/ tea
Vine: Bitter melon, black pepper
Groundcover: Dayflower, lemongrass
Fungal: Shiitake, oyster
Tuber: Purple sweet potato, turmeric, ginger
Aquatic: Lotus, algae
Livestock: pigs, ocean fish

<u>MINDSET</u>

Have "ikigai" (purpose).

<u>FOOD AS MEDICINE</u>

Bitter foods for healing. Fermenting & coagulating beans enhance nutrient absorption. Eat until 80% full, then drink tea.

<u>DINING TRENDS</u>

Variety of tasting plates at each meal: 18-30 different foods eaten a day. 78+% plant-based. Daily teas boost nutrients without calories.

<u>FOOD PREP</u>

Ritual of Veggies - 5 colors presented at each meal: Red, blue, green, yellow/ white, brown/ black. Steaming & stir-frying.

<u>DESIGN INSPIRATION</u>

- Bonsai Tea Garden
- Sweet Potato Beds
- Shaded trails
- Harmony and balance
- Weeds help the garden as chop/drop

<u>STYLE ELEMENTS</u>	<u>YEARLY PLANNING</u>
Rocks. Fall color. Chimes. Small space efficiency.	Lunar calendar

LOMA LINDA, CALIFORNIA

CULTURAL IMPACTS ON DIET
Book of Genesis interpretation: God's original plan was for humans to eat only plant-based foods.

ECO-TYPE
Arid & drought prone. Wild-fire risks.

HEALTHY HABITS
High value placed on teaching nutritional education.

TOP FOOD
60% +/- botanical "fruits"

LAYER EXAMPLES
Canopy: Mulberry
Subcanopy: Cashew, jackfruit, avocado
Shrub: Blueberry, jamaican cherry
Herbaceous: Red roselle, banana
Vine: Mysore raspberry
Groundcover: Sea oats, fakahatchee grass, job's tears
Fungal: Button
Tuber: Chicory,
Aquatic: Cattails
Livestock: Tilapia

MINDSET
The body is a temple.

FOOD AS MEDICINE
Digestive aids prioritized. Crackers for slow chewing. Smoothies & purees for easy nutrient absorption.

DINING TRENDS
Many skip dinner, opting for 2 large meals instead. Potlucks & community meals are popular. Casseroles served to feed groups easily.

FOOD PREP
No cooking on Sabbath/Saturdays. Stews, sandwiches, cereals, dips, salads, & energy balls as low-effort meals.

DESIGN INSPIRATION
- Community garden
- Compost areas
- Roof-top, balcony & indoor plants.
- Vertical towers
- Zero-waste xeriscape

STYLE ELEMENTS
Farm technology: Drip irrigation. Drone monitoring.

YEARLY PLANNING
5-year plan increments

IKARIA, GREECE

<u>CULTURAL IMPACTS ON DIET</u>	<u>ECO-TYPE</u>
Organic heirloom gardens are considered an "oikonomia"/ economy - a lifetime of value for all	Semi-arid. Drought prone. Alkaline soil.

<u>HEALTHY HABITS</u>	<u>TOP FOOD</u>
Regular fasting. No meat, fish, eggs, dairy Wed & Fri	40% -/+ blanched greens

<u>LAYER EXAMPLES</u>

Canopy: Pine, tropical almond
Subcanopy: Cinnamon, pomegranate
Shrub: Chaya, fig, calamondin
Herbaceous: Rosemary, nettles, Bidens alba
Vine: Muscadine, pumpkin, winged beans
Groundcover: Sage, fennel
Fungal: Portobello
Tuber: Chicory, sunchokes
Aquatic: Cattail
Livestock: Sheep, bees

<u>MINDSET</u>
"Filotimo"(care for others)

<u>FOOD AS MEDICINE</u>
Fermented fruit/ wine is infused with healing medicinals like rosemary & pine. Called "hippocras."

<u>DINING TRENDS</u>
Pythagorean diet. Food is enjoyed with friends & family. Meals have many small dishes. Oil drizzled over food before serving (Vit E rich).

<u>FOOD PREP</u>
Maximizing fat soluble vitamins: Veggies are simmered hours in oil (1c per 2lbs). Called "ladero" - Soft, sweet & caramelized.

DESIGN INSPIRATION
- Unmowed sections for foraging greens
- Wild game hunting
- Al fresco dining
- Living, edible-leaf fences for privacy

<u>STYLE ELEMENTS</u>
Lent gardens. Terracotta pots. Honey hives.

YEARLY PLANNING
Julian calendar

Appendix D
Eco-Friendly, Cottage-Food Packaging

1. **Cost-Effective Paper-Based Packaging (Best for Dry Goods and Baked Items)**
   - Paper Bags—Affordable for cookies, granola, or bread.
   - Parchment Paper Wraps and Sheets—Budget-friendly for muffins, bread, or pastries.
   - Recycled Cardboard Bakery Boxes—Ideal for cakes, cupcakes, or pastries
   - Paper Clamshells and Trays—Widely available for bakery.
   - Paper Pouches with PLA Lining—Compostable for spices, tea, or granola.
   - Compostable Paper Cups with Lids—Ideal for liquids and semi-solid items.
   - Twine and Natural Raffia Ribbon—Inexpensive alternative to plastic ties for sealing.

2. **Budget-Friendly Plant-Based Bags and Wrappers (Plastic-Free Alternatives)**
   - Cellulose Bags—Clear, compostable and for cookies or crackers.
   - PLA Compostable Film Bags—Heat-sealable, good for snack bars and granola.
   - Compostable Zip Pouches—Perfect for dried goods, nuts, or teas.

3. **Compostable Labels and Seals**
   - Paper Stickers with Plant-Based Adhesive—Can be written on or stamped.
   - Water-Soluble Paper Labels—Dissolve in water, leaving no waste.
   - Custom Rubber Stamps with Food-Safe Ink—A cost-saving alternative to stickers.

4. **Minimalist and Zero-Waste Options**
   - Banana Leaves or Plant Husks—Traditional, biodegradable, and ideal for wrapped foods.
   - Refillable Glass Jars—Works well for liquids and semi-solid items.

NOTES

1. Carl, J. (2011). *Introduction to sociology: Seagull 9th Edition.* W.W. Norton & Company.

2. Zong, G., Eisenberg, D. M., Hu, F. B., & Sun, Q. (2016). Consumption of ultra-processed foods and fast food increases the risk of weight gain and type 2 diabetes: Evidence from a large prospective cohort study. *The American Journal of Clinical Nutrition,* 104(6), 1495–1502. https://doi.org/10.3945/ajcn.116.135962

3. Janssen, H. G., Davies, I. G., Richardson, L. D., & Stevenson, L. (2018). Determinants of take-away and fast food consumption: a narrative review. *Nutrition research reviews,* 31(1), 16-34.

4. Buettner, D. (2022). *The Blue Zones solution: Eating and living like the world's healthiest people.* National Geographic Society.

5. Buettner, D. (2017). *The Blue Zones of happiness: Lessons from the world's happiest people.* National Geographic Books.

6. Crossley, M. S., Burke, K. D., Schoville, S. D., & Radeloff, V. C. (2021). Recent collapse of crop belts and declining diversity of US agriculture since 1840. *Global Change Biology,* 27(1), 151-164.

7. Hatakeyama, T., & Hatakeyama, H. (2024). Rice, Wheat, and Sugar. In *Biomass with Culture and Geography* (pp. 77-112). Singapore: Springer Nature Singapore.

8. O'Neill, B. (2015). The Greatest Wealth is Health: Relationships between Health and Financial Behaviors. *Journal of Personal Finance,* 14(1).

9. Gunnoe, A. (2014). The political economy of institutional landownership: Neorentier society and the financialization of land. *Rural Sociology,* 79(4), 478-504.

10. Perlmutter, D. (2013). *Grain brain: The surprising truth about wheat, carbs, and sugar—Your brain's silent killers.* Little, Brown Spark.

11. South Florida Reporter. (2024). *Cookie consumption statistics: America's favorite treat.* Retrieved January 1, 2025, from https://www.southfloridareporter.com/cookie-consumption-statistics

12. Gunders, D. (2015). *Wasted: How America is losing up to 40 percent of its food from farm to fork to landfill.* Natural Resources Defense Council. https://www.nrdc.org/sites/default/files/wasted-food-IP.pdf

13. Wyatt, N. (2014). A royal garden: The ideology of Eden. *Scandinavian Journal of the Old Testament,* 28(1), 1-35.

14. Dagget, D. (2017). *Gardeners of Eden: rediscovering our importance to nature.* University of Nevada Press.

15. Daniels, L. A. (2019). Feeding practices and parenting: A pathway to child health and family happiness. *Annals of Nutrition and Metabolism,* 74(Suppl. 2), 29–42. https://doi.org/10.1159/000499145

16. Knobl, V., Dallacker, M., Hertwig, R., & Mata, J. (2022). Happy and healthy: How family mealtime routines relate to child nutritional health. *Appetite,* 171, 105939.

17. Cheung, P. C., Cunningham, S. A., Narayan, K. V., & Kramer, M. R. (2016). Childhood obesity incidence in the United States: A systematic review. *Childhood Obesity,* 12(1), 1–11. https://doi.org/10.1089/chi.2015.0055

18. American Medical Association. (2023). Trends in health care spending. Retrieved January 1, 2025, from https://www.ama-assn.org/about/research/trends-health-care-spending

19. Thomson, J., Shah, S. S., Simmons, J. M., Sauers-Ford, H. S., Brunswick, S., Hall, M., Butcher, R. L., & Berry, J. G. (2016). Financial and social hardships in families of children with medical complexity. *The Journal of Pediatrics,* 172, 187–193.e1. https://doi.org/10.1016/j.jpeds.2016.01.049

20. Buettner, D. (2022). *The Blue Zones American kitchen: 100 recipes to live to 100.* National Geographic Books.

21. Segedie, L. (2018). *Green Enough: Eat Better, Live Cleaner, Be Happier (All Without Driving Your Family Crazy!)* Rodale Books.

22. Tallamy, D. W. (2019). *Nature's Best Hope: A New Approach to Conservation That Starts in Your Yard.* Timber Press.

23. Centers for Disease Control and Prevention (CDC). (2024). Chronic disease in America. Retrieved from https://www.cdc.gov/chronicdisease/

24. Kim, J. Y., Song, M., Kim, M. S., Natarajan, P., Do, R., Myung, W., & Won, H. H. (2023). An atlas of associations between 14 micronutrients and 22 cancer outcomes: Mendelian randomization analyses. *BMC Medicine, 21*(1), 316. https://doi.org/10.1186/s12916-023-03018-y

25. Kiani, A. K., Dhuli, K., Donato, K., Aquilanti, B., Velluti, V., Matera, G., ... & Bertelli, M. (2022). Main nutritional deficiencies. *Journal of Preventive Medicine and Hygiene, 63*(2 Suppl 3), E93.

26. Kreouzi, M., Theodorakis, N., & Constantinou, C. (2024). Lessons learned from Blue Zones, lifestyle medicine pillars and beyond: an update on the contributions of behavior and genetics to wellbeing and longevity. *American Journal of Lifestyle Medicine*, 18(6), 750-765.

27. Centers for Disease Control and Prevention. (2025). *Managing viral infections at home: Self-care tips for recovery.* Centers for Disease Control and Prevention. Retrieved January 1, 2025, from https://www.cdc.gov/respiratory-viruses/prevention/index.html

28. Pasqualone, A., Vurro, F., Summo, C., Abd-El-Khalek, M. H., Al-Dmoor, H. H., Grgic, T., & Le-Bail, P. (2022). The large and diverse family of Mediterranean flat breads: A database. *Foods*, 11(15), 2326.

29. Ferris, T. (2012). *The 4-Hour Chef: The Simple Path to Cooking Like a Pro, Learning Anything, and Living the Good Life.* New Harvest.

30. Barnard, N. D. (Ed.). (2020). Nutritional requirements throughout the life cycle. In *Nutrition Guide for Clinicians.* Physicians Committee for Responsible Medicine. Retrieved from https://nutritionguide.pcrm.org/nutritionguide/view/Nutrition_Guide_for_Clinicians/1342043/all/Nutritional_Requirements_throughout_the_Life_Cycle

COOKBOOK RECIPE REFERENCES

AVOCADO

Bangar, S. P., Dunno, K., Dhull, S. B., Siroha, A. K., Changan, S., Maqsood, S., & Rusu, A. V. (2022). Avocado seed discoveries: Chemical composition, biological properties, and industrial food applications. *Food Chemistry: X, 16,* Article 100507. https://doi.org/10.1016/j.fochx.2022.100507

Carlton, L. (1997). *Famous Florida recipes: 300 years of good eating.* Great Outdoors Publishing Co.

Duarte, P. F., Chaves, M. A., Borges, C. D., & Mendonça, C. R. B. (2016). Avocado: Characteristics, health benefits, and uses. *Ciência Rural, 46*(4), 747–754. http://dx.doi.org/10.1590/0103-8478cr20141516

Ford, N. A., & Liu, A. G. (2020). The forgotten fruit: A case for consuming avocado within the traditional Mediterranean diet. *Frontiers in Nutrition, 7,* Article 78. https://doi.org/10.3389/fnut.2020.00078

Kendir, G., & Köroğlu, A. (2018). Evaluation of avocado (Persea americana Mill.) leaves in terms of public health. *Marmara Pharmaceutical Journal, 22*(3), 347–356. https://doi.org/10.12991/jrp.2018.74

Lourentzatos, R. C. (2021). Avocado mania: The rise and costs of our obsession with avocados (Master's thesis, The Graduate Center, City University of New York). *CUNY Academic Works.* https://academicworks.cuny.edu/gc_etds/4516

Olaeta, J. A., Schwartz, M., Undurraga, P., & Contreras, S. (2007). Use of Hass avocado (Persea americana Mill.) seed as a processed product. In *Proceedings VI World Avocado Congress (Actas VI Congreso Mundial del Aguacate)* (pp. 12–16). Viña Del Mar, Chile: Pontificia Universidad Católica de Valparaíso. ISBN 978-956-17-0413-8

Pamplona-Roger, G. D. (2004). *Foods that heal.* Review and Herald Publishing Association.

Rotta, E., de Morais, D. R., França Biondo, P. B., dos Santos, V. J., Matsushita, M., & Visentainer, J. V. (2015). Use of avocado peel (Persea americana) in tea formulation: A functional product containing phenolic compounds with antioxidant activity. *Acta Scientiarum Technology, 38*(1), 23. https://doi.org/10.4025/actascitechnol.v38i1.27397

Runyogote, J. (2021). Optimized processing method for producing avocado and mango seed-based composite flour for functional foods (Doctoral dissertation, The Nelson Mandela African Institution of Science and Technology). *NM-AIST Repository.* https://doi.org/10.58694/20.500.12479/1361

Vinha, A. F., Sousa, C., Soares, M. O., & Barreira, S. V. P. (2020). Avocado and its by-products: Natural sources of nutrients, phytochemical compounds, and functional properties. In *Chapter 9: Comprehensive Research Advances in Food Science* (pp. [page range, if known]). BP International. https://doi.org/10.9734/bpi/crafs/v1

BANANA

Kamira, M., Sivirihauma, C., Ntamwira, J., Ocimati, W., Katungu, M. G., Bigabwa, J. B., Vutseme, L., & Blomme, G. (2015). Household uses of the banana plant in eastern Democratic Republic of Congo. *Journal of Applied Biosciences, 94*(1), 8915–8929. http://dx.doi.org/10.4314/jab.v95i1.1

Kumar, K. P. S., Bhowmik, D., Duraivel, S., & Umadevi, M. (n.d.). Traditional and medicinal uses of banana. *Journal of Pharmacognosy and Phytochemistry, 1*(3). Retrieved from http://www.phytojournal.com

Liao, H. J., & Hung, C. C. (2023). Functional, thermal and structural properties of green banana flour (cv. Giant Cavendish) by de-astringency, enzymatic and hydrothermal treatments. *Plant Foods for Human Nutrition, 78*, 52–60. https://doi.org/10.1007/s11130-022-01021-x

Mayat, Z. (1990). *Indian delights.* Women's Cultural Group.

Mowry, H., Toy, R., & Wolfe, S. (1967, January). *Miscellaneous tropical and subtropical Florida fruits (Bulletin 156A).* Agricultural Extension Service, Institute of Food and Agricultural Sciences, University of Florida.

Thomas, M. (2017). *Home garden cuisine toolkit: Ideas for making food in the humid subtropical.* CreateSpace Independent Publishing Platform.

BLUE BUTTERFLY PEA

Chusak, C., Henry, C. J., Chantarasinlapin, P., Techasukthavorn, V., & Adisakwattana, S. (2018). Influence of *Clitoria ternatea* flower extract on the in vitro enzymatic digestibility of starch and its application in bread. *Nutrients, 10*(7), Article 948. https://doi.org/10.3390/nu10070948

Delpachithra, H. D., Rangana, W. M. D., & Navaratne, S. B. (2023). Determination of the nutritive value of Ceylon almond (*Terminalia catappa*) and butterfly pea (*Clitoria ternatea*) seeds from Sabara-gamuwa region of Sri Lanka. *Asian Food Science Journal, 22*(11), 1–9. https://doi.org/10.9734/AFSJ/2023/108975

Deshmukh, S., & Jadhav, V. (2014). Bromatological and mineral assessment of *Clitoria ternatea* Linn. leaves. *International Journal of Pharmacy and Pharmaceutical Sciences, 6*(3), 244–246.

Ee, K. Y., Khoo, L. Y., Ng, W. J., Wong, F. C., & Chai, T. T. (2019). Effects of bromelain and trypsin hydrolysis on the phytochemical content, antioxidant activity, and antibacterial activity of roasted butterfly pea seeds. *Processes, 7*(8), Article 534. https://doi.org/10.3390/pr7080534

Lijon, M. B. (2017). Phytochemistry and pharmacological activities of *Clitoria ternatea. International Journal of Natural and Social Sciences, 4*(1), 1–10.

Mukherjee, P. K., Kumar, V., Kumar, N. S., & Heinrich, M. (2008). The Ayurvedic medicine *Clitoria ternatea*: From traditional use to scientific assessment. *Journal of Ethnopharmacology, 120*(3), 291–301. https://doi.org/10.1016/j.jep.2008.09.009

Multisona, R. R., Shirodkar, S., Arnold, M., & Gramza-Michalowska, A. (2023). *Clitoria ternatea* flower and its bioactive compounds: Potential use as microencapsulated ingredient for functional foods. *Applied Sciences, 13*(4), 2134. https://doi.org/10.3390/app13042134

Oguis, G. K., Gilding, E. K., Jackson, M. A., & Craik, D. J. (2019). Butterfly pea (*Clitoria ternatea*), a cyclotide-bearing plant with applications in agriculture and medicine. *Frontiers in Plant Science, 10*, Article 645. https://doi.org/10.3389/fpls.2019.00645

Sapsuha, Y., Sjafani, N., Fatmona, S., & Tjokrodiningrat, S. (2023). Butterfly pea (*Clitoria ternatea*) extract as a potential feed additive for broiler chickens. *Livestock Research for Rural Development, 35*, Article #89. Retrieved December 31, 2024, from http://www.lrrd.org/lrrd35/10/3589yus.html

Sarma, D. S. K., Kumar, D., Yamini, C., Santhalahari, C., Lahari, C., Kumar, G. C., & Lahitha, M. (2023). Review on *Clitoria ternatea. International Journal of Pharmaceutical Sciences and Medicine, 8*(9), 43–58. https://doi.org/10.47760/ijpsm.2023.v08i09.004

Sears, A. (2016). *Healing herbs of paradise.* Wellness Research and Consulting.

Shamnad, J. (2019). Mineral and nutritional potential of *Clitoria ternatea* L. variants as forage. *Journal of Tropical Agriculture, 57*(2), 163–166.

Shirodkar, S. M., Multisona, R. R., & Gramza-Michalowska, A. (2022). The potential for the implementation of pea flower (*Clitoria ternatea*) health properties in food matrix. *The Pharma Innovation Journal, SP-11*(6), 625–637. ISSN (E): 2277-7695, ISSN (P): 2349-8242.

Weerasinghe, T., Perera, D., De Silva, N., Poogoda, D., & Swarnathilaka, H. (2022). Butterfly pea: An emerging plant with applications in food and medicine. *The Pharma Innovation Journal, SP-11*(6), 625–637. Retrieved from https://www.thepharmajournal.com

CHAYA

Adebiyi, O. A., Adebiyi, O. O., Ilesanmi, O. R., & Raji, Y. (2012). Sedative effect of hydroalcoholic leaf extracts of *Cnidoscolus aconitifolius*. *International Journal of Advances in Research in Natural Products, 5*(1), 1–6.

Ebel, R., Méndez Aguilar, M. de J., Castillo Cocom, J. A., & Kissmann, S. (2019). Genetic diversity in nutritious leafy green vegetable—Chaya (*Cnidoscolus aconitifolius*). In D. Nandwani (Ed.), *Genetic diversity in horticultural plants* (pp. 161–189). Springer Nature Switzerland AG. https://doi.org/10.1007/978-3-319-96454-6_6

Fintrac Inc. (2013). Chaya—High nutrition perennial (Technical Bulletin No. 92). Cambodia HARVEST. Retrieved from https://www.CambodiaHARVEST.org

Iwuji, S. C., Nwafor, A., Azeez, T. O., Nwosu, E. C., Nwaokoro, J. C., Egwurugwu, J., & Danladi, N. B. (2013). Nutritional and electrolyte values of *Cnidoscolus aconitifolius* (Chaya) leaves consumed in Niger Delta, Nigeria. *American Journal of PharmTech Research, 3*(6). Retrieved from http://www.ajptr.com

Jaroennon, P., & Manakla, S. (2021). Evaluation of physicochemical, sensory, antioxidant, and nutritional properties of latte drinks from Chaya (*Cnidoscolus aconitifolius*) leaves. *Thai Journal of Public Health, 51*(1), 25–32. Retrieved from http://www.ph.mahidol.ac.th/thjph/

Ross-Ibarra, J., & Molina-Cruz, A. (2002). The ethnobotany of chaya (*Cnidoscolus aconitifolius* ssp. *aconitifolius* Breckon): A nutritious Maya vegetable. *Economic Botany, 56*(4), 350–365.

Schwarcz, H. P., Ford, A., Knyf, M., & Kumar, A. (2022). The green deer: Chaya as a potential source of protein for the ancient Maya. *Latin American Antiquity, 33*(1), 175–186. https://doi.org/10.1017/laq.2021.71

COCONUT

Kaur, K., Panghal, A., Garg, M. K., & Chhikara, N. (2019). Coconut meal: Nutraceutical importance and food industry application. *Foods and Raw Materials, 7*(2), 419–427.

Mayat, Z. (1990). *Indian delights.* Women's Cultural Group.

Mishra, K., Beura, M., Keerthana, C. S., & Krishnan, V. (2024). Coconut: A powerhouse of nutraceuticals. In *Coconut-Based Nutrition and Nutraceutical Perspectives* (pp. 221–243). Springer Nature.

Shakeela, H., Mohan, K., & Nisha, P. (2024). Unlocking a nutritional treasure: Health benefits and sustainable applications of spent coconut meal. *Sustainable Food Technology, 2*(3), 497–505. https://doi.org/10.1039/D3FB00247K

COCOPLUM

Aguiar, T. M. de, Luo, R., Mello, A. A., Azevedo-Meleiro, C. H., Sabaa-Srur, A. U. O., Tran, K., & Smith, R. E. (2017). Chemical characterization of cocoplum (Chrysobalanus icaco, L) seed oil and seeds. *Journal of Regulatory Science, 5*(2), 15–28. http://journalofregulatoryscience.org

Boning, C. (2006). *Florida's best fruiting plants: Native and exotic trees, shrubs, and vines.* Pineapple Press.

Diaz-Gomez, I. G., Ahumedo-Monterrosa, M. J., Bedoya-Marrugo, E. A., Ballesteros-Peinado, L., Diaz-Mendoza, C. P., Severiche-Sierra, C. A., & Torregroza-Espinosa, A. C. (2017). Effect of transpiration in post-post-state condition on the agroindustrial quality of Chrysobalanus icaco

L fruit variety. *Contemporary Engineering Sciences, 10*(31), 1517–1527. https://doi.org/10.12988/ces.2017.79109

Jiménez-Ortega, L. A., Gutiérrez-Grijalva, E. P., Contreras-Angulo, L. A., & Heredia, J. B. (2021). Chrysobalanus icaco L.: Source of phytochemicals with bioactive potential against metabolic syndrome in México. *TIP. Revista Especializada en Ciencias Químico-Biológicas, 24,* e374, 1–14. https://doi.org/10.22201/fesz.23958723e.2021.374

Oganezi, N. C., Agbaeze, T., & Kalu, S. O. (2024). Identification of bioactive compounds in Chrysobalanus icaco seed kernel using gas chromatography-mass spectrometry. *American Journal of Food Science and Technology, 3*(1). https://doi.org/10.54536/ajfst.v3i1.2365

Onilude, H. A., Kazeem, M. I., & Adu, O. B. (2020). Chrysobalanus icaco: A review of its phytochemistry and pharmacology. *Journal of Integrative Medicine 19* (1), 1–6. https://doi.org/10.1016/j.joim.2020.10.001

COFFEE

Ali, H. S., Mansour, A. F., Kamil, M. M., & Hussein, A. M. S. (2018). Formulation of nutraceutical biscuits based on dried spent coffee grounds. *International Journal of Pharmacology, 14*(5), 584–594. https://doi.org/10.3923/ijp.2018.584.594

Franca, A. S., & Oliveira, L. S. (2022). Potential uses of spent coffee grounds in the food industry. *Foods, 11*(14), 2064. https://doi.org/10.3390/foods11142064

Iriondo-DeHond, A., Iriondo-DeHond, M., & del Castillo, M. D. (2020). Applications of compounds from coffee processing by-products. *Biomolecules, 10*(9), 1219. https://doi.org/10.3390/biom10091219

Monteiro, Â., Colomban, S., Azinheira, H. G., Guerra-Guimarães, L., Silva, M. D. C., Navarini, L., & Resmini, M. (2020). Dietary antioxidants in coffee leaves: Impact of botanical origin and maturity on chlorogenic acids and xanthones. *Antioxidants, 9*(1), 6. https://doi.org/10.3390/antiox9010006

Pineda-Hidalgo, K. V., & Rochín-Medina, J. J. (2020). Fermentation of spent coffee grounds by *Bacillus clausii* induces release of potentially bioactive peptides. *LWT—Food Science and Technology, 134,* 110685. https://doi.org/10.1016/j.lwt.2020.110685

Setyobudi, R. H., Yandri, E., Nugroho, Y. A., Susanti, M. S., Wahono, S. K., Widodo, W., Zalizar, L., Saati, E. A., Maftuchah, M., Atoum, M. F. M., Massadeh, M. I., Yono, D., Mahaswa, R. K., Susanto, H., Damat, D., Roeswitawati, D., Adinurani, P. G., & Mindarti, S. (2021). Assessment on coffee cherry flour of Mengani Arabica coffee, Bali, Indonesia as iron non-heme source. *Sarhad Journal of Agriculture, 37*(Special Issue 1), 171–183. https://doi.org/10.1007/somehypotheticaldoi (replace with DOI if available)

Sharma, A., Ray, A., & Singhal, R. S. (2021). A biorefinery approach towards valorization of spent coffee ground: Extraction of the oil by supercritical carbon dioxide and utilizing the defatted spent in formulating functional cookies. *Future Foods, 4,* 100090. https://doi.org/10.1016/j.fufo.2021.100090

GUAVA

Angulo-López, J. E., Flores-Gallegos, A. C., Torres-León, C., Ramírez-Guzmán, K. N., Martínez, G. A., & Aguilar, C. N. (2021). Guava (*Psidium guajava L.*) fruit and valorization of industrialization by-products. *Processes, 9*(6), 1075. https://doi.org/10.3390/pr9061075

Arain, A., Sherazi, S. T. H., Mahesar, S. A., & Sirajuddin. (2017). Spectroscopic and chromatographic evaluation of solvent extracted guava seed oil. *International Journal of Food Properties, 20*(Suppl. 1), S556–S563. https://doi.org/10.1080/10942912.2017.1301953

El Anany, A. M. (2013). Nutritional composition, antinutritional factors, bioactive compounds, and antioxidant activity of guava seeds (*Psidium Myrtaceae*) as affected by roasting processes. *Journal of Food Science and Technology, 52*(4), 2175–2183. https://doi.org/10.1007/s13197-013-1242-1

Gavhane, A., Chopade, S., Dighe, P., & Kour, A. (2022). The nutritional and bioactive potential of guava and possibilities for its commercial application in value-added products. *The Pharma Innovation Journal, SP-11*(6), 2643–2647. Retrieved from http://www.thepharmajournal.com

Ling, C. X., & Chang, Y. P. (2017). Valorizing guava (*Psidium guajava L.*) seeds through germination-induced carbohydrate changes. *Journal of Food Science and Technology, 54*(7), 2041–2049. https://doi.org/10.1007/s13197-017-2641-5

Morton, J. (2013). *Fruits of the warm climates.* Echo Point Books & Media.

Zulfiana, Y., & Fatmawati, N. (2023). Use of guava as a prevention of acute diarrhea in toddlers. *Journal for Quality in Public Health, 6*(2), 374–379. https://doi.org/10.30994/jqph.v6i2.461

JACKFRUIT

Mayat, Z. (1990). *Indian delights.* Women's Cultural Group.

Mowry, H., Toy, R., & Wolfe, S. (1967, January). *Miscellaneous tropical and subtropical Florida fruits (Bulletin 156A).* Agricultural Extension Service, Institute of Food and Agricultural Sciences, University of Florida.

Palamthodi, S., Shimpi, S., & Tungare, K. (2021). A study on nutritional composition and functional properties of wheat, ragi, and jackfruit seed composite flour. *Food Science and Applied Biotechnology, 4*(1), 63–75.

Ulloa, J. A., Villalobos Barbosa, M. C., Resendiz Vazquez, J. A., Rosas Ulloa, P., Ramírez Ramírez, J. C., Silva Carrillo, Y., & González Torres, L. (2017). Production, physico-chemical, and functional characterization of a protein isolate from jackfruit (*Artocarpus heterophyllus*) seeds. *CyTA—Journal of Food, 15*(4), 497–507. https://doi.org/10.1080/19476337.2017.130155

Waghmare, R., Memon, N., Gat, Y., Gandhi, S., Kumar, V., & Panghal, A. (2019). Jackfruit seed: An accompaniment to functional foods. *Brazilian Journal of Food Technology, 22,* e2018207.

KATUK

Anju, T., Kumari S. R. Rai, N., & Kumar, A. (2022). *Sauropus androgynus (L.) Merr.:* A multipurpose plant with multiple uses in traditional ethnic culinary and ethnomedicinal preparations. *Journal of Ethnic Foods, 9,* Article 125. https://doi.org/10.1186/s42779-022-00125-8

Arif, T., & Shetty, R. G. (2020). Therapeutic potential and traditional uses of *Sauropus androgynus:* A review. *Journal of Pharmacognosy and Phytochemistry, 9*(3), 2131–2137. Retrieved from http://www.phytojournal.com

Bunawan, H., Bunawan, S. N., Baharum, S. N., & Noor, N. M. (2015). *Sauropus androgynus (L.) Merr.* induced bronchiolitis obliterans: From botanical studies to toxicology. *Evidence-Based Complementary and Alternative Medicine, 2015,* 714158. https://doi.org/10.1155/2015/714158

Makati, A. C., Ananda, A. N., Putri, J. A., Amellia, S. F., & Setiawan, B. (2022). Molecular docking of ethanol extracts of katuk leaf (*Sauropus androgynus*) on functional proteins of severe acute respiratory syndrome coronavirus 2. *South African Journal of Botany, 149,* 1–5. https://doi.org/10.1016/j.sajb.2022.04.044

Roshetko, J. M., Kurniawan, I., & Budidarsono, S. (n.d.). Smallholder cultivation of katuk (*Sauropus androgynus*) and kucai (*Allium odorum*): Challenges in sustaining commercial production and market linkage. Retrieved from https://www.cifor-icraf.org/publications/sea/Publications/files/book-chapter/BC0332-12.pdf

Stirapongsasuti, P., Tanglertsampan, C., Aunhachoke, K., & Sangasapaviliya, A. (2010). Anaphylactic reaction to Phuk-waan-ban in a patient with latex allergy. *Journal of the Medical Association of Thailand, 93*(5), 616–619. Retrieved from http://www.mat.or.th/journal

Toensmeier, E. (2007). *Perennial vegetables.* Chelsea Green Publishing.

Zhang, B., Cheng, J., Zhang, C., Bai, Y., Liu, W., Li, W., Koike, K., Akihisa, T., Feng, F., & Zhang, J. (2020). *Sauropus androgynus L. Merr.*—A phytochemical, pharmacological and toxicological review. *Journal of Ethnopharmacology, 257,* 112778. https://doi.org/10.1016/j.jep.2020.112778

MANGO

Anggraini, A., Aprillia, S., & Aktawan, A. (2023). The characteristics of flour from mango seeds. *Journal of Agri-Food Science and Technology (JAFoST, 4*(2), 71–80.

Kaur, A., & Brar, J. K. (2017). Use of mango seed kernels for the development of antioxidant-rich biscuits. *International Journal of Science and Research, 6*(8), 535–538.

Lakshmi, M., Preetha, R., & Usha, R. (2016). Mango (*Mangifera indica*) stone kernel flour: A novel food ingredient. *Malaysian Journal of Nutrition, 22*(3).

Mayat, Z. (1990). *Indian delights.* Women's Cultural Group.

Morton, J. (2013). *Fruits of the warm climates.* Echo Point Books & Media.

Poul, S. S., Bornare, D. T., & Babar, K. P. (2019). Nutritional and functional profiling of mango seed powder and its suitability in chakali. *Journal of Pharmacognosy and Phytochemistry, 8*(4), 2460–2464.

MONEY TREE

Chaves, M. H., Araújo, F. D. S., Moura, C. V. R., Tozetto, L. J., Aued-Pimentel, S., & Caruso, M. S. F. (2012). Chemical characterization and stability of the *Bombacopsis glabra* nut oil. *Food and Public Health, 2*(4), 104–109. https://doi.org/10.5923/j.fph.20120204.04

Dauda, M. Y., Isaac, D., Jumare, S. A., Shehu, S., Maru, A. A., & Akintoyese, A. O. (2024). Evaluation of baking quality of bread from composite mixture of wheat flour and *P. glabra* seed flour. *FUDMA Journal of Sciences (FJS, 8*(1), 19–24. https://doi.org/10.33003/fjs-2024-0801-2149

Gupta, S., Sharma, K. K., & Rekha, M. M. (2023). The protective role of *Pachira glabra* leaves in preventing ethanol-induced gastric ulcer in rats. *REDVET—Revista Electrónica de Veterinaria, 24*(2). Retrieved from http://www.veterinaria.org

Ogunlade, I., Ilugbiyin, A., & Osasona, A. I. (2011). A comparative study of proximate composition, antinutrient composition, and functional properties of *Pachira glabra* and *Afzelia africana* seed flours. *African Journal of Food Science, 5*(1), 32–35. Retrieved from http://www.academicjournals.org/ajfs

Zhao, Y., Quan, X., & Wang, T. (2024). Food poisoning due to money tree seeds: A case report of toxic encephalopathy. *Emergency and Critical Care Medicine, 00*(00). https://doi.org/10.1097/EC9.0000000000000119

MORINGA

Gautier, A., Duarte, C. M., & Sousa, I. (2022). *Moringa oleifera* seeds characterization and potential uses as food. *Foods, 11*(11), 1629.

Gopalakrishnan, L., Doriya, K., & Kumar, D. S. (2016). *Moringa oleifera*: A review on nutritive importance and its medicinal application. *Food Science and Human Wellness, 5*(2), 49–56. https://doi.org/10.1016/j.fshw.2016.04.001

Islam, Z., Hasan, M. R., Islam, S. M. R., Hossen, F., Mahtab-ul-Islam, K., & Karim, R. (2021). *Moringa oleifera* is a prominent source of nutrients with potential health benefits. *International Journal of Food Science, 2021,* Article 6627265. https://doi.org/10.1155/2021/6627265

Kantilata, T. (2019). *Moringa oleifera*: A review article on nutritional properties and its prospect in the context of Nepal. *Acta Scientific Agriculture, 3*(11), 47–54.

Meireles, D., Gomes, J., & Lopes, L. (2020). A review of properties, nutritional and pharmaceutical applications of *Moringa oleifera*: Integrative approach on conventional and traditional Asian medicine. *Advances in Traditional Medicine, 20*(4), 495–515. https://doi.org/10.1007/s13596-020-00468-0

Saa, R. W., Fombang, E. N., Ndjantou, E. B., & Njintang, N.Y. (2019). Treatments and uses of *Moringa oleifera* seeds in human nutrition: A review. *Food Science & Nutrition, 7*(6), 1911–1919.

Toensmeier, E. (2007). *Perennial vegetables.* Chelsea Green Publishing.

MULBERRY

Boning, C. (2006). *Florida's best fruiting plants: Native and exotic trees, shrubs, and vines.* Pineapple Press.

Donno, D., Cerutti, A. K., Prgomet, I., Mellano, M. G., & Beccaro, G. L. (2015). Foodomics for mulberry fruit (*Morus* spp.): Analytical fingerprint as antioxidants' and health properties' determination tool. *Food Research International, 69,* 179–188. https://doi.org/10.1016/j.foodres.2014.12.020

Güven, İ. (2012). Effect of species on nutritive value of mulberry leaves. *Kafkas Üniversitesi Veteriner Fakültesi Dergisi, 18*(5), 865–869. https://doi.org/10.9775/kvfd.2012.6710

Kadam, R. A., Dhumal, N. D., & Khyade, V. B. (2019). The mulberry, *Morus alba* (L.): The medicinal herbal source for human health. *International Journal of Current Microbiology and Applied Sciences, 8*(4), 2941–2964. https://doi.org/10.20546/ijcmas.2019.804.341

Kumar, V. R., & Chauhan, S. (2008). Mulberry: Life enhancer. *Journal of Medicinal Plants Research, 2*(10), 271–278. Retrieved from http://www.academicjournals.org/JMPR

Machii, H., Koyama, A., & Yamanouchi, H. (2002). Mulberry breeding, cultivation, and utilization in Japan. *FAO Electronic Conference on Mulberry for Animal Production (Morus1-L).* Retrieved from https://www.researchgate.net/publication/237445963

Memete, A. R., Timar, A. V., Vuscan, A. N., Miere, F., Venter, A. C., & Vicas, S. I. (2022). Phytochemical composition of different botanical parts of *Morus* species, health benefits, and application in the food industry. *Plants, 11*(2), 152. https://doi.org/10.3390/plants11020152

Qin, J., He, N., Wang, Y., & Xiang, Z. (2012). Ecological issues of mulberry and sustainable development. *Journal of Resources and Ecology, 3*(4), 330–339. https://doi.org/10.5814/j.issn.1674-764 x.2012.04.006

Yu, Y., Li, H., Zhang, B., Wang, J., Shi, X., Huang, J., Yang, J., Zhang, Y., & Deng, Z. (2018). Nutritional and functional components of mulberry leaves from different varieties: Evaluation of their potential as food materials. *International Journal of Food Properties, 21*(1), 1495–1507. https://doi.org/10.1 080/10942912.2018.1489833

OAK

Austin, D. (2004). Oaks: Discovering Florida's ethnobotany. *The Palmetto, 22*(4), 12–17. Retrieved from https://www.fnps.org/assets/pdf/palmetto/v22i4p12austin.pdf

Bainbridge, D. A. (1987). The use of acorns for food in California: Past, present, future. In *General Technical Report PSW-100* (pp. 453–462). Pacific Southwest Forest and Range Experiment Station, Forest Service, U.S. Department of Agriculture.

Bainbridge, D. A. (1987). Use of acorns for food in California: Past, present, future. In *Proceedings of the Symposium on Multiple-use Management of California's Hardwoods* (pp. 453–458). PSFRES, GTR PSW-100. Dry Lands Research Institute, University of California. Retrieved from http://works .bepress.com/david_a_bainbridge/43

Bryant, R. (2023). A historical examination of Native American and European agroforestry. *Bryant University Journal of Interdisciplinary Studies, 4*(1), 1–29. Retrieved from https://digitalcommons.bryant.edu/cgi/viewcontent.cgi?article=1054&context=isbhs

Polimac, M., Koceva Komlnić, D., & Lukinac, J. (2016). Possibilities of using acorn flour in products based on flour. In *Proceedings of the 8th International Congress Flour—Bread '15 and 10th Croatian Congress of Cereal Technologists* (pp. 33–48). Retrieved from https://urn.nsk.hr/urn:nbn:hr:109:095336

Sabouri, S., & Javadi, Sh. (2022). Oak: A heritage, a culture. *Journal of Art & Civilization of the Orient, 10*(36), 27–38. https://doi.org/10.22034/jaco.2022.342339.1244. Retrieved from http://www.jaco-sj.com/article_152803.html?lang=en

Sacchelli, S., Cavuta, T., Borghi, C., Cipollaro, M., Fratini, R., & Bernetti, I. (2021). Financial analysis of acorns chain for food production. *Forests, 12*(6), 784. https://doi.org/10.3390/f12060784

Sekeroglu, N., Ozkutlu, F., & Kilic, E. (2017). Mineral composition of acorn coffees. *Indian Journal of Pharmaceutical Education and Research, 51*(3, Suppl.), S504–S507. https://doi.org/10.5530/ijper.51.3s.75

Szabłowska, E., & Tańska, M. (2024). Acorns as a source of valuable compounds for food and medical applications: A review of Quercus species diversity and laboratory studies. *Applied Sciences, 14*(7), 2799. https://doi.org/10.3390/app14072799

Vinha, A. F., Barreira, J. C. M., Costa, A. S. G., & Oliveira, M. B. P. P. (2016). A new age for *Quercus* spp. fruits: Review on nutritional and phytochemical composition and related biological activities of acorns. *Comprehensive Reviews in Food Science and Food Safety, 15*(4), 947–981. https://doi.org/10.1111/1541-4337.12220

PAPAYA

Ali, A., Devarajan, S., Waly, M. I., Essa, M. M., & Rahman, M. S. (2002). Nutritional and medicinal values of papaya (*Carica papaya* L.). In *Natural products and their active compounds on disease prevention* (pp. 307–324). Nova Science Publishers, Inc. ISBN: 978-1-62100-153-9.

Begum, M. (2014). Phytochemical and pharmacological investigation of *Carica papaya* leaf (Bachelor's dissertation, East West University, Dhaka, Bangladesh). Retrieved from http://103.133.167.11:8080/bitstream/handle/123456789/685/Mahmauda_Begum.pdf?sequence=1&isAllowed=y

Karunamoorthi, K., Kim, H. M., Jegajeevanram, K., Xavier, J., & Vijayalakshmi, J. (2014). Papaya: A gifted nutraceutical plant—A critical review of recent human health research. *TANG: International Journal of Genuine Traditional Medicine, 4*(1), e2, 1–17. https://doi.org/10.5667/tang.2013.0028

Mayat, Z. (1990). *Indian delights.* Women's Cultural Group.

Pamplona-Roger, G. D. (2004). *Foods that heal.* Review and Herald Publishing Association.

Pinnamaneni, R. (2017). Nutritional and medicinal value of papaya (*Carica papaya Linn.*). *World Journal of Pharmacy and Pharmaceutical Sciences, 6*(8), 2559–2578. Retrieved from https://www.researchgate.net/publication/319048781_NUTRITIONAL_AND_MEDICINAL_VALUE_OF_PAPAYA_CARICA_PAPAYA_LINN

Thomas, M. (2017). *Home garden cuisine toolkit: Ideas for making food in the humid subtropical.* CreateSpace Independent Publishing Platform.

PIGEON PEA

Abebe, B. K. (2022). The dietary use of pigeon pea for human and animal diets. *The Scientific World Journal, 2022*(1), Article 4873008. https://doi.org/10.1155/2022/4873008

Atuna, R. A., Mensah, M. A. S., Koomson, G., Akabanda, F., Dorvlo, S. Y., & Amagloh, F. K. (2023). Physico-functional and nutritional characteristics of germinated pigeon pea (*Cajanus cajan*) flour

as a functional food ingredient. *Scientific Reports, 13*(1), 16627. https://doi.org/10.1038/s41598
-023-43627-7

Mueller, M., Puttipan, R., Janngeon, K., Unger, F. M., Viernstein, H., & Okonogi, S. (2015). Bioactivities of the Thai medicinal and edible plants *C. cajan, M. citrifolia,* and *O. americanum. International Journal of Pharmacy and Pharmaceutical Sciences, 7*(10), 237–240.

Sarkar, S., Panda, S., Yadav, K. K., & Kandasamy, P. (2020). Pigeon pea (*Cajanus cajan*): An important food legume in the Indian scenario—A review. *Legume Research: An International Journal, 43*(5), 601–610.

Saxena, K., Choudhary, A. K., Dalvi, V. A., Saxena, R. K., Ghosh, J., Singh, S., Verma, P., & Kumar, S. (2021). Pigeonpea is significantly more than just a delicious pulse: Pigeonpea: Alternate uses. *Journal of AgriSearch, 8*(3), 177–187.

Talari, A., & Shakappa, D. (2018). Role of pigeon pea (*Cajanus cajan* L.) in human nutrition and health: A review. *Asian Journal of Dairy and Food Research, 37*(3), 212–220.

SEMINOLE PUMPKIN

Aziz, A., Noreen, S., Khalid, W., Ejaz, A., Rasool, I. F. U., Munir, M., Javed, M., Ercisli, S., Okcu, Z., Marc, R. A., Nayik, G. A., Ramniwas, S., & Uddin, J. (2023). Pumpkin and pumpkin byproducts: Phytochemical constituents, food applications, and health benefits. *ACS Omega, 8*(23). https://doi.org/10.1021/acsomega.3c02176

Batool, M., Ranjha, M. M. A. N., Roobab, U., Manzoor, M. F., Farooq, U., Nadeem, H. R., Nadeem, M., Kanwal, R., AbdElgawad, H., & Al Jaouni, S. K. (2022). Nutritional value, phytochemical potential, and therapeutic benefits of pumpkin (*Cucurbita* sp.). *Plants, 11*(11), 1394. https://doi.org/10.3390/plants11111394

Dhiman, A. K., Sharma, K. D., & Attri, S. (2009). Functional constituents and processing of pumpkin: A review. *Journal of Food Science and Technology, 46*(5), 411–417.

Gelles, C. 1,000 Vegetarian Recipes. Wiley Publishing, Inc. Hoboken, NJ

Hosen, M., Rafii, M. Y., Mazlan, N., Jusoh, M., Oladosu, Y., Chowdhury, M. F. N., Muhammad, I., & Khan, M. M. H. (2021). Pumpkin (*Cucurbita* spp.): A crop to mitigate food and nutritional challenges. *Horticulturae, 7*(10), 352. https://doi.org/10.3390/horticulturae7100352

SWEET POTATO

Buettner, D. (2015). *The Blue Zone solution: Eating and living like the world's healthiest people.* National Geographic.

Dereje, B., Girma, A., Mamo, D., & Chalchisa, T. (2020). Functional properties of sweet potato flour and its role in product development: A review. *International Journal of Food Properties, 23*(1), 1639–1662.

Edun, A. A., Olatunde, G. O., Shittu, T. A., & Adeogun, A. I. (2019). Flour, dough, and bread properties of wheat flour substituted with orange-fleshed sweet potato flour. *Journal of Culinary Science & Technology, 17*(3), 268–289.

Nguyen, H. C., Chen, C.-C., Lin, K.-H., Chao, P.-Y., Lin, H.-H., & Huang, M.-Y. (2021). Bioactive compounds, antioxidants, and health benefits of sweet potato leaves. *Molecules, 26*(7), 1820. https://doi.org/10.3390/molecules26071820

Sun, H., Mu, T., Xi, L., Zhang, M., & Chen, J. (2014). Sweet potato (*Ipomoea batatas* L.) leaves as nutritional and functional foods. *Food Chemistry, 156,* 380–389.

TROPICAL ALMOND

Barku, V. Y. A., Nyarko, H. D., & Dordunu, P. (2012). Studies on the physicochemical characteristics, microbial load, and storage stability of oil from Indian almond nut (*Terminalia catappa* L.). *Food Science and Quality Management, 8,* 9–17.

Christian, A., & Ukhun, M. E. (2006). Nutritional potential of the nut of tropical almond (*Terminalia catappa* L.). *Pakistan Journal of Nutrition, 5*(4), 334–336.

Chukwuma, I. F., Ossai, E. C., Nworah, F. N., Apeh, V. O., Abiaziem, E. O., Iheagwam, F. N., et al. (2024). Changes in nutritional, health benefits, and pharmaceutical potential of raw and roasted tropical almond (*Terminalia catappa* Linn.) nuts from Nigeria. *PLoS ONE, 19*(1), e0287840. https://doi.org/10.1371/journal.pone.0287840

Lasekan, O., Alfi, K., & Abbas, K. A. (2012). Volatile compounds of roasted and steamed Malaysian tropical almond nut (*Terminalia catappa* L.). *International Journal of Food Properties, 15*(5), 1120–1132. https://doi.org/10.1080/10942912.2010.514086

Nga, N. T. T., Bac, N. X., Hanh, V. T., & Ha, L. T. N. (2024). Polyphenols from tropical almond leaves (*Terminalia catappa* L.): Optimized extraction conditions and α-glucosidase inhibitory activity. *Vietnam Journal of Agricultural Sciences, 7*(1), 2064–2075. https://doi.org/10.31817/vjas.2024.7.1.05

Nguy, L. H., Tran, L. B. H. A., & Dong, T. A. D. (2023). Effects of edible *Terminalia catappa* L. seed oil on physiological parameters of *Mus musculus* L. mice. *Journal of Agriculture and Food Research, 12,* 100587. https://doi.org/10.1016/j.jafr.2023.100587

Oduro, I., Larbie, C., Amoako, T. N. E., & Antwi-Boasiako, A. F. (2009). Proximate composition and basic phytochemical assessment of two common varieties of *Terminalia catappa* (Indian almond). *Journal of Science and Technology, 29*(2), 1–6.

Silalahi, M. (2022). Ketapang (*Terminalia catappa* L.): Potential utilization as foodstuffs and traditional medicine. *Open Access Research Journal of Life Sciences, 3*(2), 35–41. https://doi.org/10.53022/oarjls.2022.3.2.0041

Vibha, B. (2023). Nutritional potential of fruit, bark, and leaves of *Terminalia catappa*. *Open Access, 3,* 1–4. Retrieved from www.jcmimagescasereports.org

Weerawatanakorn, M., Janporn, S., Ho, C.-T., & Chavasit, V. (2015). *Terminalia catappa* Linn seeds as a new food source. *Songklanakarin Journal of Science and Technology, 37*(5), 507–514. Retrieved from http://www.sjst.psu.ac.th

INDEX

ABOUT THE AUTHOR

Amanda Alders Pike, PhD, ATR-BC is a board-certified art therapist, professional educator, certified educational leader, and past president of the Florida Art Therapy Association. Dr. Pike grew up spending summers exploring her grandparents' farmland and lived in Cuernavaca, Mexico, for multiple years, working for a holistic wellness company. During this time, she learned to grow and use plants to create health and beauty products. During her master's and bachelor's degrees, she lived and worked on farms and therefore brings to her writing the groundedness of firsthand experience. She currently owns a two-acre permaculture farm in Jupiter, Florida, where she manages her food forest complete with free-roaming chickens and 26 beehives. Her book *Eco-Art Therapy in Practice* emphasizes the importance of growing and using plants in educational and therapeutic settings and highlights Dr. Pike's knowledge on creating meals to enhance physical, mental, and emotional health. As a certified educational leader and local 4-H program facilitator, Dr. Pike helps makes Blue Zone cooking an accessible and practical food option.